Frommer's

Seattle
day BY day®
4th Edition

by Donald Olson

Contents

Published by:

Frommer Media LLC

Copyright © 2018 FrommerMedia LLC, New York, NY. All rights reserved. No part of this publication may be reproduced, stored in a retrieval system, or transmitted in any form or by any means, electronic, mechanical, photocopying, recording, scanning or otherwise, except as permitted under Sections 107 or 108 of the 1976 United States Copyright Act, without the prior written permission of the Publisher. Requests to the Publisher for permission should be addressed to Support@FrommerMedia.com.

ISBN: 978-1-628-87382-5 (paper); 978-1-628-87383-2 (ebk)

Editorial Director: Pauline Frommer
Development Editor: Elizabeth Heath
Production Editor: Kelly Dobbs Henthorne
Photo Editor: Meghan Lamb
Cartographer: Roberta Stockwell
Indexer: Kelly Dobbs Henthorne

Front cover photos, left to right: emperorcosar, Courtesy of Visit Seattle/ Tim Thompson, Courtesy of Visit Seattle/ Carriann Alabastro

Back cover photo: cdrin / Shutterstock.com

For information on our other products and services, please go to Frommers.com.

Frommer's also publishes its books in a variety of electronic formats. Some content that appears in print may not be available in electronic formats.

Manufactured in China

5   4   3   2   1

About This Guide

Organizing your time. That's what this guide is all about.

Other guides give you long lists of things to see and do and then expect you to fit the pieces together. The Day by Day guides are different. These guides tell you the best of everything, and then they show you how to see it *in the smartest, most time-efficient way*. Our authors have designed detailed itineraries organized by time, neighborhood, or special interest. And each tour comes with a bulleted map that takes you from stop to stop.

Hoping to explore Seattle's iconic Pike Place Market or tour the city's eerie underground past? Want to try some of the country's finest coffee while strolling through Seattle's hip shopping districts? Whatever your interest or schedule, the Day by Days give you the smartest routes to follow. Not only do we take you to the top attractions, hotels, and restaurants, but we also help you access those special moments that locals get to experience— those "finds" that turn tourists into travelers.

The Day by Days are also your top choice if you're looking for one complete guide for all your travel needs. The best hotels and restaurants for every budget, the greatest shopping values, the wildest nightlife—it's all here.

Why should you trust our judgment? Because our authors personally visit each place they write about. They're an independent lot who say what they think and would never include places they wouldn't recommend to their best friends. They're also open to suggestions from readers. If you'd like to contact them, please send your comments our way at feedback@frommers.com, and we'll pass them on.

Enjoy your Day by Day guide—the most helpful travel companion you can buy. And have the trip of a lifetime.

About the Author

Donald Olson is a travel writer, novelist and playwright. His travel stories have appeared in *The New York Times*, *National Geographic*, and other national publications. He has written many bestselling travel guides for Frommer's, including most recently *Easy Guide to Seattle, Portland & the Oregon Coast*; *Seattle Day by Day* and *Portland Day by Day*.

Donald's book *The Pacific Northwest Garden Tour—The 60 Best Gardens to Visit in Oregon, Washington and British Columbia* (Timber Press) was named by *Library Journal* as one of the best reference books of 2014. His newest book, *The California Garden Tour—The 50 Best Gardens to Visit in California*, was published by Timber Press in 2017. In addition to his published novels, some written under the pen name Swan Adamson, Donald has had plays produced in London, Amsterdam, New York and Portland. He is a popular speaker on garden topics. Donald lives, writes and gardens in Manhattan and Portland, OR. You can visit him at www.donaldstevenolson.com and follow him on Facebook and Instagram @ donald_steven_olson.

An Additional Note

Please be advised that travel information is subject to change at any time—and this is especially true of prices. We therefore suggest that you write or call ahead for confirmation when making your travel plans. The authors, editors, and publisher cannot be held responsible for the experiences of readers while traveling. Your safety is important to us, however, so we encourage you to stay alert and be aware of your surroundings.

Star Ratings, Icons & Abbreviations

Every hotel, restaurant, and attraction listing in this guide has been ranked for quality, value, service, amenities, and special features using a **star-rating system.** Hotels, restaurants, attractions, shopping, and nightlife are rated on a scale of zero stars (recommended) to three stars (exceptional). Within each tour, we recommend cafes, bars, or restaurants where you can take a break. Each of these stops appears in a shaded box marked with a coffee-cup-shaped bullet ☕.

A Note on Prices

In the "Take a Break" and "Best Bets" sections of this book, we have used a system of dollar signs to show a range of costs for 1 night in a hotel (the price of a double-occupancy room) or the cost of an entree at a restaurant. Use the following table to decipher the dollar signs:

Cost	Hotels	Restaurants
$	under $100	under $10
$$	$100–$200	$10–$20
$$$	$200–$300	$20–$30
$$$$	$300–$400	$30–$40
$$$$$	over $400	over $40

Frommers.com

Now that you have this guidebook to help you plan a great trip, visit our website at **www.frommers.com** for additional travel information on more than 3,600 destinations. We update features regularly to give you instant access to the most current trip-planning information available. At Frommers.com, you'll find scoops on the best airfares, lodging rates, and car rental bargains. You can even book your travel online through our reliable travel booking partners. Other popular features include:

• Online updates of our most popular guidebooks
• Vacation sweepstakes and contest giveaways
• Newsletters highlighting the hottest travel trends
• Online travel message boards with featured travel discussions

An Invitation to the Reader

In researching this book, we discovered many wonderful places—hotels, restaurants, shops, and more. We're sure you'll find others. Please tell us about them, so we can share the information with your fellow travelers in upcoming editions. If you were disappointed with a recommendation, we'd love to know that, too. Please write to: Support@FrommerMedia.com.

16 Favorite
Moments

16 Favorite **Moments**

Previous page: The Space Needle dominates Seattle's skyline.

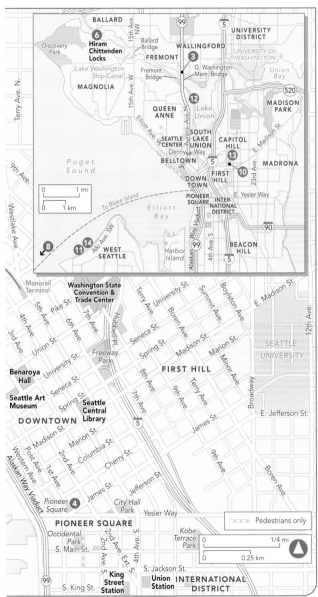

Perched near the edge of the continent, Seattle is a city that has always reached for the stars. A place of extremes, the Emerald City is caffeine-driven yet laid-back, practical yet dreamy, sophisticated but casual, soggy yet obsessive with the great outdoors. The pioneer-spirit of Seattle reflects in its mix of the old and the new: from the sturdily ornate buildings in Pioneer Square that date from the Gold Rush era, to the take-your-breath-away architecture of the Central Library designed by Rem Koolhaas and the gleaming towers that surround it. Where else will you find folks planted at a crosswalk in the pouring rain, nary a car in sight, clutching their lattes and waiting patiently for the crossing signal? Though it has changed dramatically in the 150-plus years of its existence, and reinvented itself countless times, Seattle remains an endearing and fascinating city. Here are a few things I like best about it.

❶ **Dodging the flying fish.** Working the crowds just behind Rachel, the giant piggybank that guards Seattle's beloved Pike Place Market, fishmonger-entertainers shout and toss giant silvery salmon back and forth across the counter. Watch out for the "snapping" monkfish—and the market staffer hiding behind the counter, string in hand, waiting for the next unsuspecting tourist. *See p 54.*

❷ **Spinning at the Space Needle.** On a clear day—or even a cloudy one—head to the Space Needle's SkyCity revolving restaurant for an overpriced but uniquely Seattle dining experience. A trip to the observation deck is included in the price of your meal. Diners view the Emerald City from every angle as they rotate their way through lunch or dinner. Top off your meal with a fudgy Lunar Orbiter—complete with dry ice Seattle "fog." *See p 132.*

❸ **Climbing on the troll.** Hunkered under the Aurora Bridge in the funky Fremont neighborhood is a menacing, shaggy-haired troll, clutching a replica Volkswagen Beetle in his gnarly left hand. Ill-tempered he may be, but he's never harmed any of the tourists who scramble up for photo-ops. *See p 78.*

The Freemont Troll may look menacing, but he tolerates paparazzi.

❹ **Going down under.** Seattle wasn't always on the level—at least, not the level folks walk on today. Down below historic Pioneer Square, tour guides will lead you through underground passages that were once Seattle streets and relate spicy and hilarious tales of the city's quirky, corrupt, and often naughty early history. *See p 51.*

❺ **Riding a ferryboat.** Gliding across the Puget Sound is one of the best ways to enjoy this city, which is all about water. The passengers tapping away at their laptops are local commuters, taking advantage of the free Wi-Fi. Grab a scone and a latte on board; then head out on deck and enjoy the view. You can walk aboard, bring your bike, or drive your car. *See p 101.*

❻ **Watching the fish climb.** At the Hiram M. Chittenden Locks, see the

The Seattle skyline as seen from a ferry on Elliott Bay

world's smartest salmon climb the ladders, determined to get from Puget Sound to the lakes and streams where the next generation will begin a journey of its own. Be sure to wave at the boats going up and down in the locks. It's a Seattle tradition. *See p 106.*

⑦ Partying at Bumbershoot. Seattle celebrates summer like nobody's business. The mother of all the non-stop festivals is Bumbershoot, held at Seattle Center on Labor Day weekend to "welcome" back the rainy season. Expect most anything at eclectic Bumbershoot, from stilt-walkers to impromptu parades to sculptures made of "junk." *See p 101.*

⑧ Savoring salmon at Tillicum Village. The Coast Salish Native Americans greeted Seattle's pioneer families warmly, and you'll get a taste of that hospitality here. As your boat lands, you'll be handed a bowl of steaming clams, then set free to explore Blake Island while salmon roasts in the longhouse. After lunch, enjoy a sophisticated and entertaining show of tribal dances and legends. The high-tech special effects are not exactly

traditional, but still pretty cool. Afterwards, you can explore a bit of the island before heading back to Seattle. *See p 25.*

⑨ Ringing in the New Year at the Needle. You've never seen fireworks like these. Exuberant explosions of color "climb" their way up the Needle as festive music booms in the background. Get to Seattle Center around 10:30pm and stake out the highest spot you can find on the west side of the Center House, near the front. Then send someone inside to fetch hot cocoa and popcorn. *See p 179.*

⑩ Curling up with a book at Elliott Bay Book Company. Get lost in Seattle's favorite bookstore on Capitol Hill. You'll find an enormous selection of titles as well as knowledgeable, book-loving staff, and you can grab a bite at the Elliott Bay Café. *See p 88.*

⑪ Soaking up the sun at Alki Beach. The Denny Party knew a good thing when they saw it, which is why they made Alki Beach, in what is today West Seattle, the "Birthplace of Seattle" in 1851. Today, you can gaze across Elliott Bay at the Seattle skyline as you bike, skate or walk along a 2-mile path skirting the sandy beach. Bikes and blades are available for rent.

Consider scheduling your visit to coincide with Bumbershoot, Seattle's famous city-wide fest.

Seattle's famed houseboats

Word of warning: The water's chilly! Taking the fast, inexpensive King County Water Taxi to get to Alki Beach is part of the fun. *See p 17.*

⓬ **Visiting the "neighbors."** Rent a kayak and explore the charming floating "neighborhoods" on Lake Union. About 500 Seattleites live on the water, in boats of every size and shape—including the one featured in the movie "Sleepless in Seattle." Just like any "city," there are some upscale areas and others populated by funky little vessels. *See p 102.*

⓭ **People-watching on Capitol Hill.** The grunge era lives on—sort of—in this colorful neighborhood, where college students and hangers-on from the '90s still cling to the heyday of Seattle's music scene. Piercings and tattoos abound, as do funky consignment shops, great little ethnic cafes with student-friendly prices, and some of the best lattes in town. *See p 66.*

⓮ **Ogling the pirates.** Seafair is a month of merriment and mischief, kicked off in early July by the Landing of the Pirates at Alki Beach. That's right, pirates—as in Vikings, whose blood coursed through the veins of Seattle's mostly Scandinavian settlers. Nearly every neighborhood has its own Seafair festival. The zany Torchlight Parade in downtown Seattle is my personal favorite. *See p 101.*

⓯ **Riding the monorail.** Built for the 1962 World Fair, it's only a mile-long ride, but gliding above downtown is truly a Seattle experience. The monorail runs from Seattle Center to the upper floor of the Westlake Center mall, and back again. In between, you zoom through the center of a Frank Gehry building that now houses the Museum of Pop Culture. *See p 47.*

⓰ **Sipping a whole lotta lattes.** You can't get a better cuppa joe anywhere in the world than right here, where the nation's espresso craze began. Even if you don't know your double-tall-skinny-no-whip from your venti-soy-half-caff, it's fun to make a pilgrimage to the original Starbucks at Pike Place Market. It's standing-room-only, so carry your cup with you as you browse the market stalls. *See p 39.* ●

The Seattle monorail as it runs through the Museum of Pop Culture

The Best in One Day

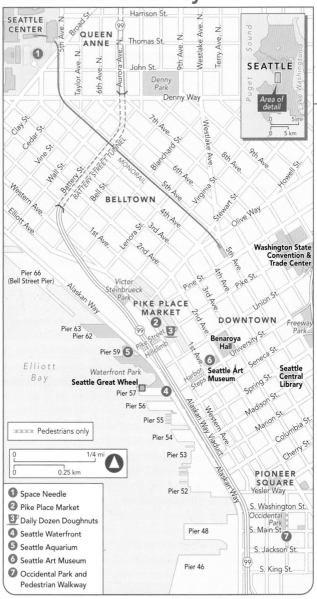

Pedestrians only

0 ——— 1/4 mi
0 ——— 0.25 km

1 Space Needle
2 Pike Place Market
3 Daily Dozen Doughnuts
4 Seattle Waterfront
5 Seattle Aquarium
6 Seattle Art Museum
7 Occidental Park and Pedestrian Walkway

Previous page: Seattle's iconic Public Market sign at Pike Place Market

One of the most compact big cities in the country, the Emerald City is easy—and just plain fun—to navigate on foot. (Sure you can drive, but parking spots are scarce—and pricey.) This sampler-platter tour roams from one end of town to the other. As you wander, always check out the incline. If it's steep ahead, walk a block farther and you'll likely find flatter ground. But don't worry too much about tiring yourself out—there are plenty of places to rest your weary feet while enjoying the eclectic street scene. START: **Monorail or bus 3, 4, 8, 16 or 30 to Seattle Center.**

❶ ★★★ Space Needle. Part retro, part futuristic, more than a touch eccentric, the Needle is the perfect symbol for Seattle. It was built for the World's Fair in 1962 after an artist sketched out a space-age focal point for the event on a placemat at—where else?—a local coffee shop. Lines for the glass elevator ride up to the observation deck can be long in summertime, but it's worth the wait—just try not to get shoved to the back of the elevator, or you'll miss the view on the way up. The typical Seattle mist only makes the view from the top that much dreamier. Your ticket to the top includes a free digital download from the Space Needle's photography department. You can also have lunch or dinner at the revolving SkyCity restaurant (reservations highly recommended; see p. 115) and rotate around the town while you dine. *Bonus:* Pick up a dining ticket on the ground floor, and you won't have to pay to go to the top. ⏱ *1 hr. Summer weekends*

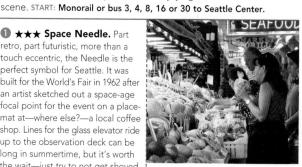

Vast and colorful Pike Place Market is must-see attraction.

are busiest. 400 Broad St. ☎ 206/905-2100. www.spaceneedle.com. Observation deck tickets: $19–$26 adults, $16–$22 seniors, $13–$18 ages 4–13. Mon–Thurs. 10am–9pm; Fri–Sat 9:30am–10:30pm; Sun 9:30am–9:30pm.

❷ ★★★ Pike Place Market Main Arcade. The heart and soul of Seattle, Pike Place is home to those famous flying fish, which you'll spot right behind Rachel the Pig. With just one day, you won't

Travel Tip

Seattle really is fun to walk, but sometimes your feet need a break! To get downtown from Seattle Center—home of the Space Needle—hop on the monorail ($2.25 one-way for adults, $1 for seniors and ages 5–12) at Westlake Center for the short ride. From there, take a metro bus ($2.75 adult peak one-zone fare, $1.50 seniors and ages 6–18) anywhere in the downtown, Pioneer Square, Pike Place Market, and waterfront neighborhoods. You can catch a bus on the street, or in the bus tunnel, conveniently located underneath Westlake Center.

The Seattle Great Wheel at Pier 57

have time to go Down Under, but there's plenty to overwhelm the senses on the Market's main street-level floor. Street musicians play, farmers hawk a spectacular assortment of locally grown produce, which you can taste at many of Seattle's finest restaurants, and local artists display an eclectic array of talents, from kazoo-making to wood-carving. The Market is a great place to sample some tasty fare and shop for high-quality souvenirs. My weakness is for the lavish bouquets of flowers, fresh from the fields in nearby lush valleys. They cost half what you'd pay at a florist. ① *1 hr. Pike Place & Pike St.* ☎ *206/ 682-7453. www.pikeplacemarket.org. Mon–Sat 10am–6pm; Sun 11am–5pm.*

3 **Daily Dozen Doughnuts.** Around the corner from the Main Arcade, in the Economy Building, follow your nose to this heavenly kiosk. Don't let the line discourage you! These light confections, fresh from the fryer, are nothing like their heavier cousins you've encountered at some doughnut shops. Might as well buy a dozen while you're at it! *93 Pike St.* ☎ *206/467-7769.*

4 ★★★ **Seattle Waterfront.** From Pike Place Market, take the elevator downhill and cross the street to Seattle's sparkling Elliott

Bay, where you can amble from pier to pier along the freshly spiffed-up waterfront. Eventually, when the Alaska Way Viaduct finally comes down (it's that 1950s-era elevated highway you see and hear above you, and it's scheduled to be dismantled and replaced by an underground traffic tunnel in 2019), the waterfront will be transformed into a giant bayside park. The area is always lively, and there are places to stop for a coffee or nosh along the way. If you have little ones, a stop at Pier 57's Bay Pavilion with its antique carousel and game room offer a fun break. The waterfront's newest attraction, the **Seattle Great Wheel** (☎ 206/623-8607; www.seattlegreat wheel.com; $14 adults, $12 seniors, $9.50 ages 4–11), is a 175-foot-tall observation wheel, with 42 fully enclosed "gondolas." But the harbor is not all about play; it's a real working waterfront, and one of the busiest in the nation. To get a good look at all the action, stop by Waterfront Park, which stretches between Piers 57 and 61, and peer through the free telescopes at the barges, tugboats, and ferryboats coming and going on the bay. ① *1 hr.*

5 ★★★ **Seattle Aquarium.** This is a sealife-lover's dream come true. The aquarium's pride and joy, a 40-foot-by-20-foot viewing window, gives visitors a glimpse of the intriguing creatures that swim in

Puget Sound. Divers interact with fish in the tank several times a day, while volunteers explain what's going on. The aquarium is perched on a pier overhanging the bay, so many of these animals are also swimming under your feet. Don't miss the giant Pacific octopus—the largest in the world. ⓘ *2 hr. 1483 Alaskan Way on Pier 59.* ☎ *206/386-4300. www.seattleaquarium.org. $30 adults, $20 ages 4–12. Daily 9:30am–5pm (last entrance at 4:30pm).*

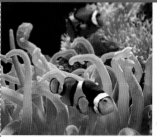

Sealife from Puget Sound and beyond is on view at the Seattle Aquarium.

⑥ ★★★ Seattle Art Museum. SAM's eclectic global collections include Northwest Native American, Pan Asian, African, European, and American modern art. The museum also hosts first-rate traveling shows and special exhibits, and offers lots of kids' activities in conjunction with the displays. Despite its world-class reputation, SAM has a friendly feel, with a passionate staff that treats visitors as honored guests. SAM's permanent collections are on display at no charge the first Thursday of every month; free to seniors the first Friday. ⓘ *2 hr. 1300 1st Ave.* ☎ *206/654-3100. www.seattleart museum.org. $20 adults, $18 seniors over 62, $13 students & kids 13–17, free for kids 12 & under. Wed & Sat-Sun 10am–5pm; Thurs-Fri 10am–9pm.*

⑦ Occidental Park and Pedestrian Walkway. From the Seattle Art Museum, walk or take bus 131 to 3rd Ave. S. and Main Street and walk from there to Occidental Square at S Washington St. The brick walkway occupies 1 block; the park claims the block to the north. In this area you'll find a sampling of Seattle's old and trendy art galleries, Victorian-Romanesque buildings constructed hurriedly during the Gold Rush, and **Glasshouse Studio,** 311 Occidental Ave. S. (www.glsshouse-studio.com), where you can watch skilled glassblowers at work. Several totem poles tower over visitors, and the Fallen Firefighter's Memorial pays tribute to those who have lost their lives battling Seattle's fires. This area has been spruced up considerably since Weyerhaeuser moved its headquarters here. ⓘ *1 hr. Occidental Ave. & Jackson St.*

Good Deal

One of the best deals in town is CityPass (www.citypass.com); with it, you can visit five popular Seattle destinations for half price (if you go to all five). Better yet, you don't have to wait in line. The passes are good for 9 days and include the Space Needle, Seattle Aquarium, Pacific Science Center or Chihuly Garden & Glass, the Museum of Pop Culture or the Woodland Park Zoo, and a seat on an Argosy Cruises harbor tour of Elliott Bay. A CityPass costs $79 for adults and $59 for kids ages 4–12. You can buy them at any of the included attractions, or order them ahead from the website.

The Best in Two Days

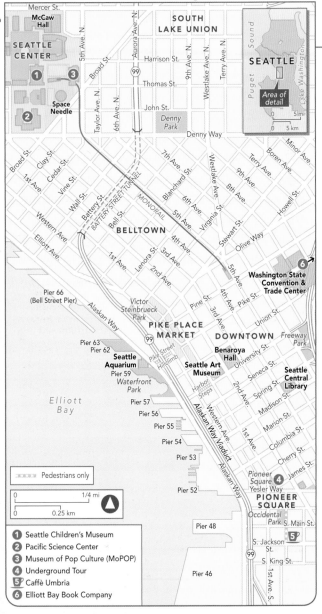

Mercer St.

McCaw Hall

SEATTLE CENTER

1 **3**

2

Space Needle

SOUTH LAKE UNION

Harrison St.

Thomas St.

John St.

Denny Park

Denny Way

SEATTLE

Puget Sound

Lake Washington

Area of detail

0   5mi
0   5 km

5th Ave. N.

Aurora Ave. N.

9th Ave. N.

Westlake Ave. N.

Terry Ave. N.

Broad St.

Taylor Ave. N.

6th Ave. N.

Broad St.

Clay St.

Cedar St.

1st Ave.

Vine St.

Wall St.

Battery St.

Bell St.

BELLTOWN

4th Ave.

Lenora St.

3rd Ave.

2nd Ave.

1st Ave.

Western Ave.

Elliott Ave.

BATTERY STREET TUNNEL

MONORAIL

7th Ave.

Westlake Ave.

6th Ave.

5th Ave.

Blanchard St.

Virginia St.

Stewart St.

Olive Way

Minor Ave.

Boren Ave.

Terry Ave.

9th Ave.

8th Ave.

Howell St.

6
Washington State Convention & Trade Center

Pier 66 (Bell Street Pier)

Alaskan Way

Victor Steinbrueck Park

PIKE PLACE MARKET

99

Pier 63
Pier 62

Seattle Aquarium

Pier 59

Waterfront Park

Elliott Bay

Pier 57

Pier 56

Pier 55

Pier 54

Pier 53

Pier 52

Pine St.

4th Ave.

3rd Ave.

Pike St.

DOWNTOWN

Union St.

Freeway Park

Benaroya Hall

Seattle Art Museum

Pike Street Hillclimb

Harbor Steps

University St.

Seneca St.

Spring St.

Madison St.

Marion St.

Columbia St.

Cherry St.

James St.

Seattle Central Library

2nd Ave.

1st Ave.

Western Ave.

Alaskan Way Viaduct

Alaskan Way

Pioneer Square **4**

Yesler Way

PIONEER SQUARE

Occidental Park S. Main St.

5

S. Jackson St.

S. King St.

99

1st Ave. S.

Pier 48

Pier 46

⋯⋯ Pedestrians only

0 _____ 1/4 mi
0 _____ 0.25 km

1 Seattle Children's Museum
2 Pacific Science Center
3 Museum of Pop Culture (MoPOP)
4 Underground Tour
5 Caffè Umbria
6 Elliott Bay Book Company

With just 1 day in Seattle you can visit only some of Seattle highlights; with a second day you can go back and spend some quality time at Seattle Center, the city's favorite hangout, and also visit two other stops that offer the quintessential Seattle experience. START: Monorail or bus 3, 4, 8, 16 or 30 to Seattle Center.

A dinosaur on the prowl at the Pacific Science Center

1 ★ **Seattle Children's Museum.** Inside the Center House, near the Space Needle at Seattle Center, you'll see the children's museum below, visible through a railed opening in the floor. The bright colors and enchanted forest are irresistible to kids, so hop on the glass elevator and ride down to the museum. In the popular Imagination Studio exhibit, parents and kids can create projects with paint, clay, and recycled materials. *Note:* If you don't have kids in tow, give this museum a pass and start your day at the Pacific Science Museum (below). ⏱ *1 hr. 305 Harrison St.* ☎ *206/441-1768. www.thechildrensmuseum. org. $10.50 adults and children, free under age 1. Mon–Fri 10am–5pm, Sat-Sun 10am-6pm.*

2 ★★ **Pacific Science Center.** *Do touch!* is the rule at this museum at Seattle Center. There's plenty here to interest all ages, but this is mainly a youth-focused museum. Kids love the animatronic dinosaurs, the butterfly garden, and the Body Works area, where they can put their own physical abilities to the test. There are buttons to press, levers to pull, animals to touch, a playground for tiny tots, and special exhibits ranging from bubbles to snakes. You can gaze at the stars in the planetarium, and watch exciting laser shows (Thurs–Sun nights, plus Sat–Sun afternoons) set to music by the Beatles, Michael Jackson, Led Zeppelin, and more. The IMAX theaters show movies for varying ages. ⏱ *2 hr. 200 2nd Ave. N.* ☎ *206/443-2001. www.pacsci.org. $31 adults, $28 seniors, $23 ages 6–15; includes IMAX; discounts available for combination passes. Daily 10am–6pm.*

3 ★ **Museum of Pop Culture.** This museum started out as the Experience Music Project, Microsoft billionaire Paul Allen's monument to homegrown Seattle rock legend

Explore the remains of old Seattle, a full story beneath the modern city, on the Underground Tour.

Jimi Hendrix. Some of the music-related exhibits are still in place, but in 2017 the museum rebranded itself as MoPOP, raised its prices, and greatly expanded its Science Fiction exhibits, with movie clips, costumes, and props from sci-fi movies and television series over the decades. The museum is housed in a Frank Gehry–designed building meant to look, from above, like one of Hendrix's guitars. From the street, it looks more like an undulating blob of metal with a monorail running through it. ① *90 min. 325 5th Ave. N. (at Seattle Center).* ☎ *206/770-2700. www.mopop.org. $28 adults, $25 seniors, $14 ages 5–17 (discount if purchased online). Late May–early Sept daily 10am–7pm; early Sept–late May 10am–5pm.*

Exhibits at MoPop chronicle the world of pop culture icons, Sci-Fi, and TV.

④ ★★★ **Underground Tour.** The historic Pioneer Building at 1st and Yesler now houses the popular Underground Tour, which takes you beneath sidewalks of Seattle to view remnants of the original pioneer town, a full story lower than the city that was rebuilt after a huge fire in the 1880s. You'll get the fascinating lowdown (literally) on the era's get-rich-quick schemers, gold-crazy prospectors, and colorful women who listed their occupation as "seamstress,"

though they seldom produced a stitch. Some of the content is mature, but it should go right over the heads of the little ones. In any case, they'll be more fascinated by the stories of the rats that once roamed the streets and the toilets that exploded with incoming tides. The guides are witty, often hilarious, and they know their stuff. There isn't really too much to see as you walk through the tunnels, but it's atmospheric and fun. ① *90 min. 608 1st Ave.* ☎ *206/682-4646. www.undergroundtour.com. $22 adults, $20 seniors & ages 13–17, $10 ages 7–12. Tours offered several times daily Apr–Sept 10am–7pm, Oct–Mar 10am–6pm; check the website for tour times; no tours Thanksgiving & Christmas day).*

The Pacific Science Center offers hands-on exhibits, special events, and a planetarium.

The Elliott Bay Book Company is housed in an historic 1917 building on Capitol Hill.

5 ★ The Emerald City is not exactly known for balmy weather, but that's never kept a Seattleite from indulging in a frozen treat—like the sinfully creamy gelato at **Caffè Umbria.** My favorites are cappuccino and pistachio. Sit at the window bar and gaze out at the passersby, or nab an outside table on a sunny day. The panini and croissants are fresh and delicious. Italian beer and wine available, too. *320 Occidental Ave. S.* ☎ *206/624-5847. www. caffeumbria.com. Mon–Fri 6am–6pm; Sat 7am–6pm; Sun 8am–5pm.*

6 ★★★ **Elliott Bay Book Company.** Located in a 20,000-square-foot historic 1917 building on quirky Capitol Hill, Elliott Bay still feels like Seattle's comfy living room. An old Ford truck service center, the space has fir floors and massive ceiling beams. Seattleites love to while away the hours here, perusing more than 150,000 books. Your challenge: not to bring home more than you can fit in your carry-on! And to stay off your phone while perusing the stacks. ☉ *1 hr. 1521 10th Ave.* ☎ *206/624-6600. www.elliottbay book.com. Mon–Thurs 10am–10pm; Fri–Sat 10am–11pm; Sun 11am–9pm.*

Seattle Makes Music

The Kingsmen, Jimi Hendrix, Heart, Queensrÿche, Pearl Jam, Nirvana, Alice in Chains, Death Cab for Cutie, Modest Mouse— Seattle seems to spawn great music. Since the 1950s, the Emerald City has been famous for its garage bands that end up going big-time. The "Louis Louis" phenomenon began when the Wailers from Tacoma (just south of Seattle) recorded the song in 1960, and it became a radio hit. (A couple of years later, two Northwest bands from a bit further south—Portland, Oregon—recorded the same song: The Kingsmen and Paul Revere and the Raiders.) In the 1990s, Seattle's Kurt Cobain and his band Nirvana kicked off the grunge era that made Seattle arguably the hippest place on the planet. The tradition lives on in Seattle's contemporary rockers, like Modest Mouse.

The Best **in Three Days**

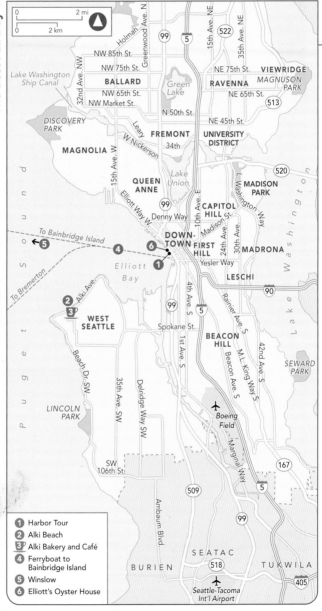

1 Harbor Tour
2 Alki Beach
3 Alki Bakery and Café
4 Ferryboat to Bainbridge Island
5 Winslow
6 Elliott's Oyster House

To fully appreciate Seattle, you need to get out on the water. After all, nearly half the city is surrounded by it. Plenty of fun awaits, whether you want to row, paddle, or sit back and relax while someone else navigates the lakes, canals and bays. START: **Bus 99, 16, 66 to Seattle Waterfront, Pier 55.**

The Alki Beach Promenade gives walkers and bikers a gorgeous view of the Seattle skyline.

1 ★★ **Harbor Tour.** This lively, informative tour of Seattle's working harbor, offered by Argosy Cruises, lasts just an hour—perfect to keep the kids enthralled as the boat cruises past dry docks, tugboats, and one of the world's largest shipping terminals—offering great views of Seattle's distinctive downtown skyline. The popular tour has been drawing crowds since 1949 and leaves around noon every day (with additional tours depending on the day and season; check the website). If an hour isn't long enough, choose from a variety of longer cruises, including a 2½-hour cruise to the locks on Lake Union and (my favorite) a 4-hour cruise to Tillicum Village on Blake Island that includes a delicious salmon bake and native dances performed by members of Coast Salish tribes. ⏱ *1 hr.* ☎ *888/ 623-1445. www.argosycruises.com. Cruises depart from Pier 55, Seattle Waterfront. 1-hr cruise $27 adults, $22 seniors, $13 ages 5–12.*

2 ★★★ **Alki Beach.** Located in West Seattle, where the first white settlers from the East arrived, this is the best beach in the city. The mood is festive, the view of Elliott Bay and the Seattle skyline breathtaking, and the water is always—even in the summertime—very chilly. That doesn't keep the locals from taking a dip, even in the cooler months when a wetsuit is needed. I recommend zipping across Elliott Bay from the Seattle Waterfront on the fast and inexpensive King County Water Taxi. Otherwise, you'll need to drive over the West Seattle Bridge and take the Harbor Avenue/Avalon Way exit, and then turn right onto Harbor Avenue and bear left at Alki Avenue. This wide, sandy beach has a great promenade for walkers, joggers, and inline skaters, and you can rent bikes or go-carts at shops across from the beach. Cafes and shops line the street across from the water. ⏱ *2½ hr.*

The ferry ride is half the fun of a trip to Bainbridge Island.

3 Alki Bakery Cafe. If all that salt air makes you hungry, head across the street to Alki Bakery and Café for pastries and coffee or something more substantial—sandwiches, pastas, or seafood. Enjoy your snack outside, with splendid ocean and mountain views thrown in for free! *2738 Alki Ave. SW. ☎ 206/935-1352. www.alkibakery.com. $*

4 ★★★ Ferryboat to Bainbridge Island. Washington State runs the largest ferry system in the country, and this line is very popular with commuters. You could plug in your laptop and check email for free, but don't. Instead, grab a cup of coffee and a raspberry scone at the onboard cafe, and go out on deck and enjoy the 35-minute ride. If you walk onto the ferry, arrive 15 minutes early; if you drive your car on (not recommended), arrive at least 20 to 30 minutes ahead of time. Drive-on wait times can be much longer during rush hours. *Catch the ferryboat at the Seattle Ferry Terminal at Pier 52. ☎ 206/464-6400. www.wsdot.wa.gov/ferries. Roundtrip fares for walk-on passengers $16.40 for adults, $8.20 for seniors & children 6–18, $28.40 for car & driver roundtrip; check schedules for departure times).*

5 ★★ Walk around Winslow. Once you're on the island, follow the crowds walking into the charming town of Winslow, where you can roam the art galleries, taste some wine, and do some shopping on Winslow Way. A great place to see the work of area artists—both new and seasoned—is the non-profit Bainbridge Arts and Crafts gallery at 151 Winslow Way E. (☎ 206/842-3132; Mon–Sat 10am–6pm, Sun 11am–5pm). For a good cup of coffee, turn left (toward the water) at Madison Avenue South, then right onto Parfitt Way Southeast, and stroll over to Pegasus Coffee House and Gallery (131 Parfitt Way SW; ☎ 206/842-6725), a picturesque, ivy-covered brick shop on the waterfront that roasts its own tasty beans. If you are a garden lover, drive or take the #90 bus to the Bloedel Reserve (7571 NE Dolphin Dr., 6 miles north of Winslow ferry terminal; www.bloedelreserve.org. $15 adults, $10 seniors/students, $8 ages 13–18; Sept–May Tues–Sun 10am–4pm; June-Aug Tues-Wed 10am-4pm, Thurs-Sun 10am-6pm), one of the great gardens of the Pacific Northwest. ⏱ 3 hr.

6 ★★ Elliott's Oyster House. Back in Seattle, this is a great place to stop for fresh local seafood. Or head for the raw bar if you just need an oyster fix. It's the perfect place to wrap up a day on the water. *1201 Alaskan Way, Pier 56. ☎ 206/623-4340. www.elliottsoyster house.com. $$. See p 125.* ●

Seattle **Heritage**

1 Museum of Flight
2 Klondike Gold Rush National Historical Park
3 Wing Luke Asian Museum
4 Museum of History & Industry (MOHAI)
5 Burke Museum
6 Nordic Heritage Museum
7 Larsen's Danish Bakery
8 Tillicum Experience

Previous Page: Stunning Chihuly Garden and Glass includes galleries, a 100-ft-long sculpture in a light-filled glass house, and a magical glass garden.

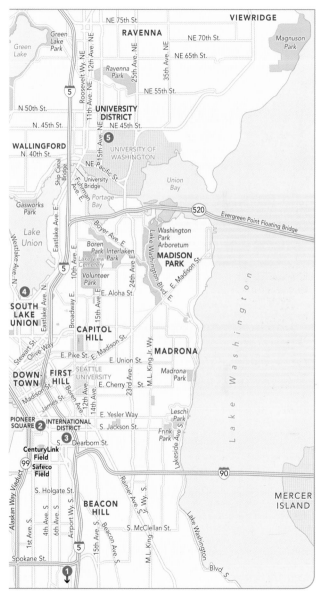

When it comes to historic roots, Seattle may not compare to a city like Boston. But, the Emerald City has such a colorful past that kids and adults alike get caught up in the fun. This tour will take you on an exploration from the days before the arrival of Europeans to the birth of the aerospace industry that helped modern Seattle take flight. START: **Bus 124, 154, 173 to the Museum of Flight.**

Gemini space suit gloves from the Destination Moon: The Apollo 11 Mission exhibit, which runs through 2019 at the Museum of Flight.

❶ ★★★ Museum of Flight.
The history of aviation, and the presence of aircraft giant Boeing, goes back pretty far in Seattle. Though it's some distance from downtown, this top-flight museum will amaze anyone intrigued by the human species' dream of escaping the bonds of earth. The historic Red Barn (Boeing's first manufacturing building), houses exhibits on early aviation, including the mail bag carried by William E. Boeing and Eddie Hubbard on the first international U.S. Air Mail flight from Vancouver, B.C., to Seattle in 1919. The exhibit ends with the Boeing 707, which ushered in the jet age. The cavernous Great

Gallery features dozens of historic aircraft, many of them suspended from the ceiling as though in flight. Visitors can climb into the cockpit of a real Blackbird, the fastest jet ever made. The Personal Courage Wing tells the stories of fighter aviators in World Wars I and II. At the Airpark, you can walk through legendary aircraft including the Concorde and the first jet Air Force One. The simulator exhibit lets you try virtual flight and hang-gliding. The museum's Space Gallery displays NASA and Russian spacecraft (and mock-ups). ① *90 min. 9404 E. Marginal Way S.* ☎ *206/764-5720. www.museumofflight.org. $23 adults, $19 seniors, $14 ages 5–17, free 4 & under. Free 5–9pm 1st Thurs of every month. Daily 10am–5pm. Bus: 124. Driving: take exit 158 off I-5*

❷ ★ Klondike Gold Rush National Historical Park. You're bound to catch Gold Fever (or shake your head in disbelief) as you listen to the tales and look at the pictures of Yukon-bound prospectors and their families who passed through Seattle on their way to strike it rich in the Alaskan gold fields. This is both a museum and a national park. Kids can earn honest-to-gosh Junior Ranger badges by filling in an activity book based on information gleaned from the two floors of exhibits. This keeps them conveniently busy while the grown-ups enjoy the displays. Films on the Gold Rush and Seattle's role in the mania are shown frequently. In the summer, you can watch

The interactive Klondike Gold Rush International Historical Park chronicles a formative period in Seattle's history.

gold-panning demonstrations, and there's also a self-guided walking tour of Pioneer Square that opens up more of the Gold Rush era's history. ◷ 1 hr. 319 2nd Avenue S. ☎ 206/220-4240. www.nps.gov/klse. Free. Daily 9am–5pm.

③ ★★ Wing Luke Asian Museum.

The Wing Luke celebrates the many Asian cultures that have immigrated to the Pacific Northwest and contributed to its growth. The main exhibit, "Honoring Our Journey," tells the 150-year-old story of Asians and Pacific Islanders settling in Washington. Other exhibits include one called "Camp Harmony D-4-44," which recreates a livestock stall converted into a family holding cell, barbed wire and all, in a West Coast Japanese-American internment camp in 1942. The museum is housed in the historic Freeman Hotel, where many early Asian immigrants lived while working in the canneries and lumber mills. Tours of the hotel and Chinatown-Japantown neighborhood are given daily. The museum is named for

Wing Luke, the first Asian-American to hold public office in the Northwest. ◷ 1 hr. 719 S. King St. (South King St. & 8th Ave. South). ☎ 206/623-5124. www.wingluke.org. $15 adults, $12.50 seniors & students, $10 ages 5–12. Includes tour of

Explore the influence of Asian immigrants to Seattle at the Wing Luke Asian Museum.

Learn about Seattle's past, including the Great Fire that destroyed much of the city, at the Museum of History & Industry (MOHAI).

historic building/former hotel. Tues–Sun 10am–5pm, 1st Thurs of month & 3rd Sat of month 10am–8pm.

④ ★★ Museum of History & Industry (MOHAI). It may not have the most exciting name, but there is nothing dull about this museum. It's a great way to learn about Northwest history through riveting, often hands-on exhibits and historic photos. You can amble along the "sidewalks" of pre-fire Seattle, which would soon be reduced to ashes by the Great Fire of 1889. Every aspect of Seattle's scientific and industrial history is covered, right up to the arrival of Microsoft and Amazon. The museum is housed in the historic Naval Reserve Building on the shores of Lake Union. ⏱ *1 hr. 820 Terry Ave. N. ☎ 206/324-1126. www.mohai.org. $20 adults, $16 seniors, $14 students, free ages 14 & under. Free first Thurs of the month. Daily 10am–5pm, Thurs until 8pm.*

⑤ ★★ Burke Museum. This museum devoted to the natural history of Washington State has always had fascinating exhibits, and it's always been too cramped to show off its holdings. The good news is that a new Burke Museum will open in 2019, and when it does, it will be a marvel of modern museum transparency and interactivity, with windows that allow visitors to watch and interact with researchers working in their labs. The extensive collection of dinosaur and prehistoric mammal skeleton will be dramatically displayed and includes the oldest and most complete T-Rex skull ever found Even though the old Burke will be closed in 2018, I'm including the new Burke here because its opening will be a highlight of 2019. ⏱ *1 hr. 17th Ave. NE & NE 45th St. ☎ 206/543-5590. www.burke museum.org. New prices and opening times unavailable at press time.*

⑥ ★★ Nordic Heritage Museum. This museum in the Ballard neighborhood is the only one in the country that celebrates the history, art and traditions of the five Nordic countries whose immigrants settled in Seattle (particularly Ballard) and the Pacific Northwest. Each country—Denmark, Finland, Iceland, Norway, and Sweden—has a room to tell its story and show off its art and culture. My favorite exhibit brings to life the arrival of early Scandinavian immigrants, via Ellis Island, to the land of their dreams. In 2018 the museum moved to a brand-new building that dramatically invigorated its exhibits. ⏱ *1 hr. 2655 NW Market St. ☎ 206/789-5707. www.nordic museum.org. $8 adults, $7 seniors & students, $6 children over 5. Tues–Sat 10am–4pm, Sun noon–4pm.*

Seattle Takes Shape

In 1852, a windy, rain-drenched winter prompted Seattle's first European settlers to move from Alki Point (now in West Seattle), where they had landed the previous year, to the more sheltered eastern shore of Elliott Bay. The reason for the zany layout of the town they created—now the Pioneer Square neighborhood—was the lack of agreement among the city fathers (and possibly the chronic drunkenness of at least one) about which direction the roads should go. Perhaps not surprisingly, squabbling over roads became a Seattle tradition. Thirty-five years later, Seattle struck it rich when gold was discovered in the Yukon. Would-be prospectors stocked up on supplies here before they headed out to the gold fields; on the way back, those who had struck it rich dropped a large percentage of their profits here. After the fire in 1889, Seattle's businessmen, frantic at missing out on profits, scrambled to rebuild their city. They built fast, but they built to last.

7 ★ **Larsen's Danish Bakery.** After your visit to the Nordic Heritage Museum, enjoy some home-made Danish pastries with a cup of coffee at this long-established bakery. Here's your chance to sample a real Danish kringle or smorkaka. *8000 24th Ave NW. www.larsens bakery.com. $*

8 ★★★ **Tillicum Experience.** Rewind to pre-European times in the Northwest. The local Coast Salish Indian tribes may have lived to regret their initial hospitality to the white settlers who landed at Alki Point and who, many years later, drove the Native Americans onto second-rate reservation land. But at Tillicum Village, the hospitality is in full force as a number of local tribes cooperatively present a warm clam-and-broth to welcome you and a salmon bake buffet served in a recreated longhouse. After the buffet lunch, they perform traditional dances illustrating creation stories. The entire experience is informative, fun and very well done. The setting is deeply forested Blake Island, believed to be an ancient campground of the Duwamish and Suquamish tribes, and the likely birthplace of Chief Seattle. Now a state park, it can be reached only by a boat operated by Argosy cruises. ⏱ *4 hr.* ☎ *206/933-8600. www.argosycruises.com. Boat operated by Argosy Cruises leaves from Pier 55 on the Seattle waterfront. Price with the cruise and buffet lunch: $84 adults, $75 seniors, $32 ages 5–12; free age 4 & under; dates & times vary by month.*

Seattle for Art Lovers

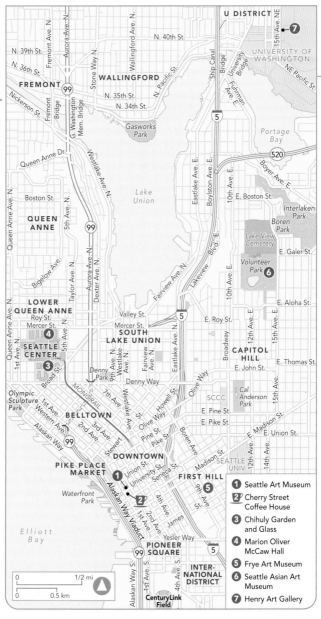

1 Seattle Art Museum
2 Cherry Street Coffee House
3 Chihuly Garden and Glass
4 Marion Oliver McCaw Hall
5 Frye Art Museum
6 Seattle Asian Art Museum
7 Henry Art Gallery

The Emerald City has always supported the arts with its extra cash, whether from gold, aerospace, butcher shops (the Frye) or tech mania. The Pacific Northwest is known for its public art, particularly outdoor sculptures, and for its Venetian-influenced glass. Renowned homegrown glass artist Dale Chihuly launched an American glass-art movement in the late 1960s that is still going strong in Seattle. START: **Bus 212, 216, 217, 255, 256 to Seattle Art Museum.**

Jonathan Borofsky's "Hammering Man" looms over the Seattle Art Museum.

❶ ★★★ **Seattle Art Museum.** You'll know you're there when you see the hardworking "Hammering Man," a 48-foot tribute to the working classes that shaped Seattle's character. Appropriately, the arm of the animated outdoor sculpture, designed by Jonathan Borofsky, gets a rest every year on Labor Day. Entrance to the first two floors of this noteworthy museum is free of charge, and includes the Brotman Forum, which features changing exhibits and a large-scale sculpture by John Grade called "Middle Fork" inspired by a 140-year-old western hemlock tree located in the Cascade Mountains east of Seattle. Traveling exhibits of art created by Pacific Northwest Native American tribes, and regional art from or about the Pacific Northwest and around the world fill the rest of the museum. ⏱ *2 hr. 1300 1st Ave.* ☎ *206/654-3100.*

www.seattleartmuseum.org. $20 adults, $18 seniors 62 & over, $13 students & children 13–17, free children 12 & under. Wed–Sun 10am–5pm; Thurs–Fri 10am–9pm. See p 65.

❷ ★ **Cherry Street Coffee House.** While you're in an arty mood, stop for a snack at this chic cafe, which showcases the works of local artists. The coffee is great, and so are the soups and sandwiches. If you're a carnivore, try their famous BLT; if not, you'll love the homemade veggie burgers. *1212 1st Ave.* ☎ *206/264-9372.* www.cherryst.com. $

❸ ★★★ **Chihuly Garden and Glass.** Not many artists are given a museum in their lifetime, but world-famous Seattle glass artist Dale Chihuly has one devoted entirely to his work, and it's right next to the Space Needle. Chihuly's work is so intensely colorful and inventive it seems to transcend the limits of glass. The museum presents a chronological portrait of his life and work, and ends in a garden with fabulous glass plants. ⏱ *45 min. 305 Harrison St.* ☎ *206/743-4940. www.chihuly gardenandglass.com. $29 adults, $222 seniors, $18 ages 4–12. Sun–Thurs 11am–7pm, Fri–Sun 11am–8pm.*

❹ ★ **Marion Oliver McCaw Hall.** Seattle has seen a burgeoning of art houses and expansions since the '90s, and this was one of the most notable. Home to the Seattle Opera and the Pacific Northwest Ballet, this remodeled performance

A whimsical installation at Chihuly Garden and Glass.

hall—resplendent with color and drama—has drawn rave reviews for its acoustic excellence and stunning art exhibits. Outside, a contemporary fountain blends in seamlessly with the walkway; at night, colored lights create swirls of color. If you're in town over the holidays, the PNB's "Nutcracker"—complete with Maurice Sendak costumes and sets—is not to be missed. ⏱ *15 min. 321 Mercer St.* ☎ *206/ 389-7676. www.seattleopera.org. Ticket prices for performances vary.*

⑤ ★★ Frye Art Museum.
Charles and Emma Frye, German immigrants who made a fortune in Seattle meat-packing during the Klondike Gold Rush, left their immense collection of then-contemporary art to the city to be displayed to the public in one location free of charge. Thus was born the Frye. Its collected representational works—portraits, still-lifes,

landscapes—are by 19th- and 20th-century French, German, and American painters. But in recent years, the museum has reinvented itself, adding modern and abstract art to the collection. These new works are often intriguingly juxtaposed with paintings that once hung in the Fryes' living room or meat house. ⏱ *1 hr. 704 Terry Ave.* ☎ *206/622-9250. www.fryemuseumt.org. Free. Tues–Sun 11am–5pm; Thurs to 7pm.*

Though the building is closed for renovation until 2019, kids can still climb on the stone camels outside the Seattle Asian Art Museum.

Olympic Sculpture Park

You won't have to be cooped up indoors to enjoy this relative newcomer to Seattle's art scene. Run by the Seattle Art Museum, the **Olympic Sculpture Park** (2901 Western Ave.; www.seattleart museum.org) is a unique, 9-acre outdoor sculpture park that features very large permanent and traveling exhibits. Added bonus: It's all right on the waterfront and has a great on-site cafe. From "Father and Son," a double fountain by Louise Bourgeois that captures a sometimes problematic relationship, to "Eagle" by Alexander Calder, an abstract work on wings of fancy, the creations are both fun and thought-provoking. Admission is free, and the park is open daily from 30 minutes before sunrise to 30 minutes after sunset. Free hour-long tours are available through the **Seattle Art Museum** (☎ 206/654-3100) at varying times throughout the year.

The Henry Art Gallery offers a wide collection of old masters to contemporary works.

⑥ ★ Seattle Asian Art Museum.

This museum is undergoing a major renovation and will be closed for an indefinite period. In the meantime, some of the collection and programs will be relocated (check website for latest details). Set in the middle of lovely **Volunteer Park** (p 67) and operated by the Seattle Art Museum, SAAM holds a noteworthy collection of historic and contemporary art from a variety of Asian cultures. Kids love climbing on the life-size camel statues that kneel on either side of the entrance of this Art Deco gem. Isamu Noguchi's captivating "Black Sun" sits outside the museum. A photo of the Space Needle taken through the sculpture's open center makes a great souvenir. ⓘ *1 hr. 1400 E. Prospect St. (in Volunteer Park).* ☎ *206/654-3100. www.seattleartmuseum.org.*

Museum is closed for renovations. New hours and prices unavailable at press time.

⑦ ★★ Henry Art Gallery.

Old world meets new at the Henry, where you can find works by masters such as Rembrandt, but also avant-garde photography and sculpture. The Henry's solid reputation has soared since its mega-expansion in 1997. One of its most popular permanent exhibits is James Turrell's riveting "Skyspace," which turns light—both natural and artificial—into ever-changing art. ⓘ *1 hr. University of Washington campus, 15th Ave. NE & NE 41st St.* ☎ *206/543-2280. www.henryart.org. Wed-Sun 11am–4pm; Thurs until 9pm. $10 adults, $6 seniors, free for students & ages 13 & under, free for everyone on Sun and first Thurs of the month.*

The Olympic Sculpture Park is operated by the Seattle Art Museum.

Seattle Film & Theater

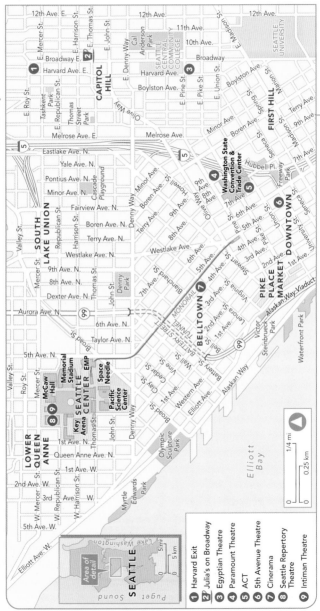

1 Harvard Exit
2 Julia's on Broadway
3 Egyptian Theatre
4 Paramount Theatre
5 ACT
6 5th Avenue Theatre
7 Cinerama
8 Seattle Repertory Theatre
9 Intiman Theatre

eattleites spend those long-awaited summer days outdoors, but come fall, it's time to head for the theater or the movies. So perhaps the gray winters have played a role in making this an important film and theater town. The month-long Seattle International Film Festival (☎ 206/324-9996; www.seattlefilm.org), held in May at several venues throughout the city, is one of the largest film festival in the country and has launched a number of world premieres. The city also boasts several magnificent theaters built in the Roaring Twenties or earlier, as vaudeville houses, playhouses, movie palaces, or clubs. START: **Bus 9 or 49 to E. Roy St. & Harvard Ave.**

❶ ★ **Harvard Exit.** Tucked away in an unassuming brick building on a side street in the artsy Capitol Hill neighborhood, this art theater specializes in independent and foreign-language films. Built in 1925 as a clubhouse for The Woman's Century Club, it was converted in the '60s to a movie theater. In addition to the cozy fireplace, grand piano, and comfy chairs, its huge lobby houses a 1919 movie projector used for silent films. Parking can be tricky, so leave yourself plenty of time if you come for a show. ① *15 min. 807 E. Roy at Harvard.* ☎ *206/781-5755. www.landmark theatres.com/Market/Seattle/Harvard ExitTheatre.htm. Free admission to see the lobby.*

A detail from the Egyptian Theatre's elaborate lobby art

❷ **Julia's on Broadway.** The spotlight is on Broadway at this light-hearted themed restaurant, complete with show-monikered cocktails. It's the perfect spot to grab a bite during a theater tour. I love their "afternoon breakfast"—try the Huevos Rancheros. The emphasis is on fun—and fresh, healthy ingredients. *300 Broadway E.* ☎ *206/860-1818. $*

❸ **Egyptian Theatre.** Though built in 1915, this former Masonic Temple didn't adopt its Egyptian theme until the '80s, when it became home to the Seattle International Film Festival. It features a wide-reaching program of independent films, foreign movies, documentaries and restored classics. ① *15 min. 805 E Pine St. www.siff. net/egyptian-theater.* ☎ *206/781-5755.*

❹ ★★★ **Paramount Theatre.** My one complaint about this opulent theater: I often find myself transfixed by the ceiling instead of the stage. Not that the shows aren't compelling. The Broadway series, silent movies, comedy shows, and diverse range of concerts are first-rate. It's just that the French Renaissance architecture is so lavish, and the intricate ceiling so intriguing, that the architecture *almost* steals the show. Built in 1928 as Seattle's most spectacular theater, the Paramount treated guests to stage shows and silent films, shown to the accompaniment of a custom-made Wurlitzer organ. Not a bit of its former splendor has been lost, a fact often noted by

The 1928 Paramount Theatre retains its original splendor.

affluent Seattle brides, who make their entrances down the grand staircase in the lobby. At wedding receptions, the theater's sloped seating area converts to a flat hardwood floor for tables and dancing. ① 15 min. 911 Pine St. ☎ 206/467-5510. www.stgpresents.org. Free admission to the lobby.

⑤ ★★ ACT (A Contemporary Theatre). The focus at this nationally recognized theater is on

ACT Theatre stages mostly contemporary works.

presenting contemporary and new plays, a number of which have gone on to New York. However, one of its most popular performances is the classic "Christmas Carol." The beautiful 1924 terracotta building became home to the ACT in 1973. The theater doesn't have a parking lot, but ample parking is available across the street, in the Convention Center Garage. ① 15 min. 700 Union St. ☎ 206/292-7676. www.acttheatre.org.

⑥ ★★★ 5th Avenue Theatre. The 5th was one of the first vaudeville houses built with an Asian design in the 1920s, when all things Eastern were in vogue. Architect Robert Reamer intended the magnificent interior to look like three Imperial Chinese masterpieces: the Forbidden City, the Temple of Heaven, and the Summer Palace. The theater has undergone two transformations since its vaudeville days: first, to a movie palace; then, after a major renovation in the '80s, to a playhouse. Its stage has been graced by an array of personalities including Katharine Hepburn, Robert Goulet, and Carol Channing. The 5th hosts more than 100 live performances each year, including touring Broadway musicals and Broadway-bound shows. Nearby parking garages offer evening discounts. ⏱ *15 min. 1308 5th Ave.* ☎ *206/625-1900. www. 5thavenue.org.*

⑦ ★★ Cinerama. If you recall the old wraparound Cinerama films (like *Lawrence of Arabia*), you're in for a treat at the historic Seattle Cinerama Theatre, one of only three venues in the world that can show the classic three-panel Cinerama films. Once sentenced to demolition, Cinerama was saved in 1999 by former Microsoft co-founder Paul Allen. And, as you might expect, the renovation was done in high-tech fashion, with a 90-foot-long louvered screen and cutting-edge acoustics. There's also a smaller screen for contemporary films. The theater also underwent a major renovation that brought better digital sound and a 3D experience. ⏱ *15 min. 2100 4th Ave.* ☎ *206/441-3080. www. cinerama.com.*

⑧ Seattle Repertory Theatre. This Tony Award–winning regional venue has two stages, both housed in a graceful curved building in the northwest corner of Seattle Center. The focus here is on serious art theater. ⏱ *15 min. 155 Mercer St.* ☎ *206/443-2222. www.seattle rep.org.*

⑨ Intiman Theatre. Specializing in international drama—both classics and contemporary plays—this intimate Tony-winning regional theater, sandwiched between the Seattle Repertory Theatre and the Seattle opera's McCaw Hall, has launched world premieres. ⏱ *15 min. 201 Mercer St.* ☎ *206/ 269-1900. www.intiman.org.*

The elaborate ceiling of the 5th Avenue Theatre

Seattle for Kids

1 Seattle Aquarium
2 Seattle Children's Theatre
3 Seattle Center Armory Food Court
4 Seattle Children's Museum
5 Pacific Science Center
6 Seattle Center Skatepark
7 Center for Wooden Boats
8 Northwest Puppet Center
9 Woodland Park Zoo
10 Green Lake Park

Though Seattle is heavy on young professionals with dogs instead of kids, it is an unusually child-friendly town. Glaring shopkeepers and condescending waiters are rare. Kids love the natural beauty of Puget Sound, the mountains, and parks; and there is a wealth of activities to keep youngsters busy any time of the year. START: **Bus 99 to Pier 59.**

"Immersive" exhibits at the Seattle Aquarium reveal the beauty of undersea life.

① ★★ **Seattle Aquarium.** A perennial favorite, the aquarium offers stories for tots, crafts for older kids, and animal feedings and presentations. At the tide pool exhibit, kids love to get their hands on anemones and sea stars. There's also a huge aquarium with creatures from Puget Sound. ⏱ *2 hr. 1483 Alaskan Way on Pier 59.* ☎ *206/386-4300. www.seattle aquarium.org. $30 adults, $20 ages 4–13. Daily 9:30am–5pm. See p 99.*

② ★★★ **Seattle Children's Theatre.** It's hard to say who's having more fun, the kids or their parents. The sets are clever, the costumes ingenious, and the acting first rate. The season runs September through June. You can get a healthy snack at intermission, but hurry or you'll spend the whole time waiting in line—in which case you'll miss out on the gift area, stocked with books and clever items that relate to the show.

Afterward, the characters chat with kids and sign autographs. *201 Thomas St. at Seattle Center.* ☎ *206/441-3322. www.sct.org. Ticket prices vary.*

③ **Seattle Center Armory Food Court.** You'll find lots of quick and tasty options here, from Thai noodles to fish and chips. There are plenty of treats as well, from warm, sugar-dusted beignets to homemade taffy. The perfect "grown-up" outing for kids is dinner at the food court, followed by a play at the Seattle Children's Theatre. *305 Harrison St.* ☎ *206/684-7200. $*

④ ★ **Seattle Children's Museum.** Most of the special exhibits here are geared toward the 6-and-under crowd, but children up to 10 will enjoy the hands-on science section and Imagination Studio, where they create art projects. Make that an early stop, in case

Adults and children alike love the inventive performances at the Seattle Children's Theatre.

paint needs to dry, and then pick up the finished product on your way out. In the Lil' Green Thumbs outdoor exhibit, kids learn about growing flowers and veggies and plant their own seed to take home. ⏱ *90 min. 305 Harrison St.* ☎ *206/441-1768. www.thechildrensmuseum. org. $12 adults and children. See p 115.*

⑤ ★★ Pacific Science Center. Older kids will love the interactive exhibits, such as Adventures in 3Dimensions, which shows how 3D technology involves our brains to create special effects. Younger ones go for the crawl-and-climb area, which includes a treehouse and a table-height "stream" for water play. At the Insect Village, kids of all ages thrill and chill to the giant robotic insects and live animal displays. The IMAX shows are outstanding. ⏱ *90 min. 200 2nd Ave. N.* ☎ *206/443-2001. www.pacsci. org. $31 adults, $28 seniors, $23 ages 6–15, $19 ages 3–5; includes IMAX. Price about $10 less without IMAX. Mon, Wed–Fri 10am–5pm; Sat–Sun 10am–6pm. See p 116.*

⑥ ★ Seattle Center Skatepark. Let the kids loose at this 10,000-square-foot, cutting-edge skateboard park. Known to local skateboarders as Sea Sk8, it features a fully skateable plaza, steps and a vertical glass wall. Bring your own board because there are no rentals. ⏱ *1 hr. 2nd Ave. N. & Thomas St.* ☎ *206/684-7200. www. seattlecenter.com/skatepark. Free. Daily during daylight hours.*

⑦ ★ Center for Wooden Boats. A wooden boat festival, fishing derbies, sailing lessons, the Halloween haunted boathouse, storytelling—check the website for all kinds of year-round programs for kids of all ages. You might want to stop by this place on Lake Union just to admire the collection of wooden boats. ⏱ *15 min. 1010 Valley St.* ☎ *206/382-2628. www.cwb. org. Free admission. Prices vary for special events.*

⑧ ★★ Northwest Puppet Center. The Carter Family Marionettes, a local multi-generational family of puppeteers, present high-quality performances geared toward

Hands-on activities at the Pacific Science Center make it a sure bet for kids.

The Carter Family Marionettes are the stars at the Northwest Puppet Center.

children of various ages. The artistry is remarkable, and the genial Carters bring in puppeteers from around the world, and the stories are often based on books or folk tales. After the show, puppets are often brought out on stage for children to come up and touch. There's a puppet museum, too. *9123 15th Ave. NE.* ☎ *206/523-2579. www. nwpuppet.org. Tickets: $11 adults, $9 seniors, $8.50 children. Public shows are on weekend afternoons.*

❾ ★★★ Woodland Park Zoo. Woodland Park has won awards for several exhibits, including the primate area and the African Savanna. The newest exhibits are the Humboldt penguin habitat, where an underwater viewing area gives guests a close-up view of frolicking penguins from Peru, and the fun-loving meerkats area. At Zoomazium, an indoor play area, kids 8 and under can explore nature, listen to stories and burn off a little energy. Special programs are offered for toddlers in the morning and school-aged kids in the afternoon. The zoo also has a

beautiful 1918 carousel; rides cost $2. ⏱ *2 hr. 750 N. 50th St.* ☎ *206/ 684-4800. www.zoo.org. May–Sept: $21 ages 13–64, $15 ages 3–12; Oct– Apr: $15 ages 13–64, $10 ages 3–12. May–Sept daily 9:30am–6pm; Oct– Apr: daily 9:30am–4pm.*

❿ Green Lake Park. Seattle's favorite place to walk, the 2.8-mile path around lovely Green Lake draws moms with strollers, joggers, dog-walkers, bicyclists, and nature-lovers. An **indoor warm-water pool** (☎ 206/684-4961; $5.50 ages 18-64, $3.75 ages 1–17 and 65+, free under 1) offers family, public and lap swimming. Tots can splash away in a large outdoor wading pool, open daily 11am–8pm from mid-June to Labor Day. This is a great playground for younger kids, because it's divided into separate areas for toddlers and their rowdier older siblings. ⏱ *1 hr. 7201 E Green Lake Dr. N.* ☎ *206/684-4075. www.seattle.gov/parks. The park is open 24 hr.*

The Woodland Park Zoo is famous for its tigers, as well as lions, bears and primates.

Caffeinated Seattle

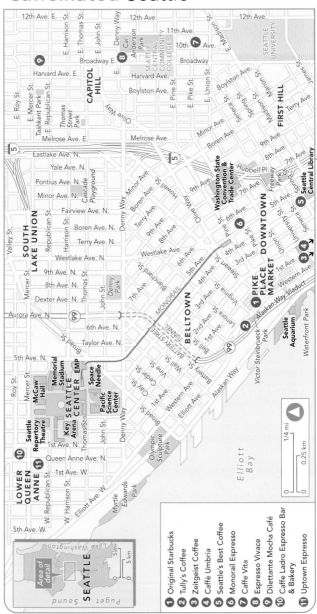

1 Original Starbucks
2 Tully's Coffee
3 Zeitgeist Coffee
4 Caffè Umbria
5 Seattle's Best Coffee
6 Monorail Espresso
7 Caffe Vita
8 Espresso Vivace
9 Dilettante Mocha Café
10 Caffe Ladro Espresso Bar & Bakery
11 Uptown Espresso

SEATTLE

Area of detail

Puget Sound

Lake Washington

Even inveterate tea-drinkers can't help but get caught up in the coffee frenzy that permeates Seattle. Pumpkin-spice lattes, peppermint mochas, white chocolate lattes with raspberry, caramel macchiatos—who could resist their favorite flavors blended tastefully with the drug that keeps Seattleites going through the drizzle? Purists may opt for espresso or a simple cappuccino. If you just don't like coffee, try a chai tea latte. There's no coffee in it, just creamy, delightfully spiced tea that makes the world seem warm and cozy. In the summer, order your favorite drink served over ice. Don't worry about being picky; the person in line ahead of you is likely to demand a double short half-caff extra-hot soy no-foam latte. Watch the barista's face; he or she won't blink an eye. START: **Bus 10, 99, 113, 121 or 122 to Pike Place Market.**

❶ ★ Starbucks. You must begin, of course, where Seattle's—and, arguably, America's—coffee culture began back in 1971. The very first Starbucks, at Pike Place Market, still features the chain's original mascot, the topless mermaid, an image that has been toned down over the years in other locations. Many coffee-lovers gripe that Starbucks stores are ubiquitous; but their flavored drinks are consistently good from store to store and the stores are always good places to stop when you need to check your email or work on the internet. The original location is stand-up only and the lines can be long. *The original: 1912 Pike Pl.* ☎ *206/448-8762. www.starbucks.com.*

The first latte vento was served at this original Starbucks coffee house—and the rest is history.

Zeitgeist offers an urbane oasis from busy city life.

❷ ★ Tully's Coffee. With shops in several Western states—including a number in Seattle—Tully's still roasts its coffee painstakingly, in small batches in antique roasters. The stores are friendly and welcoming, the drinks and baked goods terrific, and they usually have tables where kids can read and draw while the grown-ups sit by the fireplace and chat. My favorite is the one near Pike Place Market (2001 Western Ave. # 110A; ☎ 206/443-1915). *The original: 1401 4th Ave.* ☎ *206/ 625-0600. www.tullyscoffeeshops. com.*

❸ ★★ Zeitgeist Coffee. This spacious, hip European-style coffeehouse serves up film screenings and rotating works by up-and-coming artists along with its popular Italian beans, illy caffè. *See p 52.*

❹ ★★★ Caffè Umbria. The Bizzarri family has been roasting beans since Emanuele's grandfather Ornello opened his first shop in Perugia, Italy. Five blends are available, including fair-trade beans. Umbria's Italian-style coffee almost makes you feel like you're in Italy. You can enjoy a heavenly extra-foamy cappuccino right here in Pioneer Square. *See p 15.*

❺ ★ Seattle's Best Coffee. An early player on the local coffee scene, Seattle's Best Coffee was bought out by Starbucks a few years ago. But SBCs are still allowed to serve their own coffee blends. The chain got its name many years ago, after winning a contest for the best cuppa joe in town. *Downtown: 1100 4th Ave.* ☎ *206/623-0104; Pike Place Market: 1530 Post Alley.* ☎ *206/467-7700. www.seattlesbest.com.*

❻ ★ Monorail Espresso. Back in 1980, even before Starbucks began selling coffee drinks at its original store (just beans before that), Chuck Beek came up with the idea of running a little espresso cart in Seattle. It was the first espresso cart in the world it was located beneath the monorail track. Fifteen years later, with a greatly expanded coffee menu (are you up for a maple bacon latte?), Chuck opened a permanent shop a few blocks away. It's a great spot to drink in a little history with your double latte. *520 Pike St. (at 5th).* ☎ *206/625-0449.*

❼ ★ Caffe Vita. This roastery also claims many devotees who swear by its beans and blends from around the world. Vita forms relationships with coffee growers in Africa, Indonesia, and the Americas, and offers a wide variety of tastes. Locations include Capitol Hill: *1005 E. Pike St.* ☎ *206/709-4440. Queen Anne: 813 5th Ave. N.* ☎ *206/285-9662. www.caffevita.com.*

❽ ★★★ Espresso Vivace. David Schomer's slow-roasting

Is this really Seattle's best? You'll have to try all the stops on our tour, then decide.

Cozy Café Vita serves coffee brewed from beans sourced all over the world.

process is designed to produce a sweet caramel flavor, and the roasting is stopped early to keep the oils in and prevent a burned flavor. For many coffee aficionados, this is as good as it gets. *Capitol Hill cafe location: 532 Broadway Ave. E.* ☎ *206/860-2722. Capitol Hill Stand: 321 Broadway Ave. E. www.espresso vivace.com.*

⑨ ★★ Dilettante Mocha Café. Silky-smooth, top-quality chocolate makes for sinfully rich mochas, and the presentation is style. The chocolate melts in pots right beside the espresso machine. *Locations include 538 Broadway E.* ☎ *206/329-6463. Map p 89.*

⑩ ★★★ Caffe Ladro Espresso Bar & Bakery. Serving only organic, fair-trade, shade-grown coffee, Caffe Ladro has about a dozen locations around metro Seattle. The urban-hip shops serve delicious quiche and baked goods. Try a Medici latte with orange peel. *600 Queen Anne Ave. N.* ☎ *206/ 282-1549. Downtown: 801 Pine St.* ☎ *206/405-1950. www.caffeladro. com.*

⑪ ★★ Uptown Espresso. This is a serious coffeeshop, with rough wood tables occupied by quietly chatting friends and furiously typing computer-users. The coffee and baked goods are excellent. Lattes come topped with a layer of Uptown's heavenly Velvet Foam. *525 Queen Anne Ave N.* ☎ *206/ 285-3757. Belltown: 2504 4th Ave.* ☎ *206/441-1084. https://velvet foam.com/.*

A cappuccino at Espresso Vivace—almost too pretty to drink

Architecture & Design

1. Safeco Field
2. CenturyLink Field
3. Union Station
4. King Street Station
5. Pioneer Building
6. Pioneer Square Pergola
7. Smith Tower
8. Arctic Building
9. Specialty's Café & Bakery
10. Seattle Central Public Library
11. Seattle Art Museum
12. Banana Republic
13. Amazon Biospheres
14. Museum of Pop Culture (MoPOP)
15. Space Needle

Although a city this young may not have the widest range of architectural styles, there are many historic gems to be found, and Seattleites have put a great deal of cash into preserving their colorful past. Most of the renovations have been undertaken with care, and it is delightful to see the modern uses to which these old buildings have been put, with all due respect paid to their history. But architecture here is hardly stuck in the past. The city's rapid growth and penchant for adventure has attracted world-renowned architects, who have designed a number of cutting-edge buildings. START: **Bus 106, 123, 124, 131 or 132 to Safeco Field.**

CenturyLink Field, home to the Seattle Seahawks

1 ★ Safeco Field. The Seattle Mariners' stadium, erected after the team demanded a new facility to replace the not-so-old but leaky Kingdome, was built amid even more controversy than usual in Seattle. But it has won the hearts of Seattleites, partly because it keeps the rain off but lets the fresh air in. It has one of the few retractable stadium coverings in the country, and the only one that doesn't fully enclose the field. On a perfect sunny day when the roof is open, baseball doesn't get better than this. If you can't make a game, take the hour-long tour offered year-round—you'll get to see off-limits areas such as the private suites and press box, if they're not in use. Even if you're not a sports fan, you'll enjoy the views of the city and sound, and the baseball-inspired art on display by Northwest artists. ⏱ *1 hr. 1250 1st Ave. S.* ☎ *206/346-4001. www.mariners. mlb.com. Tour: $10 adults, $9 seniors, $7 ages 3–12, free under 3. Check website for tour days and times.*

Baseball's Seattle Mariners make ultra-modern Safeco Field their home base.

②ᐧ★ CenturyLink Field. The Mariners weren't the only sports team to demand a new stadium. The Seahawks also insisted on moving out of the ill-fated Kingdome. So it was destroyed in a fantastic implosion and replaced by Century-Link Field. Its graceful double-arched roof, studded with blue lights that glow as you fly into the city or drive along I-5, has become a treasured part of the city's skyline. The roof also overhangs most of the bleachers, keeping about 70% of the fans dry. The field is open-air, and so is the north end, which allows drop-dead views of downtown. If you want to taste the luxury suite experience—and walk right onto the field—take a tour. They're offered all year long. ⏱ *90 min. 800 Occidental Ave. S.* ☎ *206/381-7555. www.centurylinkfield.com. Tours: $14 adults, $10 seniors, $8 ages 4–12; Check website for tour dates and times.*

③ ★ Union Station. Opened in 1911, this was a transcontinental train station for 60 years. Sadly, the vast Beaux Arts building was abandoned and sat around deteriorating until Microsoft billionaire Paul Allen came to the rescue in the 1990s. It landed a National Preservation Award in 2000, and now it serves as the headquarters for Sound Transit, a regional commuter train. Its spectacular hall, which features a beautifully lighted barrel-vaulted ceiling, is rented out for weddings and other grand occasions, and it's easy to see why. In the daytime, natural light pours in through an enormous semi-circular window. The elegant architecture is worth an admiring look. ⏱ *15 min. 401 S. Jackson St.* ☎ *206/682-7275. Free.*

④ ★ King Street Station. This bustling Amtrak and Sound Transit commuter station was built in 1906 for the Great Northern Railway and Northern Pacific Railway. An extensive restoration, completed in 2013, returned it to its former glory. Its elaborate high ceilings were uncovered—hidden since the 1960s by drab suspended tiles. The entry hall, dubbed the Compass Room because of marble-tiled directional points on the floor, has also been refurbished, as has the station's clock tower, once the tallest structure in Seattle. And its clock is once again keeping time. ⏱ *15 min. 303 S. Jackson St.* ☎ *206/382-4125. Free.*

⑤ ★★ Pioneer Building. This elegant, Romanesque-style structure, hurriedly built right after the Great Fire, was named the "finest building west of Chicago" by the American Institute of Architects when it was completed in 1892. The Underground Tour (see p 51) offers a fascinating look at the building and at Seattle's colorful history, if you have the time (tours last 90 min.) ⏱ *15*

The elegant barrel-vaulted interior of Seattle's Union Station, built in 1911

The Victorian-era Pioneer Square Pergola

min. 1st Ave. & Yesler Way. Underground Tour, 610 1st Ave., #200.
☎ 206/682-4646. www.underground
tour.com. $22 adults, $20 seniors,
$10 children 7–12. Tours offered
daily, throughout the day. See p 51.

⑥ ★ Pioneer Square Pergola.
You wouldn't know it today, but
Seattle's eye-catching iron-and-glass
pergola gained its fame for what
once lay beneath: elegant public
restrooms made of marble and
bronze, widely considered the most
luxurious in the world in 1910. People would enter the restrooms on
stairways leading from the pergola.
It was a project in keeping with
Seattle's traditional egalitarian eth-
ics. The "comfort stations" have
long since closed, and the graceful
Victorian pergola itself was crushed
by a veering truck in 2001. Fortu-
nately, it was restored using as much
of the original materials as possible.
🕐 15 min. 1st Ave. & Yesler Way.

⑦ ★★★ Smith Tower. The tallest building west of the Mississippi
when it was built for Mr. Smith of
Smith-Corona typewriter fame in
1914, this impeccably restored and

gleaming 42-story neoclassical
office building is a grand old dame,
worth a visit to see original features
like solid onyx banisters and to ride
in its 1914 brass-caged elevators.
They're the last manually operated
ones on the West Coast. The elaborate Chinese Room, with its ornately
carved teak ceiling, is on the 35th
floor, as is the observation deck.
The panoramic view is spectacular.
Afterwards you can dine, snack or
have a cocktail in the Chinese
Room. 🕐 30 min. 506 2nd Ave.
☎ 206/622-4004. www.smithtower.
com. Observation deck $17 adults,
$13.50 kids 6–12, free 5 & under.
Daily 10am–5pm. (Check first to make
sure no private events are scheduled.)

⑧ ★ Arctic Building. Fondly
dubbed the "Walrus Building," this
eight-story art deco structure was
once an exclusive club for the relatively few gold-miners who struck it
rich in the Yukon. In homage to the
land where the riches were made,
the building featured Alaskan marble hallways and a row of sculpted
walrus heads around the third floor
of the colorful terracotta exterior.
Members could do everything from

Walruses adorn the art deco Arctic Building, in homage to the Alaskan Gold Rush.

sip tea to go bowling here. A few years ago, it was transformed into the Arctic Club Hotel Seattle, featuring period décor. ⏱ *15 min. 700 3rd Ave.* ☎ *206/340-0340. Free admission to the lobby. See p 157.*

🍴 **Specialty's Café & Bakery.** Grab a hearty sandwich or a healthy Cobb salad, followed by a delicious, oven-fresh peanut butter cookie. For the bargain-minded, the day-old baked goods are a good value. *1023 3rd Ave.* ☎ *206/264-0882. $*

⑩ ★★★ **Seattle Central Public Library.** In 2004, Seattle's new, $165 million central public library designed by Dutch architect Rem Koolhaas was the most talked-about building in Seattle, and it remains a modern architectural showpiece. This is not your staid, turn-of-the-century or midcentury-modern library. Architecture aficionados from around the world come specifically to see it. Outside, its odd, asymmetrical glass and steel angles jut over the sidewalk. Inside, patrons walk up a spiraling ramp that gradually leads to the top floor. Elevators and neon-hued escalators are another option. On your way up, stunning views of the surrounding downtown buildings can be seen through the netlike steel structure. And it's a real library, too. ⏱ *30 min. 1000 4th Ave.* ☎ *206/386-4636. www.spl.org. Free. Mon–Thurs 10am–8pm, Fri–Sat 10am–6pm, Sun noon–6pm.*

⑪ ★★★ **Seattle Art Museum.** This museum, with its ungainly cliché of a postmodern façade, was designed by Robert Venturi. The museum moved to this location after spending its first 60 years in that art-deco building in Volunteer Park that now houses the Seattle Asian Art Museum (see p 29). The outside of the building—the upper 12 floors of which are office space—already looks dated, but the interior galleries are impressive.

Completed in 2004, the Seattle Central Public Library is an architectural landmark.

1 hr. ☎ 206/654-3100. www.
seattleartmuseum.org. $20 adults,
$18 seniors over 62, $13 students &
kids 13–17, free for kids 12 & under.
1300 1st Ave. Wed–Sun 10am–5pm,
Thurs-Fri until 9pm. See p 65.

⑫ ★ **Banana Republic.** Yes, it's
a chain store, but it's set in a beautiful building that once housed the
old Coliseum Theatre, built in 1916
by renowned Seattle architect B.
Marcus Priteca as a movie palace
for showing silent films. The original
grandeur is preserved in the building's white terracotta exterior. 🕐 15
min. 500 Pike St. ☎ 206/622-2303.

⑬ ★ **Amazon Biospheres.** A
work-in-progress, Amazon's corporate headquarters consists of three
rather humdrum towers with three
rounded biospheres between them.
Stroll by for a look at Seattle's newest $4 billion development in the
South Lake Union area. It's full of
hyper-trendy restaurants and eventually the plant-filled biospheres

will be open to the public. 🕐 15
min. Corner of 6th and Lenorat.

⑭ ★ **Museum of Pop Culture.**
Without question, this is the oddest
structure in Seattle, built by Microsoft co-founder Paul Allen, a huge
fan of the late local guitar legend
Jimi Hendrix. At ground level the
museum looks like amorphous
blobs of colorful sheet metal, but
from the air, designer Frank Gehry's
building is supposed to resemble
one of Hendrix's famed smashed
guitars. (But who can look at a
building from the air?) Originally
called Experience Music Project,
the museum rebranded itself in
2017 as MoPOP, but some exhibits
from its earlier music-centric days
remain. What's big now is the
expanded Star Trek and Science
Fiction museums. I personally think
it's way overpriced for what it is.
🕐 1 hr. 325 5th Ave. N. (at Seattle
Center). ☎ 206/770-2700.
www.mopop.org. ☎ 206/770-2700.

The Museum of Pop Culture is housed in one of Seattle's most distinctive buildings.

Built for the 1962 World's Fair, the Space Needle soon became the symbol of Seattle.

$28 adults, $25 seniors, $19 ages 5–17. Daily summer 10am–7pm, winter 10am-5pm.

⓯ ★★★ **Space Needle.** In typical Seattle style, there was much disagreement over what the centerpiece for the 1962 World's Fair should look like and where it should go. The futuristic design morphed considerably from the original "Needle" sketched out on a paper placemat by a hotel chain president. By the time architect John Graham (designer of Seattle's Northgate, the first shopping mall in the world) and his team came up with something everyone agreed on, the fair was only 1½ years away. Construction went at breakneck speed, and the last elevator car arrived the day before the fair opened. The Space Needle went on to become the world-recognized symbol for Seattle, and a decade ago got a snazzy $20 million facelift. ① *1 hr. 400 Broad St.* ☎ *206/905-2100. Observation deck tickets: $19-$29 adults, $16-$22 seniors, $13-$18 ages 4–13, Mon–Thurs 10am–9pm; Fri–Sat 9:30am–10:30pm; Sun 9:30am–9:30pm. See p 115.* ●

Heads Up!

One of the best ways to sample the city's architecture is to take one of the many popular walking tours offered by the Seattle Architecture Foundation. Most tours last about 2 hours and showcase a wide variety of styles and locations, from the Seattle waterfront to the art deco district to the Craftsman bungalows north of the city. There are even tours for families, "Eye Spy Seattle" geared at adults and kids ages 5–10, and the Family Tour for grown-ups with kids ages 8–14. Check the website (www.seattlearchitecture.org) for dates and times. Most tours cost $18 in advance or $25 for same-day tickets, $10 for children 5–12 (Family Tour only).

50

Pioneer Square

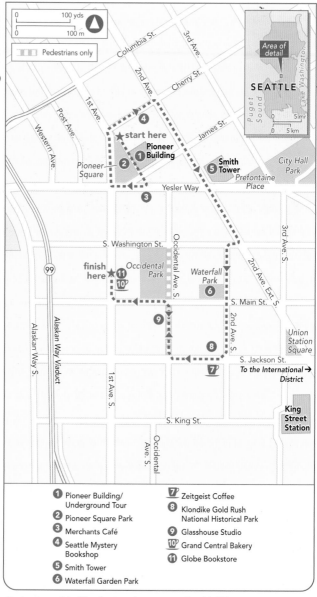

1 Pioneer Building/
Underground Tour
2 Pioneer Square Park
3 Merchants Café
4 Seattle Mystery
Bookshop
5 Smith Tower
6 Waterfall Garden Park

7 Zeitgeist Coffee
8 Klondike Gold Rush
National Historical Park
9 Glasshouse Studio
10 Grand Central Bakery
11 Globe Bookstore

Previous page: A traditional gate at the entrance to Seattle's Chinatown

For a taste of Seattle's gritty past, wander the oddly angled streets of Pioneer Square, where some of the city's finest art galleries intermingle with the shops and restaurants. The ornate Victorian brick and stone buildings were erected after the Great Fire of 1889 by local fat cats, eager to get back to selling supplies— and services of every kind—to prospectors en route to the Yukon. At night the district's clubs still spring to life. START: **Bus 10, 11, 16, 66 or 99 to Pioneer Square.**

Historic Pioneer Square Park is low-key by day and a nightlife hub after dark.

❶ ★★★ **Pioneer Building/ Underground Tour.** Begin your tour at the very spot where pioneer Henry Yesler built his sawmill in the 1850s, then rebuilt after the Great Fire. He hired famed architect Elmer Fisher—who designed more than 50 post-fire structures—to create the stylish building. Go inside and check out Doc Maynard's Pub and the entertaining Underground Tour, which gives you the insider scoop on Seattle's colorful past. This is one of my favorite ways to amuse visitors. The guides are as funny and irreverent as stand-up comics when they tell the story of Seattle's beginnings. ⏱ *90 min. 1st Avenue & Yesler Way. Underground Tour, 608 1st Ave. (☎ 206/682-4646. www.underground tour.com. $22 adults, $20 seniors & students, $10 children 7–12; offered daily, throughout the day.*

❷ ★ **Pioneer Square Park.** The pergola (see p 45), Seattle's most beloved hunk of iron, graces the south end of this triangular park— really more of a courtyard—directly in front of the Pioneer Building. It's popular with tourists, but also with vagrants looking for a bench to while away the day. Another rebuilt item in the park is a 60-foot Tlingit totem pole, a replacement for one stolen from an Alaskan village in 1938 by a group of prominent Seattle citizens. When the pole burned years later, the city hired the descendants of the original Native American carvers to produce its replacement. ⏱ *15 min. 1st Avenue & Yesler Way.*

❸ ★ **Merchants Cafe.** Step back in time at the oldest watering hole in Seattle. Back in the day, prospectors would quaff a brew at the saloon, then head upstairs to the brothel, now converted into apartments. So much gold was dropped here by prospectors on the weekends, it came to be known as the Sunday Bank. Today, you can enjoy lunch, dinner, or a beer in the remodeled restaurant. ⏱ *15 min. 109 Yesler Way. ☎ 206/935-7625. Sun–Fri 11am–midnight, Sat 11am–2am.*

Idyllic Waterfall Garden Park is one of Seattle's best-kept secrets.

④ ★★ Seattle Mystery Bookshop. Whodunit aficionados can spend hours tracking down mystery books, both collectable and current, at this terrific little shop. There are frequent author signings, and if you miss one you like, check with JB—he keeps a large number of autographed volumes on hand. ⏱ *15 min. 117 Cherry St. ☎ 206/587-5737. www.seattlemystery.com. Mon–Sat 10am–5pm, Sun noon–5pm.*

⑤ ★★ Smith Tower. Ride the antique caged elevators up to the 35th floor observation deck for a fabulous view of downtown Seattle and Mt. Rainier, though the building is now dwarfed by more modern 'scrapers. ⏱ *30 min. 506 2nd Ave. ☎ 206/622-4004. www.smith tower.com. Observation deck $17 adults, $13.50 seniors and kids 6–12, free under 6. Daily 10am–5pm (Check first to make sure no private events are scheduled). See p 45.*

⑥ ★★ Waterfall Garden Park. This little-known oasis is my favorite place to hang out with a latte. You'll know you're there by the crash of water tumbling 22 feet down a wall of boulders, drowning out the urban bustle. The two-level gem of a park was built in honor of United Parcel Service employees. At lunchtime, office workers sit among its trees and flowers to escape the concrete. ⏱ *15 min. 219 2nd Ave. S.*

⑦ ★★ Zeitgeist Coffee Drop by for a muffuletta and espresso and then enjoy people-watching or discussing world events. If the conversation turns contentious, a world globe and a monster-size dictionary are on hand to help resolve matters. *171 S. Jackson St. ☎ 206/583-0497. $*

First Thursday Gallery Walk

The country's first art walk, this monthly event is great fun, and a terrific way to catch all the latest exhibits. Best of all, it's free. First Thursday showcases the Pioneer Square area's eclectic array of galleries. The best new artists and exhibits are featured, and the art ranges from paintings to sculptures to blown glass. It all starts at Main Street and Occidental, in Occidental Park, where vendors hawk their art and street musicians entertain. The neighborhood galleries open their doors, visitors peruse the art and it usually turns into a fun, mellow scene. The art walk runs noon–8pm the first Thursday of every month (www.firstthursdayseattle.com).

Watch artisans at work at the Glasshouse Studio.

❽ ★ Klondike Gold Rush National Historical Park.

In 1897 and 1898, 120,000 fortune hunters stampeded through Seattle and headed north to Canada's Yukon Territory, where gold had recently been discovered, and the impact on the city was enormous. This indoor "park" tells the story of the Klondike Gold Rush with great attention to detail (e.g., 1 in 10 of those headed for the gold fields were women). ⏱ *1 hr. 319 2nd Ave. S. ☎ 206/220-4240. www.nps.gov/klse. Free. Daily 9am–5pm. See p 22.*

❾ ★★ Glasshouse Studio.

Seattle is home to some of the world's finest glass artists. (Dale Chihuly, famed for his outrageously colorful, fanciful works, has his own museum [p 93] near the Space

The Globe Bookstore is a fixture of Pioneer Square.

Needle.) Here, you can watch artists at work in Seattle's oldest glass-blowing studio as they shape glowing globs of molten glass into amazing things of beauty. You can buy their vases, chandeliers, jewelry, and more in the adjacent shop. ⏱ *30 min. 311 Occidental Ave. S. ☎ 206/682-9939. www.glasshouse-studio.com. Mon–Sat 10am–5pm, Sun 11am–4pm.*

❿ Grand Central Bakery.

You'll smell it before you see it. Some of the best pastries, sandwiches, and soups in town come from this bakery, which you can enter from Occidental Park or the Grand Central Arcade on 1st Avenue. Start with a basil egg sandwich, followed by a sweet-tooth-pleasing chocolate croissant, then take home a Como Loaf, one of Seattle's original artisan loaves. *214 1st Ave. S. ☎ 206/622-3644. $*

⓫ ★ Globe Bookstore.

From Beowulf to Harry Potter, you'll likely find what you're looking for in this wonderful, musty bookshop. The focus is on used and collectable books, but you'll find new titles as well. The cookbook and children's sections are especially impressive. The owner really knows his stuff, and the prices are sometimes less than half the price you'll see on eBay. ⏱ *30 min. 218 1st Ave. S. ☎ 206/682-6882. Daily 10am–6pm.*

Pike Place Market

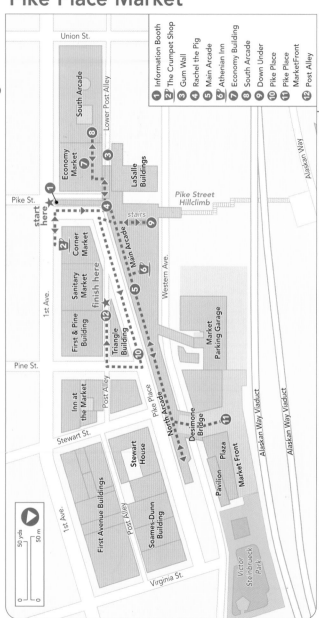

1. Information Booth
2. The Crumpet Shop
3. Gum Wall
4. Rachel the Pig
5. Main Arcade
6. Athenian Inn
7. Economy Building
8. South Arcade
9. Down Under
10. Pike Place
11. Pike Place MarketFront
12. Post Alley

Buzzing with tourists, savvy locals, and finicky restaurateurs, Pike Place Market is the heart and soul of Seattle. Kids love the street performers and the "flying" fish; adults are mesmerized by the mind-boggling variety of shops, food, and entertainment. You can find just about anything you want here, from salted herring to $4,000-a-pound Piemontese truffles to handmade mandolins. It's a wonderful place to spend a day—or two. Plus, it's the only neighborhood in town where jaywalking won't get you a ticket! START: **Bus 10, 99, 113, 121 or 122 to Pike Place Market.**

1 Information Booth. Make this your first stop—not just to pick up a market newspaper and map, but to arm yourself with coupons for tours, including the popular Argosy Cruises trips around the harbor and to the locks connecting Lake Washington and Lake Union, and discounts on current theatrical shows in town. (Also check www.goldstar.com and click on "Seattle" at the bottom of the page for deals on tickets.) *Pike St. & 1st Ave.* ☎ *206/228-7291. www.pikeplace market.org.*

Beloved Rachel the Pig holds court at Pike Place Market.

2 ★ The Crumpet Shop. Start your day off here at this British-flavored spot that's been in business for more than 40 years. Even coffee addicts will appreciate the variety of tasty whole-leaf teas served daily. Of course, there are also the mouth-watering crumpets, baked fresh daily. Crumpet purists can get one with just marmalade, but I love them with smoked salmon, cream cheese, and cucumber. Come early, and you can watch the bakers at work. *1503 1st Ave. www.thecrumpetshop.com.* ☎ *206/682-1598. $*

3 Gum Wall. If you're not too easily grossed out, take a detour down the ramp from the Information Booth before you tackle the Market proper. Hang a left and be careful not to lean against the wall! It is covered in several inches'

worth of chewed gum. After several years of futile efforts to clean it off, the city dubbed it a tourist attraction. *1530 Post Alley.*

4 ★ Rachel the Pig. Seattle's beloved bronze porker stands just under the famous neon "Public Market Center" sign and clock. Drop a few coins in the piggybank and you'll be helping to help support the Market Foundation's charities. The civic-minded folks who saved the Market in the 1970s decided the revival should include social services, such as low-income apartments for seniors. *Pike Place & Pike Street.*

5 ★★★ Main Arcade. Get ready for sensory overload! The tenderest asparagus, freshest daffodils, richest sockeye salmon, can be found here. Start right behind Rachel the Pig and elbow your way through the North Arcade. Everything sold here is required to be

The Best **Neighborhood** Walks

Spirit of the Market

Tales abound of ghosts and ghouls wandering among the narrow old hallways, stairwells, dusty corners, and nooks and crannies of Pike Place Market, looking for closure—or at least their old haunts. So many ghosts have been reported by workers and visitors to the Market that a few even have names—like Jacob, supposedly a horse groom in real life, back in the days when the Market had stables. Now, he's said to haunt the Down Under, where he reportedly mixes up the bead colors at the Bead Zone shop. Jacob favors red beads. Then there's Frank, who supposedly introduces himself to guests at the Alibi Room nightclub before fading away. And more than one ghost has been reported hanging around Kell's Irish Pub on Post Alley, the former site of a mortuary. The Market's colorful history includes brothels, orphans who worked for pennies, a deadly flu epidemic, and the old mortuary. It all adds up to fertile ground for spirits. Even if you don't believe in them, you'll enjoy taking a 75-minute Market **Ghost Tour** (www. seattleghost.com). Tours start at 5 and 7pm Thursday through Sunday, but check the website, because the company changed ownership and moved to a new location.

grown, caught or created locally. From the world-famous fish throwers at **Pike Place Fish Market** to the tulip-growers from Skagit Valley, the North Arcade is alive with scents, sounds, and colors. Salad greens with edible flowers? Chocolate pasta? Pepper jelly? You'll find them all here. Try the tasty free samples at **Sosio's Fruit &**

Be sure to dodge the flying fish as you head through the fish market.

A multi-talented street performer at Pike Place Market

Produce, and stop for a complimentary cup of specially blended MarketSpice Tea at **MarketSpice,** which has been here since 1911. Head to the back of the shop and look for the carafe. On the north end of the Main Arcade, you'll find the handmade-craft booths, where you can buy anything from clay ocarinas to watercolor paintings of umbrellas. ⓘ *90 min. Mon–Sat 10am–6pm; Sun 11am–5pm. (Fine-dining restaurants stay open later.)*

❻ ★ **The Athenian Inn.** Tucked off the Main Arcade, this is a favorite hangout of longtime Seattleites—and the tourists who remember it from "Sleepless in Seattle." You can get all-day breakfast here or seafood straight from the Market. The Athenian, now over a hundred years old, is a dark, homey kind of place with a long bar. Sit upstairs for the best views of Puget Sound. *1517 Pike Place.* ☎ *206/624-7166. www.athenianinn. com. $$*

❼ ★ **Economy Building.** On the corner of this building, beside the Information Booth, is **First and Pike News ★,** where the shelves groan under the weight of newspapers from around the world and magazines of every ilk. **DeLaurenti Specialty Food Market** is a favorite spot for Seattleites to buy wine, cheeses, and olive oil. It also has a terrific deli. On your way to the Economy Atrium, you'll pass by the nut, crepe, and doughnut kiosks. ⓘ *15 min.*

❽ ★ **South Arcade.** The Economy Building opens onto a newer row of shops and restaurants, including **Pike Pub & Brewery,** one of the area's many excellent

Dining at the Market

You won't go hungry at Pike Place Market, where dining options range from booths selling sausage, noodles, or pastries to first-rate restaurants like **Place Pigalle** (p 130), perched over the water and serving mussels to die for. For a cheap lunch, pick up sandwiches in the market, then head toward the water from Rachel the Pig, where there's a tucked-away indoor sitting area with the same panoramic view of the sound that you'll get in the high-end restaurants.

Tour the Market

There's no happier place in Seattle than the Market, where every turn brings a kaleidoscope of produce, crafts, garrulous vendors, and shoppers from around the world. On the hour-long **Market Heritage Tour** (www.publicmarkettours.com; $15 for adults, $13 for seniors/ages 13–17, $10 for children 12 and under), you can pick up some great insider tips on shopping the market, while learning the history on how it came to be in 1907, and how it almost came not to be in the 1970s. (Fortunately, Seattleites decided they couldn't bear to see their market turned into parking garages and office buildings.) The tour runs Friday through Sunday at 2pm, rain or shine, and meets at the corner of Western Avenue and Virginia Street. But if you're more into sampling some of the best the market has to offer, **Seattle Food Tours** (☎ 206/725-4483; www.seattlefoodtours.com) offers a daily 2½-hour walk. Delectable edibles might include smoked salmon, homemade gelato, to-die-for clam chowder, and locally grown fruit.

micro-breweries. **Northwest Tribal Art** is a great place to find colorful masks, totem poles, soapstone figurines, and silver jewelry crafted by local Native Americans. ⏱ *15 min.*

⑨ ★ Down Under. Pike Place Market is perched on the top of a hillside, with a labyrinth of eclectic stores sprawling beneath the Main Arcade. It's worth venturing down the staircase to explore them. The shops are jammed with gems, books, ethnic clothing, and jewelry, and there's even an old-fashioned barbershop. Craft stores sell unusual items, including **Afghani Crafts** women's clothing; **Hands of the World,** featuring folk art mainly from developing nations; and **Polish Pottery Place,** where beautifully detailed items are made by a handful of families who've been at it for generations. ⏱ *30 min.*

⑩ ★★ Pike Place. Once you've jostled your way through the market and out into the fresh air (or

drizzle), you're far from done. A brick street runs between the Main Arcade and several facing blocks, and brims with shops, food stands, restaurants, and yet more produce.

Pike Place Market features farm fresh fruit and veggies from all over the Northwest.

Sweet temptations at Pike Place Market

The "Big Ass Grapes" at the corner shop are appropriately named. This area is just as lively as the inside Market, with street performers entertaining the crowds. Someone might be tickling the ivories of a full-size piano on a street corner, or showing off the vocabulary of the parrot perched on his shoulder. The ethnic food stands are great places to grab a snack. Try the steamed-pork hum bao and red bean sesame balls at **Mee Sum Pastry.** Or, for more substantial fare, **Piroshky Piroshky** serves an array of delicious savory and sweet pastries. I usually order the potato and mushroom, with a marzipan piroshky for dessert. The original **Starbucks** is right in the mix, for a latte to wash it all down (see p 39). ⏱ *30 min.*

⑪ ★★ **Pike Place Market-Front.** The newest expansion of Pike Place Market, called

MarketFront, opened in June 2017. You get to it by re-entering the Market from Pike Street at Stewart Street. Cross an overpass over Western Avenue and you'll come to the new market building extension and a plaza overlooking Elliott Bay with stairs down to the Waterfront. ⏱ *15 min.*

⑫ ★★ **Post Alley.** Hike back into the Market and east up the hill for half a block and you'll find yourself on a winding little street where the din is lower but the shops and cafes still delightful. **Perennial Tearoom** (1910 Post Alley; ☎ 206/448-4054) is a lovely place to stop for a spot of tea; then pick out a few varieties from the wall of teas to enjoy later. The shop stocks teas and teapots from around the world. A block farther south on Post, you can find classy souvenirs—no kidding—at **Made in Washington.** ⏱ *15 min.*

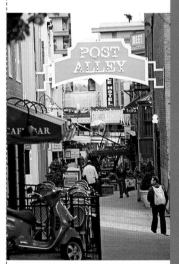

Charming Post Alley is the perfect spot to escape the hubbub of Pike Place Market.

Downtown

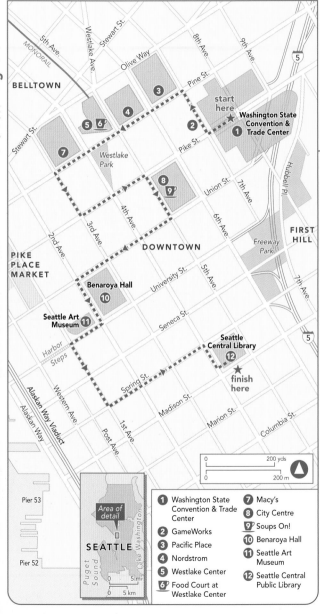

1 Washington State Convention & Trade Center

2 GameWorks

3 Pacific Place

4 Nordstrom

5 Westlake Center

6 Food Court at Westlake Center

7 Macy's

8 City Centre

9 Soups On!

10 Benaroya Hall

11 Seattle Art Museum

12 Seattle Central Public Library

Seattle's downtown core is a world-class destination, bustling with local office workers and shoppers and gawkers from all over the globe. Once in decline, this neighborhood was livened up more than two decades ago by the dotcom millionaires. That came right on the heels of the grunge rock era, which had already focused the world's attention on the Emerald City. Downtown tenants include Nordstrom, the world-famous department store that started here as a humble shoe store in 1901; the world's first Game-Works, dreamed up in part by Steven Spielberg; and Westlake Mall, which is also where you catch the monorail to Seattle Center or Central Link to Sea-Tac. Today, Seattle's downtown is vibrant, colorful, and one of the most walkable in the country. START: **Bus 306, 312, 10, 11, 14 to the Washington State Convention & Trade Center.**

❶ ★ Washington State Convention & Trade Center. Space was an issue when Seattle's convention center was built in 1988, and it was solved with a unique freeway-straddling design. Look up if you're driving on I-5 and you'll see the center's greenery draped along the overpass. Just a few years later, when the city's economy began to skyrocket, it became clear that the convention center needed to expand. The problem? There was nowhere to go, except across Pike Street. So that's just where the other half went in 2001, connected to the original building by an enormous glass skybridge. Enter on the south side of Pike Avenue and ride up the multiple escalators to check out the ever-changing local art exhibits. If it's raining, you can hang out in the underground concourse, which starts at the convention center, winds under the Seattle Hilton and past shops, cafes, and historical exhibits, and comes out at 5th Avenue Theatre and the Rainier Square Shopping Center. The Convention Center serves as the venue for, among other things, the big annual Pacific Northwest Flower & Garden Show in February, where I've given a couple of talks. ⏱ *15 min. 800*

Convention Place. ☎ *206/447-5000. www.wscc.com. Daily 6am–10pm.*

❷ ★ GameWorks. This 20,000-square-foot virtual-entertainment center is way too loud for my ears, but for kids (including many of the grown-up variety) it's a paradise with 180 video, interactive, ticket and prize games. There's a cafe, a sports bar and a pool room upstairs. On Thursday, you can play video games from 5pm to close for $10. ⏱ *15 min. 1511 7th Ave.* ☎ *206/521-0952. www.gameworks. com/locations/seattle. Mon–Thurs 11am–midnight, Fri 11am–1am, Sat 10am–1am, Sun 10am–midnight.*

Get your shopping fix at 5-story Pacific Place mall.

Shop Savvy

Shopping at Pacific Place can be a full-day experience. But if you'd rather skip the national chain stores and focus on the local highlights, stop by **Twist ★★★**, a Northwest boutique that's as colorful as it is fun. The glassware and home decor items will lure you in; the unusual jewelry by artists around the world will keep you browsing. And don't miss the chic **Sixth Avenue Wine Seller,** where owner Beverly Shimada pours wines from around the world for $6 a glass during happy hour, from 3 to 6pm weekdays. You can also grab a bite from the yummy menu of shareable plates.

❸ ★ **Pacific Place.** This downtown mall, adjacent to Nordstrom, contains five levels of upscale shop-o-tainment, including Tiffany & Co., Ann Taylor, Barney's New York, Coach, MaxMara, six restaurants, and a multiplex movie theater. A mall-wide renovation began in 2017 to make it more appealing. In-the-know Seattle drivers headed downtown park at Pacific Place because it's centrally located, owned by the city, and one of the best deals in a town where parking is at a premium. At night, after 5pm, there's a special rate of $6. ⏱ *1 hr. 6th Ave. & Pine St.* ☎ *206/405-2655. www. pacificplaceseattle.com. Mon–Sat 10am–8pm, Sun 11am–7pm.*

❹ ★★★ **Nordstrom.** The Nordstroms, one of Seattle's oldest families, moved their flagship department store in 1998 from its cramped quarters to an empty 1918 building that was the former home of the iconic Frederick & Nelson department store. Nordstrom has come a long way since Swedish immigrant John Nordstrom opened his first shoe store in 1901, using Gold Rush money he brought back from Alaska. My favorite story about the chain's legendary customer service is about a businessman who called the store from the airport, in a panic because he didn't have a tie for a business meeting. A salesperson was dispatched to the airport with a selection of ties. Considering Seattle's tangled traffic, I wouldn't count on the ties arriving in time these days, but the store's service is still hard to beat. And the shoes ★★★ are still exquisite. But before I try on a pair, I usually walk a block south to check out Nordstrom Rack (400 Pine St.), where you can save up to 75% on clothing and shoes. ⏱ *30 min. 500 Pine St.* ☎ *206/628-2111.*

The first Nordstrom store, now part of a nationwide chain, opened in Seattle in 1901.

Bronze plates at Macy's date to 1929 and depict the industries of the Northwest.

Mon–Sat 9:30am–9pm, Sun 11am–7pm.

⑤ ★ Westlake Center This, like other malls built in downtown Seattle in the 1980s, was suffering from mall fatique and looking a bit tired, so they decide to redo it to make it more appealing to today's shoppers. You'll enjoy browsing in the Northwest-based shops such as Seattle-based, women-owned Fireworks, an incredibly fun store crammed with playful art; and **Made in Washington ★★★,**

which sells souvenirs your friends will actually like. Seattle's mile-long monorail, built for the 1962 World's Fair, runs from the top floor of Westlake Center to Seattle Center. ① *1 hr. 400 Pine St.* ☎ *206/467-1600. www.westlakecenter.com. Mon–Sat 10am–8pm, Sun 11am–6pm.*

⑥ ★ Food Court at Westlake. There's something to please every palate at this food court, from quesa-dillas to sushi, all amazingly fresh and tasty. It's easy on the family budget, and wiggle worms have plenty of room to stretch when they're done eating. A few highlights: Boba-chine bubble tea & baguettes, Bombay Wala, Salena Mexicana, Noodle Zone, Sarku-Japanese Sushi, Mediterranean Avenue, and Emerald City Smoothie. *400 Pine St.* $

⑦ ★ Macy's. The famous New York–based department store is housed in the former Bon Marche department store, which for more than 100 years catered to Seattle's

Dotcom Delirium

Seattle has always been a boom-or-bust town, starting with the Gold Rush, and continuing much later with a series of massive hirings and devastating layoffs by Boeing. Then in the 1990s, strange things began happening in the once aviation-dependent economy. First, grunge rock grabbed the limelight for Seattle. Then a little company named Microsoft, started by hometown boys Bill Gates and Paul Allen, helped to spawn an entire industry of dotcom startups. By the late '90s, Seattle's economy was flying high from the glorious infusion of dotcom dollars. World-class restaurants, theater, and other cultural activities sprang up or expanded, eager to fill the after-hour entertainment needs of the newly moneyed. Though the dotcom bubble burst in Seattle, and throughout the country, just a couple of years later, Seattle's now-diversified economy quickly revived. Seattle struggled during the economic downturn, but its downtown remains vibrant, its night scene lively, and the economy got another huge boost with the arrival of Amazon, which has located its world headquarters in the South Lake Union neighborhood.

Stunning architecture at the Seattle Central Public Library

working class. Look closely and you'll find traces of the old Bon. Check beside the escalators for the intricate 1929 bronze panels depicting industries of the Northwest, from fisheries to technology. And check the sales racks for good clothing buys. This Macys, like others around the country, has recently been downsized. ○ *15 min. 1601 3rd Ave.* ☎ *206/506-6000. www.macys.com.*

❽ **City Centre.** This mixed-use building is a prestigious downtown office address, but it also houses some great little shops, including American Eagle Outfitters, Aldo (leather goods), Grace Diamonds, and Facèrè (antique and art jewelry). You can grab a veggie sub at Jimmy John's, a wrap at Sandella's Flat Bread Café, or some sushi rolls (veggie options available) at Sushi Kudasai. On the top retail floor, you'll find an excellent full-service restaurant (Palomino—with both a cafe and fine-dining room). ○ *15 min. 1420 5th Ave.* ☎ *206/624-8800. Store hours vary. Most open at 10am Mon–Sat & noon Sun & close daily between 5pm & 9pm (Palomino stays open later).*

A life-sized, glass dinosaur skeleton decorates multi-use City Centre.

9 Soups On! A bowl of soup is just the thing for a wet, chilly Seattle day. I can never decide between the chicken basil chili and the lobster bisque. Usually I ask for a sample of one, and buy a bowl of the other. This is just a small stand on the first floor of City Centre, but the taste is big, and there's plenty of room to sit and enjoy your soup. *1420 5th Ave. $*

10 ★★★ Benaroya Hall. Home to the Seattle Symphony, Benaroya is a modernist dream. I highly recommend catching a concert here, but even if you're not in the mood, the hall is worth a peek. Check out the colossal glass chandeliers by world-famous Tacoma-born glass artist Dale Chihuly. *⏱ 30 min. 200 University St. ☎ 206/215-4800. www.seattlesymphony.org. Ticket prices vary; free admission to see the chandeliers. See p 148.*

11 ★★★ Seattle Art Museum. Seattleites take their art seriously, and SAM is a reflection of that. The museum is home to an outstanding array of works from all over the world, but be sure to check out the Northwest Native American collection, which is one of the finest you'll find anywhere. *⏱ 90 min. 1300 1st Ave. www.seattleartmuseum.org. $20 adults, $18 seniors over 62. $13 students & kids 13–17, free for kids 12 & under. ☎ 206/654-3100. Wed–Sun 10am–5pm, Thurs-Fri 10am–9pm. See p 46.*

12 ★★★ Seattle Central Public Library. It's hard to say which is more fun, admiring the building or browsing its well-stocked shelves. One thing is for sure: You'll have to drag the kids out of the children's section. Of course you can get a latte! *1000 4th Ave. ☎ 206/386-4636. www.spl.org. Free. Mon–Thurs 10am–8pm, Fri–Sat 10am–6pm, Sun noon–6pm. See p 46.*

Cai Guo-Qiang's massive installation greets visitors to the Seattle Art Museum.

Capitol Hill

1 Volunteer Park

2 Harvard-Belmont Landmark District

3 Consignment Apparel Shops

4 Espresso Vivace

5 Dance Footsteps

6 Dumpling Tzar

7 Elliott Bay Book Company

8 Frye Art Museum

Remnants of the grunge era live on in this eclectic neighborhood, which is also the center of gay life in Seattle. In addition to tattoos and piercings, expect to see the occasional neon-blue Mohawk, cross-dressing shoppers, and panhandlers who may at times be a bit unsteady on their feet. The housing is also diverse, with seedy apartments sharing blocks with spectacular mansions and whole stretches of formerly gritty Broadway now gentrified into brand-new condos and upscale rentals. Likewise, the shops along Broadway range from retro-consignment to ultra-trendy fashion. It's safe to bring young children here, but there's not much of interest for them, except for Volunteer Park—far removed from the diverse Broadway street scene. START: **Bus 10 to Volunteer Park.**

A Bird of Paradise in bloom at Volunteer Park Conservatory

1 ★★★ Volunteer Park. Flush with Gold Rush money, Seattle hired the Olmsted Brothers (their father designed New York City's Central Park) in 1903 to design an elaborate series of parks, including this one. There's lots of room to run and many trails to explore in this urban oasis. If you climb the 106 steps to the top of the **Water Tower** at the south end of the park, you'll be rewarded with one of the best views in town and a permanent show about the Olmsted's contributions to Seattle's park plan. Just west of the tower is the **Seattle Asian Art Museum** (p 29). Farther west is the **Volunteer Park Conservatory ★★★**, bursting with colorful exotic plants and eye-catching seasonal floral displays. ⏱ *1 hr. 1400 E. Galer St.* ☎ *206/684-4743. www.seattle.gov/parks. Free. Conservatory Tues–Sun 10am–4pm.*

2 ★ Harvard-Belmont Landmark District. Seattle has more than its share of millionaires—both dotcom and otherwise—and quite a few live in this tree-shaded neighborhood, ensconced in graceful, sprawling mansions built in the early 20th century. The best walk is along the northern end of Broadway, between East Highland and East Roy. You can also drive, but walking affords better peeking through the hedges. ⏱ *30 min. Bounded roughly by Harvard Ave., Broadway, Bellevue Place & Boylston.*

The colorful greenhouse at Volunteer Park Conservatory

❸ ★ **Consignment Apparel Shops.** With two colleges nearby (Seattle University and Seattle Central Community College), previously worn—and retro—clothing is highly sought after. There aren't as many vintage apparel shops as there once were along Broadway, but the ones that remain are excellent (although one recently morphed into a pet supply store, another sign of the changing scene along Broadway). **Crossroads Trading Co.** (325 Broadway Ave. E.; ☎ 206/328-5867) focuses on contemporary styles. Some items are new, but the only way to tell is by their blue tags. This is not the cheapest consignment shop in town, but the merchandise is top-flight. ⏱ *1 hr. Broadway Ave. E.*

Bigfoot

The most popular legend in the Northwest, without a doubt, is that of Sasquatch, more fondly dubbed Bigfoot. Believers swear that Sasquatches roam the forests and mountains of the Pacific Northwest. Reports of an enormous hairy beast in the region have been circulating since the early 1800s. Some, but not all, of the stories have been proven fraudulent. In 1969, a man in northern Washington reported finding Sasquatch footprints in a ghost town called Bossburg. Bigfoot hunters rushed to the scene and found additional tracks nearby—more than 1,000 in all. One of them was measured at more than 17 inches long. At least one British anthropologist was impressed with the find. Sasquatch-spotters often report an awful, skunklike smell just before they see the beast or its tracks. But with no scientifically confirmed hard proof, the mystery—and perhaps the ape-man—lives on.

4 ★★ **Espresso Vivace.** This is a no-frills stand, but the coffee drinks are sublime, right down to the Rosetta pattern the barista "draws" in the foam. Sidewalk seating is available. If you like your drinks flavored, try the rich, creamy caffe caramel. *321 Broadway Ave. E. $*

5 ★ **Dance Footsteps.** One of the most unusual displays of public art you'll find is embedded in the sidewalks along Broadway. Dancers' Series: Steps consists of bronze shoeprints of dancers performing various steps. There are eight sets along the avenue, from the tango to the foxtrot, and a couple of steps that artist Jack Mackie made up just for fun. Go ahead and try them out! No need to feel self-conscious: It takes a lot to turn heads on Capitol Hill. ◷ *15 min. Along Broadway.*

6 **Dumpling Tzar.** This cozy spot serves up delicious Russian dumplings, "the people's food," in a restaurant that can be described as a proletarian setting with just enough Russian kitsch to make it fun. The bite-sized dumplings are made with egg noodles, filled with pork, beef or veg, and eaten with sour cream or a host of other toppings. *1630 12th Ave.* ☎ *206/466-6561. www. dumplingtzar.com. $*

The Dance Footsteps public art display on Broadway invites passersby to tango or foxtrot.

A contemporary art installation at the Frye Museum

7 ★★★ **Elliott Bay Book Company.** Seattleites may be tech-savvy but they still love their books, and this is the city's favorite bookstore. In its new location—a 20,000-square-foot historic 1917 building on quirky Capitol Hill—Elliott Bay still feels like Seattle's comfy living room. Peruse the shelves at your leisure in this old Ford truck service center with its fir floors and massive ceiling beams. Your challenge: not to bring home more than you can fit in your carry-on! ◷ *30 min. 1521 10th Ave.* ☎ *206/624-6600. www.elliottbay book.com. Mon–Thurs 10am–10pm; Fri–Sat 10am–11pm; Sun 11am–9pm.*

8 ★★ **Frye Art Museum.** A gift to the city by a prominent pioneer family that earned a fortune in the meatpacking business and used their money to buy modern art of the late-19th and early-20th centuries, the Frye is a lovely surprise of a museum. In addition to the Frye family's impressive personal art collection, which still hangs in the house they lived in, you'll see new acquisitions and intriguing installations of contemporary art. It's located on First Hill, a few minutes' walk from Capitol Hill, but well worth the brief detour to see the collection and enjoy the old Seattle neighborhood around it. ◷ *1 hr. 704 Terry Ave. See p. 28,* **5**.

Chinatown–International District

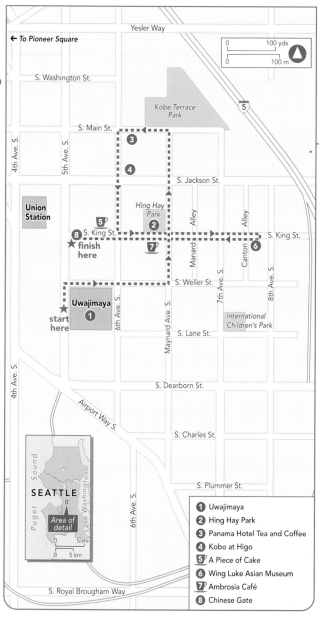

← To Pioneer Square

Yesler Way

0   100 yds
0   100 m

S. Washington St.

Kobe Terrace Park

S. Main St.

5

Union Station

S. Jackson St.

Hing Hay Park

Alley

Alley

S. King St.

finish here

Manard

Canton

S. King St.

Uwajimaya

start here

S. Weller St.

7th Ave. S.

8th Ave. S.

International Children's Park

6th Ave. S.

Maynard Ave. S.

S. Lane St.

4th Ave. S.

S. Dearborn St.

Airport Way S.

S. Charles St.

SEATTLE

Puget Sound

Lake Washington

Area of detail

0   5mi
0   5 km

S. Plummer St.

6th Ave. S.

S. Royal Brougham Way

1 Uwajimaya
2 Hing Hay Park
3 Panama Hotel Tea and Coffee
4 Kobo at Higo
5 A Piece of Cake
6 Wing Luke Asian Museum
7 Ambrosia Café
8 Chinese Gate

Although not as large as San Francisco's Chinatown, this Asian neighborhood is lively—and about as diverse as they come, with a flood of Southeast Asian immigrants joining the mix in recent years. Its name changed from Chinatown to International District and back to the current compromise. When I feel like globetrotting but can't spare the time, I'll spend an afternoon here, strolling past shops with whole barbecued ducks hanging in the window, riotously colorful vegetable markets spilling out into the streets, window displays of exotic herbs and medicines, and pastry shops hawking some of the tastiest wares in town. It's all about the smells, the colors, and the single-minded shoppers tracking down bargains. START: **Bus 3 or 4 to 5th Avenue & James Street.**

Lion dancers celebrate Chinese New Year at Seattle's Chinatown Gate.

❶ ★★ **Uwajimaya.** Yes, it's a grocery store, but this is also a bona fide tourist destination. Built by a Japanese patriarch whose family was interned during World War II, this enormous supermarket—now run by his children—is stocked with exotic Asian produce, meats, baked goods, and other products. You can check its website for recipes from eight Asian countries, then do your shopping. There is also an Asian bookstore, gift shop, and a large dine-in area that gives an entirely new meaning to the term "food court." It's easy to lose track of time in here. ① *30 min. 600 5th Ave. S.* ☎ *206/624-6248. www. uwajimaya.com. Mon–Sat 8am–10pm, Sun 9am–9pm.*

❷ ★ **Hing Hay Park.** This small but unusual park is situated on a red-bricked square. The colorful pagoda, crafted in Taipei, Taiwan, is the genuine article, as is the spectacular dragon artwork. If you have time, settle in at one of the chess tables for a leisurely game. The park is a popular gathering spot that often hosts the Lunar New Year Lion Dances in February. ① *15 min. 423 Maynard Ave. S. (King St. & Maynard).*

❸ ★ **Historic Panama Hotel Bed & Breakfast Tea & Coffee House.** You can sip Italian Lavazza coffee or choose from a global tea menu at this elegant shop in the historic Panama Hotel, which

At the Panama Hotel, trunks left behind by Japanese families sent to internment camps are a reminder of a painful past.

housed Japanese workingmen in the early 20th century. When owner Jan Johnson bought the hotel, she discovered trunks full of personal items left behind and never reclaimed by Japanese families sent off to internment camps. You can view one of these trunks through a glass window in the tea-shop's wooden floor. Many other items are on display as a history lesson and a reminder of a regrettable moment in time. ⏱ *30 min. 607 S. Main St.* ☎ *206/515-4000. www.panamahotelseattle.com.*

④ ★ **Kobo at Higo.** History stands still at this shop, housed in the former Higo Variety Store, a Japanese five-and-dime that stood in this spot for 75 years. The Murakami family had to board it up while they were sent to an internment camp, but reopened when they returned. Sadly, Mr. Murakami died very shortly afterward, but his widow and children kept the shop going until 2003, when the youngest daughter retired. Happily, the new owners, John Bisbee and

Binko Chiong-Bisbee, have preserved much of the past, including pre-war merchandise and family mementos. Be sure to check out the display wall devoted to the old Higo. But the new shop, a Japanese and Northwest fine-art and craft gallery, features stylish new treasures. ⏱ *30 min. 604 S. Jackson St.* ☎ *206/381-3000. www.koboseattle.com. Mon–Sat 11am–6pm, Sun noon–5pm.*

⑤ ★ **A Piece of Cake.** This is the favorite bakery for many cake-loving Seattleites. The cakes are feather-light, the frosting flavorful but not too sweet, and the fillings creative. In season, try the melon ball–filled cake. The cakes here are works of art, perfect for a very special occasion. ⏱ *30 min 514 S. King St.* ☎ *206/623-8284. $*

⑥ ★★ **Wing Luke Asian Museum.** This Smithsonian–affiliated museum is one of the best

Memorabilia on display at the Wing Luke Asian Museum captures the history of Asian immigrants in the Pacific Northwest.

Bathhouse Tour

When early Japanese immigrants came to the United States, they built hundreds of community bathhouses, just like they had at home. The bathhouses, or *sentos*, were culturally important places to socialize, relax in the hot waters, and clean off after a hard day's work. Only one remains intact in its original location—the marble bath in the basement of the **Historic Panama Hotel Bed & Breakfast** (see above). The bath officially closed in 1950, but is still open for historic tours. To schedule one, call the **Panama Hotel** at ☎ 206/223-9242.

of its kind in the nation, and a great community resource in the midst of a diverse neighborhood. Its library, which is open to the public during museum hours, includes a wealth of oral and video histories, photos, and books about the experiences of Asian-Pacific Americans in the Northwest. ○ *1 hr. 719 S. King St. (S. King St. & 8th Ave. S.).* ☎ *206/623-5124. www.wingluke.org. $22 adults, $20 seniors & students, $17.50 ages 5–12. Includes tour of historic building/former hotel. Tues–Sun 10am–5pm, 1st Thurs of month & 2nd Sat of month 10am–8pm. See p 23.*

7 ★ **Ambrosia Cafe.** This was the first shop in the International District to specialize in pearl tea, a craze that started in Taiwan. Now available all over town—more often called "bubble tea"—the icy drink consists of brewed tea mixed with sweetened milk and syrups, poured into a tall cup filled with pea-size tapioca balls. You drink it through a straw wide enough to suck up the "bubbles." It's an odd sensation the first time or two, but then you get hooked. Try the mango and green tea flavors. *619 S. King St.* ☎ *206/623-9028. $*

8 ★ **Chinese Gate.** After a half-century of grassroots efforts,

Seattle's Chinatown has its own traditional entrance gate, just like other major cities with large Chinese populations, such as San Francisco and Los Angeles. The eye-catching, 45-foot archway was unveiled in 2008. The $500,000 gate, according to tradition, should bring luck and strength. It also greets visitors and makes it easier to spot the district. There are hopes of building a second gate on the other end of the neighborhood. *S. King St., just east of 5th Ave. S.*

Find pre-war and family mementos, as well as modern wares for sale, at Kobo at Higo.

Wallingford

7th Ave. NE

4th Ave. NE

Latona Ave. NE

Thackery Pl. NE

2nd Ave. NE

1st Ave. NE

Eastern Ave. N.

Sunnyside Ave. N.

Corliss Ave. N.

Bagley Ave. N.

Meridian Ave. N.

Burke Ave. N.

Wallingford Ave. N.

Densmore Ave. N.

Woodlawn Ave. N.

Ashworth Ave. N.

Interlake Ave. N.

Interlake Ave. N.

Stone Way N.

Midvale Ave. N.

NE 45th St.

NE 43rd St.

NE 42nd St.

NE 40th St.

1st Ave. NE

N. 45th St.

N. 42nd St.

N. 41st St.

N. 40th St.

N. 43rd St.

N. 44th St.

N. 45th St.

N. 46th St.

NE Pacific St.

Lake Washington

Puget Sound

SEATTLE

Area of detail

5 mi
5 km

200 yds
200 m

start here

finish here

Wallingford Playfield

1 Archie McPhee
2 Alphabet Soup
3 Molly Moon's Ice Cream
4 Bottleworks
5 Fuel Coffee
6 Bad Woman Yarn
7 The Sock Monster
8 Wallingford Playfield
9 Guild 45th
10 Irwin's Neighborhood Bakery and Café
11 Wine World & Spirits

One of Seattle's most charming residential neighborhoods, Wallingford is packed with lovingly restored Craftsman bungalows on quiet, tree-lined streets. Some of the city's finest ethnic restaurants—and a few of its most eclectic shops—can be found in Wallingford's lively business district. There are parks galore for the kids to romp in, and a great little 1920s-era art deco movie house—it's an ideal spot to catch a blockbuster or, especially, an Indie film. If you're here in early July, check the neighborhood website (www.wallyhood.org) for the date of the annual Seafair Kiddies Parade & Fair. It's a day full of pirates, clowns and general merrymaking for all ages. START: **Bus 16 or 44 to Stone Way North & N. 45th Street.**

If it's weird or wacky, you'll find it at Archie McPhee.

❶ ★★ Archie McPhee. From rubber chickens to avenging narwhals to underpants for your hands—if it's weird, wacky, and fun, you'll find it. For a quarter-century, Seattleites have flocked to Archie McPhee for sensory overload—or just a giggle. And yes, there really was an Archie McPhee, a fun-loving guy. ⏱ *30 min. 1300 N. 45th St.* ☎ *206/297-0240. www.archie mcpheeseattle.com. Mon–Sat 10am–7pm, Sun 11am–6pm.*

❷ ★★ Alphabet Soup. This is a magical place for kids, well-stocked with new, used, and vintage children's books—and even a small used section for Mom and Dad. The picture books are wonderful, and the prices are low enough that you'll leave with an armful. ⏱ *15 min. 1406 N. 45th St.* ☎ *206/547-4555. Wed–Fri 11am–8pm, Sat 10am–8pm, Sun noon–6pm.*

❸ ★★ Molly Moon's Homemade Ice Cream. Sure, you can find an ice cream shop just about anywhere. But you can only find Molly Moon's in two locations on the planet, and this is one of them. The ingredients are local but the flavors are celestial. Try the maple walnut, honey lavender, or balsamic strawberry. Of course, you could order vanilla bean, but why? ⏱ *15 min. 1622 N. 45th St.* ☎ *206/547-5105. Daily noon–11pm.*

❹ ★ Bottleworks. Adults only! With 16 beers on tap and hundreds of bottled varieties from around the world, this neighborhood bottle shop, the oldest in Seattle, is a destination for beer-lovers from all over. ⏱ *15 min. 1710 N. 45th St.* ☎ *206/632-1057. www.bottleworks. com. Sun–Wed 11am–8pm, Thurs 11am–9pm, Fri–Sat 11am–11pm.*

Try the Earl Grey and maple walnut ice cream at Molly Moon's Ice Cream, where the ingredients are local and the flavors are out of this world.

5 Fuel Coffee. Friendly baristas and comfy chairs make Fuel a great spot for topping off. You might need the caffeine to keep you moving post–Molly Moon's. And if you need to catch up on email, you'll find lighted tables in the back, and free Wi-Fi. ⏱ *15 min. 1705 N. 45th S.* ☎ *206/634-2700. $*

6 ★ Bad Woman Yarn. Tucked into the Wallingford Center—a historic schoolhouse-cum-shopping-destination—is this gem of a shop, overflowing with colorful, fluffy balls and a staff that will help you find the right yarn to bring a perfect pattern to life. If you have an open afternoon or evening, join the locals for a free knitting group or sign up for a class ($17 and up). Check the schedule on the website. ⏱ *15 min. 1815 N. 45th St.* ☎ *206/ 547-5384. www.badwomanyarn.com. Mon–Fri 10am–8pm, Sat 10am–6pm, Sun 11am–5pm.*

7 ★ The Sock Monster. Footsie fashion for everyone (women, men, kids), in every conceivable color, pattern, and style, is what this playful neighborhood sock shop offers. The selection is staggering. ⏱ *15 min. 1909 N. 45th St.* ☎ *206/724-0123. www.thesock monster.com. Mon–Fri 11am–7pm, Sat 11am–8pm, Sun noon–6pm.*

8 ★ Wallingford Playfield. After a morning of shopping, the kids will be ready to burn off some energy, and Wallingford Playfield is the perfect spot. Here you'll find lots of equipment for climbing, a water play area for splashing—and a huge grassy area. ⏱ *30 min. 4219 Wallingford Ave. N.* ☎ *206/684-4075. www.seattle.gov/parks. Daily 4am–11:30pm.*

9 ★ Guild 45th. This art deco–style theater has screens in two separate buildings. The first one opened in 1919; the second in the 1980s. The Guild specializes in

Gasworks Park

Seattle's favorite place to go fly a kite, this former gas-manufacturing-plant-turned-park also boasts one of the most spectacular views in town. Take along a blanket and throw a picnic at the top of the hill, overlooking Lake Union, the Space Needle and—on a clear day—Mount Rainier. It doesn't get better than this. Years ago, the city—making lemonade out of the proverbial lemon—turned the abandoned boiler house into a picnic shelter and the old compressor building into a play area where kids can explore the now brightly painted machinery. From the parking lot, you can also access the popular Burke-Gilman Trail, a 12½-mile route following the old path of the Burlington-Northern Railroad. Walkers, joggers, cyclists and skaters share the fresh air.

screening edgy and foreign films. *2115 N. 45th St.* ☎ *206/781-5755. www.landmarktheatres.com/Market/ Seattle/Guild45thTheatre.htm.*

10 ★ **Irwin's Neighborhood Bakery and Cafe.** Right about now, a homemade pizza, soup, or chicken pot pie should hit the spot. Real men—and women—will love the quiche Diablo, chock-full of hot peppers. Go ahead, finish up with a slice of pie. *2123 N. 40th St.* ☎ *206/675-1484. $*

11 ★ **Wine World & Spirits.** The latest addition to Wallingford's shopping menu is this 23,000-square-foot superstore, the largest wine shop in the Northwest. It's packed with gleaming bottles from around the world—including at least 500 wines from Washington State, whose wineries have made a major global splash in recent years. Step up to the elegant tasting bar for daily wine samplings (Mon–Fri

Flying a kite at Gasworks Park

6–8pm, Sat–Sun 2–5pm) from up to 10 wineries. ⏱ *30 min. 400 NE 45th St.* ☎ *206/402-6086. wineworld spirits.com. Mon–Sat 10am–9pm, Sun 11am–7pm.*

Fremont

SEATTLE

Area of detail

Puget Sound

Lake Washington

Phinney Ave. N.

Fremont Ave. N.

Evanston Ave. N.

Fremont Pl.

N. 36th St.

FREMONT

N. 35th St.

start here

1 (under bridge)

Aurora Ave. N.

N. Northlake Way

N. 34th St.

Lake Washington Ship Canal

finish here

Fremont Ave. N.

George Washington Bridge

Fremont Bridge

99

Lake Union

QUEEN ANNE

0   100 yds
0   100 m

1   Fremont Troll
2   Statue of Lenin
3   Royal Grinders
4   Fremont Rocket
5   PCC Natural Markets
6   *Waiting for the Interurban* Statue
7   Lake Union Ship Canal

The self-proclaimed center of the universe (with a sign to prove it), this funky north-end neighborhood has a quirkiness that several years of gentrification have failed to destroy. Tech firms Adobe Systems and Getty have built their headquarters here, and high-end condos followed. Though some of the cottage-industry art studios have given way to higher-rent tenants, this is still an artsy kind of place. One of my favorite things about Fremont is the eccentric public art scattered about the neighborhood. When I'm not in the mood for the urban pace of downtown, I head for friendly Fremont to poke around, stroll along the ship canal connecting Lake Washington to Lake Union, and relax. START: **Under the north end of the Aurora Avenue Bridge, at N. 36th St.**

1 ★★ Fremont Troll. If you drive over the Aurora Avenue Bridge, better hope your car doesn't suffer the same fate as the Volkswagen Bug plucked off the road by the nasty-tempered troll lurking below. At least, that's how the story goes. The 18-foot-high

troll, which reflects the neighborhood's Scandinavian roots, is much friendlier if you visit him in person. You can climb on him all you want, and he's okay with family pictures, too. Back in 1989, when the Fremont Arts Council held a nationwide search for a piece of public art

The much-loved Fremont Troll resides under the Aurora Avenue Bridge.

to go under the bridge, Fremont residents overwhelming voted for the troll—and the VW held in his clutches. ① *15 min. N. 36th St.,*

Vladimir Lenin blends right into the eccentric Fremont neighborhood.

under the Aurora Avenue Bridge, also known as the George Washington Memorial Bridge.

❷ ★ **Statue of Lenin.** We're talking Vladimir. The sculpture of the former Russian revolutionary ended up in Fremont on a fluke, and here it has stayed, despite controversy. It was brought back from Slovakia by a Seattle-area bronze artist who was considering selling it for scrap when he met an untimely death. His family had the statue moved near a brass foundry in Fremont, and no one has figured out what to do with it since. Now it's become a part of this eccentric neighborhood where hardly anything seems out of place. If you're here during a holiday season, expect to see Lenin decked out in appropriate garb. ① *15 min. 36th & Evanston Ave. N.*

3 ★ **Royal Grinders.** Tucked behind Lenin's statue is a great little spot where you can cool off with a tasty gelato. The challenge is choosing from the eclectic menu of flavors—a couple of dozen, ranging from lavender to cappuccino chip. Feeling droopy? Try one "drowned" in espresso. If you're hungry, the freshly made, toasted subs come piled high with veggies and meats. *3526 Fremont Place N.* ☎ *206/545-7560.* $

4 ★ **Fremont Rocket.** It's an odd twist of fate that the statue of Lenin ended up just down the block from a 55-foot for-real Cold War-era rocket, taken from an Army surplus store, mounted on a building in Fremont and—voila!—turned into art. Stop by in the evening to see the rocket's onboard lights ablaze. ⏱ *15 min. 35th & Evanston Ave. N.*

5 ★ **PCC Natural Markets.** Fruits and veggies have never been so much fun, and these, mostly from local farms, are bursting with flavor. PCC is an organic store with a produce section that's so irresistible, some Seattleites go out of their way to shop here. This is a full-service grocery store, and all the cosmetic and fragrance products are cruelty-free. It's technically a co-op, but non-members can shop here, too. The bakery features such unusual items as Paris balsamic pear tarts and vegan carrot cake. *600 N. 34th.* ☎ *206/632-6811.*

6 ★ **Waiting for the Interurban.** Six passengers and a dog wait endlessly for their train in this castaluminum sculpture memorializing the era of the electric rail line Unless you look closely, you might mistake the riders for real people, as they are often dressed seasonally. ⏱ *15 min. South side of N. 34th St.*

7 ★★★ **Lake Union Ship Canal.** A stairway on the Fremont Bridge leads down to a wonderfully strollable pathway along the ship canal near Lake Union. High above you'll see the green span of the Aurora Bridge, and beneath and beyond that, a marina and part of the Queen Anne neighborhood. Be aware of the bicyclists as you end your Fremont tour with a lovely waterside walk. ⏱ *30 min. Access from Fremont Bridge.* ●

The statues of Waiting for the Interurban await a train that never comes.

Shopping **Best Bets**

Best **Art Jewelry**
★★★ Twist, *600 Pine St. (p 93)*

Best **Bookstore (New Books)**
★★★ Elliott Bay Book Company,
1521 10th Ave. (p 88)

Best **Bookstore (Used)**
★★ Twice Sold Tales,
1833 Harvard Ave. (p 89)

Best **Gifts**
★★★ Millstream, *112 1st Ave. S.
(p 92)*

Best **Glass**
★★★ Glasshouse Studio,
311 Occidental Ave. S. (p 93)

Best **Handcrafted Wood
Furniture**
★★ Northwest Fine Woodwork-
ing, *101 S. Jackson St. (p 91)*

Best **Pirate Booty**
Pirates Plunder, *1301 Alaskan Way,
Pier 57 (p 93)*

Best Place to **Find an Out-of-
Town Newspaper**
★ First and Pike News, *93 Pike St.
(p 88)*

Best **Rugs**
★ Palace Rug Gallery, *323 1st Ave.
S. (p 96)*

Best **Fashion Bargains**
★★★ Nordstrom Rack,
400 Pine St. (p 96)

Best Place to Find **a Manly
Skirt**
★ Utilikilts, *620 1st Ave. (p 91)*

Best **Shoes**
★★★ Nordstrom, *500 Pine St.
(p 90)*

Best **Souvenirs**
★★ Made in Washington, *400 Pine
St. (p 92)*

Best Place to **Buy a Gown for
the Opera**
★★ Mario's, *1513 6th Ave. (p 90)*

Best **Toys**
★★ Magic Mouse Toys, *603 1st
Ave. (p 96)*

Previous page: Seattle's legendary independent bookstore, Elliott Bay Book Company

Downtown Shopping

Barnes & Noble **5**	LUSH **8**
Driscoll Robbins Fine Carpets **17**	Macy's **9**
Easy Street Records & CDs **3**	Mario's **11**
E.E. Robbins **4**	Niketown **12**
Facere **13**	Nordstrom **7**
Fireworks **8**	Nordstrom Rack **8**
Fran's Chocolates **15**	Pacific Place **6**
Jeffrey Moore Gallery **14**	Pirates plunder **16**

Seattle Glassblowing Studio **2**
See's Candies **10**
Silver Platters **1**
Twist **6**
Watson Kennedy Fine Home **18**
Westlake Center **8**
Young Flowers **19**

Pioneer Square Shopping

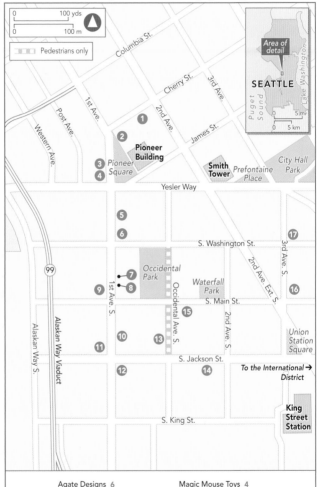

Pike Place Market Shopping

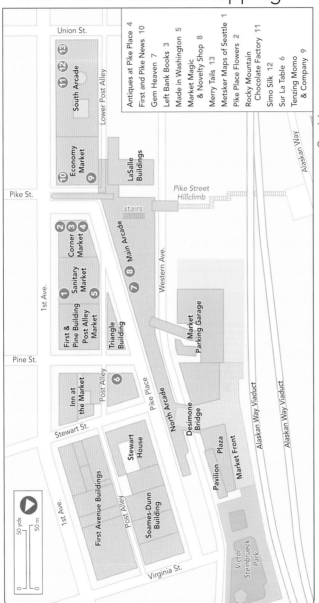

Antiques at Pike Place 4
First and Pike News 10
Gem Heaven 7
Left Bank Books 3
Made in Washington 5
Market Magic
 & Novelty Shop 8
Merry Tails 13
Metsker Maps of Seattle 1
Pike Place Flowers 2
Rocky Mountain
 Chocolate Factory 11
Simo Silk 12
Sur La Table 6
Tenzing Momo
 & Company 9

Capitol Hill Shopping

Crossroads Trading Co. 3
Dilettante Mocha Café 3
Elliott Bay Book Company 8
Kobo Shop and Gallery 1
Mud Bay Granary 4

Panache 5
Trendy Wendy 6
Twice Sold Tales 7
Wall of Sound 9

Seattle **Shopping A to Z**

Original art glass for sale at Glasshouse Studios

Antiques

Antiques at Pike Place PIKE PLACE MARKET This is a fun shop to poke around in, and you'll likely find something you can't live without, whether it's a Mickey Mantle baseball card, a toy from your past, or a gorgeous estate ring. *92 Stewart St.* ☎ *206/441-9643. Bus: 10, 99. Map p. 85.*

Vintage cameras at Antiques at Pike Place

Cutty Sark Nautical Antiques PIONEER SQUARE Nautical antiques—from compasses to ship's wheels—are sold here, making it the perfect place to grab gifts for all the old salts on your list. *320 1st Ave. S.* ☎ *206/262-1265. www.cutty antiques.com. Bus: 85, 99. Map p 84.*

★ **Flanagan & Lane Antiques** PIONEER SQUARE The French furniture is exquisite; so are the Chinese fans and dishes. Don't miss the interesting assortment of antique clocks. *165 S. Jackson St.* ☎ *206/682-0098. www.flanagan-laneantiques.com. Bus: 13, 85, 99. Map p 84.*

Art

Akanyi African & Tribal Art Gallery PIONEER SQUARE African and tribal art are showcased at this unique shop, which features a large collection of musical instruments, masks, and furniture from all over the continent. *155 S Main St.* ☎ *206/381-3133. Bus: 1, 2, 4, 13, 43, 49, 85, 99. Map p 84.*

G. Gibson Gallery PIONEER SQUARE The focus here is on fine

Jeffrey Moose Gallery specializes in indigenous art.

art photography, but you'll also find contemporary sculptures and paintings by locally and internationally important artists. *300 S. Washington St.* ☎ *206/587-4033. www.ggibson gallery.com. Bus: 1, 2, 4, 13, 43, 49. Map p 84.*

★★ **Jeffrey Moose Gallery** DOWNTOWN This eclectic shop specializes in indigenous art, including Australian aboriginal works and Native-American masks and carvings. *1333 5th Ave., Ste. 511.* ☎ *206/467-6951. www.jeffrey moosegallery.com. Bus: 85, 106, 150, 255, 545, 577. Map p 83.*

Books & Magazines

★★★ **Barnes & Noble** DOWN-TOWN B&N is the largest bookstore in downtown Seattle, and it remains a great place to browse for new titles and every other title still in print and to attend author signings and events. Another big, browsable B&N is located in Bellevue at 626 106th Ave. NE (☎ *425/451-8463). 600 Pine St.* ☎ *206/264-0156. www.bn.com. Bus: 10, 11, 14. Map p 83.*

★★★ **Elliott Bay Book Company** CAPITOL HILL Seattle's premier bookstore is a must for any bibliophile. *1521 10th Ave.* ☎ *206/ 624-6600. www.elliottbaybook.com. Bus: 10, 11, 43, 49, 60, 84. Map p 86.*

★★ **First and Pike News** PIKE PLACE MARKET This is one of the last great newsstands in the country, with hundreds of magazines and newspapers from around the world. It's Seattle best place to go to read all about it. *93 Pike St.* ☎ *206/624-0140. Bus: 10, 99, 113, 121 or 122. Map p 85.*

★ **Globe Bookstore** PIONEER SQUARE Be forewarned: It's easy to spend more time than you planned in this terrific little bookshop, packed with new and used mysteries, history books, children's books, and cookbooks. *218 1st Ave. S.* ☎ *206/682-6882. Bus: 16, 66, 86, 99. Map p 84.*

★★★ **Left Bank Books** PIKE PLACE MARKET Since 1973, this employee-owned collective has reflected Seattle's labor-movement roots. Its collections include an anarchy section, LGBT literature, short stories, an amazing collection of 'zines, and lots of clever, left-leaning T-shirts. *92 Pike St.* ☎ *206/622-0195. www.leftbank books.com. Bus: 10, 99, 113, 121 or 122. Map p. 85.*

★★★ **Metsker Maps of Seattle** PIKE PLACE MARKET Metsker's has been around since 1950 and has a map for every destination you can think of, as well as travel books and travel gear. *1522 1st Avet.* ☎ *206/623-8747. www.metskers. com. Bus: 99, 113. Map p 85.*

★★ **Seattle Mystery Bookshop** PIONEER SQUARE Skullduggery reigns supreme here. Word of warning to mystery-lovers: This will not be a quick stop for you. And good luck stumping the

Mystery buffs will want to investigate the Seattle Mystery Bookshop.

well-informed staff. *117 Cherry St.* ☎ *206/587-5737. www.seattle mystery.com. Bus: 16, 66, 99, 554, 594. Map p 84.*

★★ **Twice Sold Tales** CAPITOL HILL You'd be hard-pressed to find a deeper inventory of used books. Plan on plenty of time to browse. And if you're a cat-lover, make time to play with the kitties that roam the shop. *Locations include 1833 Harvard Ave. (☎ 206/324-2421) & 4501 University Way NE (☎ 206/ 545-4226). www.twicesoldtales.info. Bus: 8, 43, 49, 60. Map p 86.*

Candy
★★ **Dilettante Mocha Café** CAPITOL HILL Don't pass up the hand-dipped truffles, made with recipes passed down from the owners' great uncle, who prepared them for the Imperial Court of Austria. If you fall in love, you can join their chocolate club and get treats delivered to your door every month. *Locations include 538 Broadway E.* ☎ *206/329-6463. www.dilettante. com. AE, MC, V. Bus: 49, 60. Map p 86.*

★★★ **Fran's Chocolates** DOWNTOWN A Seattle success story that has nothing to do with PCs or software. Seattle native Fran Bigelow's salted caramels are so fabulously delicious that you won't believe your taste buds. *Four Seasons Hotel, 1325 First Ave. www. franschocolates.com.* ☎ *800/4122- 3726. Bus: 10, 99, 113, 121 or 122. Map p 83.*

Rocky Mountain Chocolate Factory PIKE PLACE MARKET The

Handmade chocolates from Dilettante Mocha Café

colorful rows of apples dipped in rich chocolates and caramel, then rolled in a variety of toppings, are almost painful to look at. And once you're inside, you may as well sample a piece of creamy homemade fudge. *1419 1st Ave.* ☎ *206/262-9581. www.rmcf.com. Bus: 10, 99, 113, 121 or 122. Map p 85.*

★★ **See's Candies** DOWNTOWN See's offers scrumptious gourmet candies at a good value. The company has been in business since 1921, but offers a variety of new tastes alongside its tried-and-true favorites. *Downtown location: 1518 4th Ave.* ☎ *206/682-7122. www. sees.com. Bus: 10, 11, 14, 43, 81. Map p 83.*

Department Stores

★★ **Macy's** DOWNTOWN Like other Macy's around the country, this one in a historic Seattle building has been downsized and revamped, but it's still good for brand-name clothing, jewelry, housewares, and cosmetics. *1601 3rd Ave.* ☎ *206/ 506-6000. www.macys.com. Bus: 1, 11, 13, 14, 43. Map p 83.*

★★★ **Nordstrom** DOWNTOWN The shoes! Nordstrom got its start over a century ago as a humble Seattle shoe store and, while it's hardly humble anymore, it's still those fabulous shoes that lure Seattleites in. Of course, there's much, much more, and it's high quality, with high price tags to match. *500 Pine St.* ☎ *206/628-2111. www. nordstrom.com. Bus: 10, 11, 14, 43, 83. Map p 83.*

Discount/Consignment Shopping

Crossroads Trading Co. CAPI-TOL HILL Not all the clothes here are used, but the only way to tell is by the tags, because everything looks new and hip. This is not the cheapest consignment shop, but

you'll find great stuff here, especially since its new expansion doubled the fun. *325 Broadway Ave. E.* ☎ *206/328-5847. www.crossroadstrading.com. Bus: 8, 43, 49, 60. Map p 86.*

★★★ **Nordstrom Rack** DOWN-TOWN You'll have to do some hunting, but that's part of the fun. Among the racks of marked-down designer clothes, housewares, and—yes!—shoes, quite a few treasures are usually waiting to be discovered and have your name on them. *400 Pine St.* ☎ *206/448-8522. www.nordstrom.com. Bus: 10, 11, 14, 99, 554. Map p 83.*

Fashion

★★★ **Mario's** DOWNTOWN For that perfect evening gown, if money is no object, you're sure to find a jaw-dropper here. The men's clothing is also exceptional. Everything is beautifully tailored, and the service equally impeccable. Mario's has been the go-to store for elegant, superbly tailored, mostly-Italian fashion for decades. *1513 6th Ave.* ☎ *206/223-1461. www.marios.com. Bus: 10, 11, 14, 43, 49. Map p 83.*

★ **Panache** CAPITOL HILL The name fits this quirky little shop perfectly. The clothing here is trendy but elegant, and there are plenty of options for accessorizing. They have misses' and junior sizes, plus a separate men's section. *225 Broadway E.* ☎ *206/726-3300. Bus: 9, 49, 60. Map p 86.*

★★ **Ragazzi's Flying Shuttle** PIONEER SQUARE The art is wearable at this shop, which offers hand-woven apparel and accessories, and a fun collection of original contemporary jewelry. *607 1st Ave.* ☎ *206/343-9762. www.ragazzisfly-ingshuttle.com. Bus: 10, 11, 16, 66, 99. Map p 84.*

Trendy Wendy CAPITOL HILL You'll get the red-carpet welcome

Cheerful, fragrant Pike Place Flowers

here, literally. Very hip clothes and accessories. And there's even a plus-size section. *211 Broadway E.* ☎ *206/322-6642. Bus: 8, 9, 43, 49, 60. Map p 86.*

★ **Utilikilts** PIONEER SQUARE If the slogan "Free Your Balls and Free Yourself" appeals, you'll want to check out these liberating kilts for men. There are eight basic styles, all handmade; custom orders cost extra. *620 1st Ave.* ☎ *206/282-4226. www.utilikilts.com. Bus: 10, 11, 16, 66, 99. Map p 84.*

Flowers

★ **Pike Place Flowers** PIKE PLACE MARKET This charming little corner shop, near the entrance to Pike Place Market, has been the focus of many photos of the Market. The arrangements are unique. *1501 1st Ave.* ☎ *206/682-9797. www.pikeplaceflowers.com. Bus: 10, 99, 113, 121 or 122. Map p 85.*

★ **Young Flowers** DOWNTOWN If you're looking for something sophisticated and different, you can't do better than this little shop, small in size but very big in creativity. *1111 3rd Ave.* ☎ *206/628-3077. Bus: 11, 15, 18, 121, 122. Map p. 83.*

Furniture

★ **Northwest Woodworkers Gallery** PIONEER SQUARE The one-of-a-kind furniture and decor items you'll find at this 30-year-old

cooperative are crafted by artisan woodworkers. They feature stunning blends of woods. The price tags are high, but the quality is superb. *101 S. Jackson.* ☎ *206/625-0542. www.nwfinewoodworking.com. Bus: 10, 11, 85, 99. Map p 84.*

Gems

★ **Agate Designs** PIONEER SQUARE A 300-pound amethyst geode might be a bit large for your studio apartment, but a pair of bookends or a small fountain might be just right. The items sold here

Rock hounds and non-collectors alike will enjoy Agate Designs' cool offerings.

Whimsy and inspiration are the themes at Fireworks, a specialty gift shop.

are made from dazzling gems, minerals, and fossils. There's something for every budget, and the owner is happy to share his wealth of knowledge. *120 1st Ave S.* ☎ *206/621-3063. www.agate designs.com. Map p 84.*

Gem Heaven PIKE PLACE MARKET You'll feast your eyes on gorgeous gemstones, crystals, minerals, and jewelry at this great little shop "Down Under" in the Market. *1501 Pike Place #408.* ☎ *206/381-9302. www.gemheaven.net. Bus: 10, 99, 113, 121 or 122. Map p 85.*

Gifts
★★★ Fireworks DOWNTOWN There are two themes at Fireworks: whimsy and inspiration, and often a combination of the two. Check out the revolving shadow lanterns, handmade by Northwest artists. *400 Pine St.* ☎ *206/-682-6462. www.fireworksgallery.net. Bus: 10, 14, 41, 71, 72. Map p 83.*

★ Kobo Shop and Gallery CAPITOL HILL Beautiful and sophisticated Northwest and Asian products are the focus here: pottery, teas, unusual gifts, and travel items. *814 E. Roy St.* ☎ *206/726-0704. www.koboseattle.com. MC, V. Bus: 9, 49. Map p 86.*

★★★ Made in Washington PIKE PLACE MARKET This is no

tacky souvenir shop. Take something home to your friends from Made in Washington and it's guaranteed not to end up at their garage sale. *1530 Post Alley.* ☎ *206/467-0788. Downtown location: 400 Pine St.* ☎ *206/623-9753. www.madeinwashington.com. Bus: 10, 99, 113, 121 or 122. Map p 85.*

★ Merry Tails PIKE PLACE MARKET This is a great place to find a souvenir for Fido, or for any pet lover on your list. You'll find lots of breed-specific items and unusual gifts. *1409 1st Ave.* ☎ *206/623-4142. Bus: 12, 99, 125. Map p. 85.*

★★★ Millstream PIONEER SQUARE I always feel like I'm stepping into a mountain cabin when I enter this woodsy-themed shop. Inside you'll find the talents of many serious Pacific Northwest artists—jewelry crafted from British Columbia jade and wood carvings. Millstream is back in its original location after spending a decade at Westlake Center. *112 1st. Ave. S.* ☎ *206/233-9719. www.millstream seattle.com. Bus: 10, 11, 16, 66, 99. Map p 84.*

★ Noble Horse Gallery PIONEER SQUARE True to its name, this equestrian-themed shop is filled with every horse item imaginable—and quite a few you'd never think of. You can buy equestrian-themed art, clothes, books and home

Millstream showcases the work of local artisans.

Pirate-themed booty is the stock and trade of Pirates Plunder.

decor, including horse-shaped shower hooks. And yes, you can buy a saddle here. *216 1st Ave. S. ☎ 206/382-8566. www.noblehorse gallery.com. Bus: 10, 11, 16, 66, 99. Map p 84.*

Pirates Plunder DOWNTOWN Here's where to go for everything pirate (and zombie, though that's another story)! Seriously, this shop specializes in pirate-related booty ranging from T-shirts to artwork. *1301 Alaskan Way. ☎ 206/624-5673. www.piratesplunder.com. Bus: 10, 11, 12, 99, 113. Map p 83.*

★★★ **Twist** DOWNTOWN This exuberant Northwest store, located in Pacific Place shopping mall, features whimsical hand-carved furniture, avant-garde art jewelry, and beautiful glassware. *600 Pine St., Ste. 130. ☎ 206/315-8080. www. twistonline.com. Bus: 10, 11, 14, 43, 49. Map p 83.*

Glass
★★★ **Foster/White** PIONEER SQUARE This gallery, housed in a century-old building, is more than glass; you'll also find contemporary paintings and sculptures by premier artists. Check the website for upcoming exhibitions. *220 3rd Ave. S. ☎ 206/622-2833. www.fosterwhite. com. Bus: 1, 2, 13, 14. Map p 84.*

★★★ **Glasshouse Studio** PIONEER SQUARE In addition to being a working artists' studio, Glasshouse sells the wares of many local glass artists. The colors are exuberant, and you can buy everything from a simple vase to a huge chandelier shaped like an explosion of peppers. *311 Occidental Ave. S. ☎ 206/ 682-9939. www.glasshouse-studio. com. Bus: 10, 85, 99. Map p 84.*

★★★ **Seattle Glassblowing Studio** DOWNTOWN The studio offers classes in glassblowing, and the gallery features elegant and fanciful work by a variety of artists. Be sure to check out the unique glass-art sinks. The studio is open to the public, so you can watch the artists at work. *2227 5th Ave. ☎ 206/ 448-2181. www.seattleglassblowing. com. Bus: 56, 82, 202. Map p 83.*

Housewares
★★★ **Sur La Table** PIKE PLACE MARKET Everything at this store inspires even a befuddled cook like myself to go home, put on an apron and whip up some mouthwatering fantasy concoction. Every type of pot and pan you've ever dreamed of, kitchen gadgets, fine

One-of-a-kind furniture, jewelry, and gifts are the specialty at Twist.

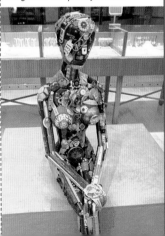

linens, glassware, exotic oils and spices—you'll find it all in this wonderfully browsable shop. *84 Pine St.* ☎ *206/448-2244. www.surlatable. com. Bus: 99, 113, 121, 122. Map p 85.*

★★ **Watson Kennedy Fine Home** DOWNTOWN You'll feel like you're shopping along the Left Bank in this charmingly eclectic store, stocked with French teas and soaps, antiques, housewares, and bath products. You might even find a decorative map of the Paris metro here. *1022 1st Ave.* ☎ *206/652-8350. www.watsonkennedy.com. Bus: 12, 16, 66, 99. Map p 83.*

Jewelry

★ **E.E. Robbins** DOWNTOWN Seattle's a romantic place (in the right light and place), and if you to decide to pop the question while you're here, head to E.E. Robbins, where the owner is a third-generation diamond expert. The staff is friendly, never pushy, and they'll offer you a glass of wine while you shop. *2200 1st Ave.* ☎ *206/826-7464. www.eerobbins. com. Bus: 81, 99. Map p 83.*

★★ **Facèré** DOWNTOWN This small store at City Centre is chock full of stylish, unique art jewelry by Northwest, national and international artists. You'll also find just the right antique or vintage piece to make your party dress sparkle. *1420 5th Ave. #108.* ☎ *206/624-6768. www.facerejewelryart.comBus: 306, 312, 522. Map p 83.*

Malls

City Centre DOWNTOWN Despite a limited number of stores, City Centre features some interesting clothing, leather goods, and jewelry shops; several excellent fast-food restaurants, and Palomino, a beautiful sit-down restaurant that happens to be among

Seattle's favorite lunch spots. *1420 5th Ave.* ☎ *206/624-8800. Store hours vary. Most open at 10am Mon–Sat & noon Sun; & closed daily btw. 5 & 9pm (Palomino stays open later). Bus: 306, 312, 522. Map p. 83.*

★ **Pacific Place** DOWNTOWN This elegant upscale mall is a great place for shopping, if your budget allows, but you can also enjoy just browsing its many unusual and artsy shops. *6th Ave. & Pine St.* ☎ *206/405-2655. www.pacific placeseattle.com. Bus: 10, 11, 14, 43, 49. Map p 83.*

★★ **Westlake Center** DOWNTOWN You'll find lots of clothing and gift stores, with merchandise in just every price range. *400 Pine St.* ☎ *206/467-1600. www.westlake center.com. Link Light Rail Westlake Station or Bus: 41, 71, 72, 301, 316. Map p 83.*

Markets

★★★ **Ballard Sunday Market** BALLARD This year-round Sunday farmer's market in the picturesque heart of the old Ballard neighborhood sells organic produce, cheeses, meats, fish, baked goods, wine, and crafts. There are ethnic food stalls, and many of Ballard's most delightful shops are open as well. A great way to spend a Sunday and explore a charming Seattle neighborhood. *Ballard Ave. NW, btw. NW 20th & 22nd Ave. www. sfmarkets.com.*

Music/CDs

★★ **Easy Street Records & CDs** QUEEN ANNE This roomy store is a music-lover's nirvana, offering a vast inventory of CDs and vinyl, and even in-store concerts. Private listening stations are scattered throughout the store. *20 Mercer St.* ☎ *206/691-3279. www. easystreetonline.com. Bus: 1, 8, 13, 15, 18. Map p 83.*

Street musicians at lively Ballard Sunday Market

★★ Silver Platters QUEEN ANNE Odds are you'll be able to find that obscure CD at this spacious independent music shop, whether you're into punk, jazz or old rock. The staff is very knowledgeable. They also have a great movie selection on DVD. Check online for in-store performances and signings. *701 5th Ave. N.* ☎ *206/283-3472. www.silver platters.com. MC, V. Bus: 3, 16, 82. Map p 83.*

★★ Wall of Sound CAPITOL HILL This eclectic shop specializes in international, avant-garde, electronic, and experimental music, and you'll also find a great selection of mainstream CDs. Check the website for visiting artists and indie movie screenings. *315 E. Pine St.* ☎ *206/441-9880. www.wosound. com. Bus: 10, 11, 14, 43, 49. Map p 86.*

Perfume/Skincare/Herbal Products

★ LUSH DOWNTOWN Who would have thought soap could be so much fun? You can suds yourself in just about any scent your heart desires. If you like, pick a sparkly

bar, with glitter that lasts as long as the soap. *400 Pine St., Ste. 100.* ☎ *206/624-5874. www.lush.com. Link Light Rail Westlake Station or Bus: 41, 71, 72, 301, 316. Map p 83.*

Tenzing Momo & Company PIKE PLACE MARKET This little shop will meet all your New Age needs: aromatherapy oils and books, incense, herbs, and tarot cards. *93 Pike St., Ste. 203.* ☎ *206/623-9837. www.tenzing-momo.com. Bus: 10, 99, 113, 121 or 122. Map p 85.*

Pets

Mud Bay Granary CAPITOL HILL The pet food is natural and healthy, and you'll find every accessory a well-heeled doggy—or feline—could dream of. *321 E. Pine St.* ☎ *206/322-6177. www.mudbay.us. Bus: 8, 43, 49 or 60. Map p 86.*

Rugs

★ Driscoll Robbins Fine Carpets DOWNTOWN Yes, there is a Driscoll Robbins, and he travels around the world in search of eye-catching hand-woven rugs—from traditional to contemporary designs—then displays them in an equally beautiful showroom. *Warning:* They are hard to resist. *1002 Western Ave.* ☎ *206/292-1115. www.driscollrobbins.com. Bus: 12, 16, 66. Map p 83.*

★ **Palace Rug Gallery** PIONEER SQUARE Colorful wool and silk rugs from Afghanistan, Pakistan, and China are stacked high in this large space. They are all hand-made, and some take up to 16 months to complete. If you're local, you can take several home and try them out. *323 1st Ave. S.* ☎ *206/382-7401. www.palacerug.com. Bus: 10, 85, 99. Map p 84.*

Shoes
★ **The Clog Factory** PIONEER SQUARE Talk about a niche! If you're in the market for clogs, this is your place. Even if you're not, you might change your mind. They've got high-quality clogs in all colors, shapes and sizes, Mary Janes to slippers. *217 1st Ave. S.* ☎ *206/682-2564. www.clogheaven. com. Bus: 10, 85, 99. Map p 84.*

There's a clog for every foot at The Clog Factory.

★★ **Niketown** DOWNTOWN You'll find all the latest Nike shoes here, and lots of tributes to the top athletes who endorse them. *1500 6th Ave.* ☎ *206/447-6453. Bus: 10, 11, 14, 81. Map p 83.*

★★★ **Nordstrom** DOWNTOWN No footwear listing is complete without the name that's synonymous with shoes in Seattle. *500 Pine St.* ☎ *206/628-2111. www. nordstrom.com. Bus: 10, 11, 14, 43, 83. Map p 83.*

★★★ **Nordstrom Rack** DOWNTOWN In addition to super bargains on men's and women's clothing, the Rack has a huge selection of shoes, all current, all at a fraction of their original price. *400 Pine St.* ☎ *206/448-8522. www. nordstrom.com. Bus: 10, 11, 14, 99, 554. Map p 83.*

Toys & Novelties
★★ **Magic Mouse Toys** PIONEER SQUARE Grown-ups have just as much trouble as kids in tearing themselves away from this wonderful, multi-level shop where the toys are built to last. Wander through rooms filled with learning-focused books, games and kits-- there's an entire room dedicated to puzzles. And of course, everyone is encouraged to play. *603 1st Ave.* ☎ *206/682-8097. Bus: 10, 99, 157, 158. Map p 84.*

★★ **Market Magic & Novelty Shop** PIKE PLACE MARKET Making magic for 30 years, this store buried deep in the Market has been visited by a number of well-known magicians over the years. There's usually some sleight-of-hand in progress; just look for the row of gawking kids. *1501 Pike Place #427.* ☎ *206/624-4271. Bus: 10, 99, 113, 121 or 122. Map p 85.* ●

5 The Best of the **Outdoors**

The Seattle **Waterfront**

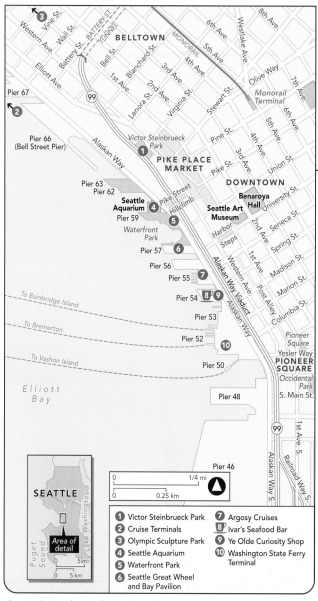

1 Victor Steinbrueck Park
2 Cruise Terminals
3 Olympic Sculpture Park
4 Seattle Aquarium
5 Waterfront Park
6 Seattle Great Wheel and Bay Pavilion
7 Argosy Cruises
8 Ivar's Seafood Bar
9 Ye Olde Curiosity Shop
10 Washington State Ferry Terminal

Previous Page: Sailing on Elliott Bay

It's nothing like it used to be back in grittier times, but Seattle's waterfront is still the watery focus of the city. The main body of water you see is Elliott Bay, which leads to Puget Sound, which leads to the Pacific Ocean. From the ferry terminals at the south end of the waterfront to the Olympic Sculpture Park at the north end, you can stroll, dine, shop, visit the aquarium, take a boat tour, ride on the giant observation wheel, and simply enjoy what made Seattle Seattle. Be prepared for transformative changes in the years ahead as the noisy elevated Alaskan Way viaduct is dismantled and the waterfront becomes a giant park connected to the city and dedicated to pedestrians. The glass panels you see in the new pavement are meant to provide light for migrating salmon as they make their way along the shoreline to and from the Pacific Ocean. START: Bus 99, 113, 121 or 122 to 1st Avenue, walk to Western Avenue.

1 ★ **Victor Steinbrueck Park.** Just north of Pike Place Market, this waterfront park is a great place for a picnic (grab your picnic supplies in the Market) or to get an overview of the waterfront area below. If the weather gods are with you, you'll be treated to a panorama of mountains—the Cascades (starring Mount Rainier) curving around to the east and the Olympics to the west and, of course, Elliott Bay. *2001 Western Ave. Daily 6am–10pm.*

2 ★ **Cruise Terminals.** Seattle is a major departure point for cruises to Alaska, and that's where most of the luxury cruise ships you'll see here are headed. Seven major cruise lines come and go from Seattle. A second terminal, Smith Cove

The Seattle waterfront at night

terminal, is at Pier 91 north of the old Bell Street terminal at Pier 66. Check the Port of Seattle's website for an up-to-date cruise schedule. *2225 Alaskan Way S., Pier 66; 2001 W. Garfield St., Pier 91.* ☎ *206/615-3900. www.portseattle.org.*

3 ★★★ **Olympic Sculpture Park.** Part of the Seattle Art Museum, this remarkable—and free—outdoor sculpture park occupies a hilly site overlooking Elliott Bay, at the north end of what many locals consider to be the most attractive part of the Seattle waterfront. Works by an international roster of major sculptors will delight, intrigue and challenge you, and the maritime/mountain views are sublime. *2901 Western Ave. See p. 28.*

4 ★★ **Seattle Aquarium.** Be sure to grab a schedule of animal feeding times when you buy your tickets. It's not every day you'll get to see a gentle, giant octopus dine! Each mealtime "show," is accompanied by a short talk by a naturalist. *1483 Alaskan Way on Pier 59.* ☎ *206/386-4300. www.seattleaquarium.org. $30 adults, $20 children 4–12. Daily 9:30am–5pm. See p 35.*

5 ★★★ **Waterfront Park.** Stretching between Piers 57 and 59, this concrete park is my favorite spot for watching all the action out in Elliott Bay. It's not a green oasis, but you can't beat the location. With the "Waterfront Fountain" sculpture splashing in the background, you can breathe in a lungful of salty Seattle air, lean over the railing, and watch the maritime parade of ferries, tugs, sailboats, fishing trawlers, cruise ships, and the occasional seal. *1301 Alaskan Way.*

❻ ★★ Seattle Great Wheel and Bay Pavilion. Seattle's newest landmark, the Seattle Great Wheel, opened in 2012. It will never rival the Space Needle for iconic supremacy, but it's quite a sight, especially when it's lit up at night. The Great Wheel takes visitors up 175 feet in enclosed pods for fabulous views of Puget Sound, the Olympic Mountains, and the city. Behind the Wheel, Bay Pavilion is a place for kids to play arcade games or take a spin on the merry-go-round. *Pier 57, 1301 Alaskan Way. $14 adults, $12 seniors, $9.50 kids 4–11. Winter Mon–Thurs 11am–10pm, Fri 11am–midnight, Sat*

The vintage carousel at Bay Pavilion

10am–midnight, Sun 10am–10pm; summer Sun-Thurs 10am-11pm, Fri-Sat 10am-midnight. See p. 10.

❼ ★★★ Argosy Cruises. In addition to its fascinating and enjoyable, 4-hour Tillicum Excursion to Blake island, and a popular 1-hour Waterfront Tour of Elliott Bay, Argosy offers brunch, lunch, and dinner cruises; a tour of lakes Washington and Union (including the famous Seattle houseboats); and a cruise through the Hiram M. Chittenden Locks. There are themed cruises, holiday cruises, musical cruises—you name it, they've got a cruise for it. ⏱ *1–2½ hr. Pier 55, Seattle Waterfront.* ☎ *206/622-8687. www.argosy-cruises.com. See p 11.*

❽ ★ Ivar's Seafood Bar. The best bowl of clam chowder in Seattle, or at least the most famous, is right here at Ivar's, which has been dishing out local seafood since 1938. You can also get clams 'n chips, oysters 'n chips and a variety of other fresh, locally caught treats for munching as you wander the waterfront. Or take a break and relax at one of the outdoor tables set up beside the bar. *Pier 54, 1001 Alaskan Way.* ☎ *206/624-6852. $*

❾ ★ Ye Olde Curiosity Shop. A reworked rendition of a century-old Seattle landmark, this is as much quirky museum as it is a tacky souvenir shop. The owner's great-grandfather gathered oddities from around the world and hired local Native Americans to carve totem poles. Shrunken heads and mummies share the shelves with Seattle T-shirts and homemade fudge. The store expanded in 2016 and lost some of its gritty old pizzazz. *Pier 54, 1001 Alaskan Way.* ☎ *206/682-5844. www.yeoldecuriosityshop.com.*

Ivar's Seafood Bar is famous for its clam chowder.

⑩ ★★★ Washington State Ferry Terminal. It's not the terminal building that's great, but where those ferries will take you from here. You can glide your way to Bainbridge Island, Bremerton, or Vashon Island. There is passenger-only service to Vashon from this spot, and if you're headed to Bainbridge Island or Bremerton you can walk on or take your car. The latter is pricier, and the lines can be much longer. If you just want to walk on a ferry, go for a ride and poke around town, Bainbridge (35 min.) is your best option. If you'd like a long, leisurely ride, take the hour-long Bremerton run. And if you want to go exploring the Kitsap or Olympic peninsulas (Olympic National Park takes you over mountains and through rainforest to the northwestern edge of the state), drive onto the Bremerton ferry and leave from the western side of Puget Sound. *801 Alaskan Way, Pier 52. See p 181.*

Seattle Celebrates Summer

When the winters are as long and gray as they are in Seattle, who can blame the locals for a little excess when summer shows up, with its picture-perfect days that stretch until 10 at night? Getting a jump on the season is the **Northwest Folklife Festival,** which is held at Seattle Center in May and showcases the region's cultures. In June, the **Seattle Pride Festival** celebrates the LGBT community. At **Bite of Seattle** in July, crowds elbow their way into Seattle Center to hear live bands and sample gourmet treats and wine from local restaurants. Summer is officially kicked off with the **Fourth of July** fireworks over Lake Union, one of the finest displays in the nation. **Seafair** is a month of parades, competitions, and hydroplane races celebrating all things maritime. The mother of all festivals, **Bumbershoot,** marks the end of summer and the return of drizzle. Fine arts, crafts, acrobats, big-name bands, and general zaniness rule supreme at Seattle Center over the Labor Day weekend.

Lake Union

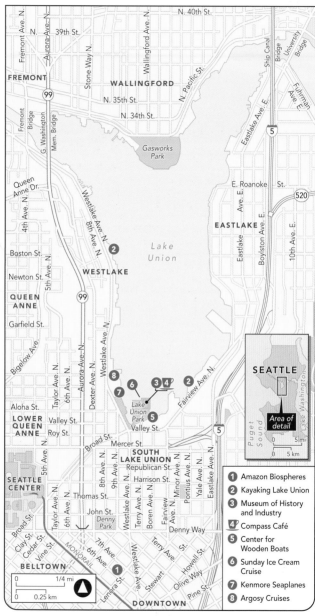

FREMONT

N. 40th St.
N. 39th St.

WALLINGFORD

N. 35th St.
N. 34th St.
N. Pacific St.

Ship Canal

University Bridge

Fuhrman Ave. E.

Gasworks Park

Fremont Ave. N.
Aurora Ave. N.
N.
Stone Way N.
Wallingford Ave. N.
N.

G. Washington Mem. Bridge

Fremont Bridge

Queen Anne Dr.
4th Ave. N.
Westlake Ave. N.
8th Ave. N.

E. Roanoke St.

Eastlake Ave. E.

Eastlake Ave. E.
Ave. E.
Ave. E.
Boylston Ave. E.
10th Ave. E.

EASTLAKE

Boston St.
Newton St.

WESTLAKE

Lake Union

QUEEN ANNE

5th Ave. N.

Garfield St.

Bigelow Ave.

Dexter Ave. N.
Westlake Ave. N.
Aurora Ave. N.
Taylor Ave. N.
6th Ave. N.

Westlake Ave. N.

Fairview Ave. N.

Aloha St.

LOWER QUEEN ANNE

Valley St.
Roy St.
Valley St.

Lake Union Park

Broad St.

Mercer St.

SOUTH LAKE UNION

Republican St.
Harrison St.

Thomas St.

SEATTLE CENTER

5th Ave.
Taylor Ave. N.
6th Ave. N.
8th Ave. N.
9th Ave. N.
Westlake Ave. N.
Terry Ave. N.
Boren Ave. N.
Fairview Ave. N.
Minor Ave. N.
Pontius Ave. N.
Yale Ave. N.
Eastlake Ave. N.

John St.
Denny Park
Denny Way

Broad St.
Clay St.
Cedar St.
Vine St.

BELLTOWN

7th Ave.
6th Ave.
MONORAIL

Terry Ave.
St.
Stewart St.
Olive Way
Howell St.
Pine St.

Lenora St.

DOWNTOWN

0   1/4 mi
0   0.25 km

SEATTLE

Area of detail

Puget Sound
Lake Washington

0   5 mi
0   5 km

1 Amazon Biospheres
2 Kayaking Lake Union
3 Museum of History and Industry
4 Compass Café
5 Center for Wooden Boats
6 Sunday Ice Cream Cruise
7 Kenmore Seaplanes
8 Argosy Cruises

Despite its prime waterfront location, this neighborhood north of downtown was until quite recently, underutilized by Seattleites. That's all changing now, as apartments, shops, and restaurants pop up along the shore, and the adjacent South Lake Union area undergoes a dramatic urban transformation with the arrival of Amazon's world-headquarter towers and biospheres. This is an entertaining and evolving neighborhood, where you'll see seaplanes gracefully taking off and landing, sailboats gliding dreamily along the lake, neighborhoods of houseboat-dwellers, and spanking-new towers and businesses. START: **South Lake Union Streetcar 98, or Bus 17, 70, 71, 72or 73 to Lake Union.**

The South Lake Union Streetcar is a fun new way to explore the area.

1 ★★ **Amazon Biospheres.** If there is anything that has driven major redevelopment of the South Lake Union neighborhood, it's the arrival of Amazon's world headquarters. The corporate towers aren't very interesting, but the plant-filled biospheres between them are worth a look. They're meant for Amazonians, but hopefully, when they're finished in 2018, they will be open to the rest of us, too. ⏱ *15 min. Corner of 6th and Lenorat.*

2 ★★★ **Kayaking Lake Union.** There's nothing quite like paddling a boat in the heart of a city, especially one as picturesque as Seattle. Seaplanes buzz overhead and splash down nearby as you explore the houseboat "neighborhoods" and enjoy the dramatic view of the Space Needle and Seattle's distinctive skyline. If you want to pay for the extra rental time, you can paddle up to the dock at one of the waterfront restaurants and enjoy a scenic lunch. *Boats may be rented at Moss Bay (1001 Fairview Ave. N., #1900;* ☎ *206/682-2031; www.mossbay.co; kayak rentals June 1–Sept 15 $16/hr. single, $22/hr. double) or Northwest Outdoor Center (2100 Westlake Ave. N., Ste. 1;* ☎ *206/281-9694; www.*

nwoc.com; kayak rentals $16/hr. single, $25/hr. double, or $30/hr. triple). Standup paddleboards are also available at Northwest Outdoor Center.

③ ★★ Museum of History & Industry (MOHAI). This gem of a museum housed in the refurbished Naval armory building provide a fascinating overview of Seattle's history, including major events, iconic personalities, and original artifacts. ① 1 hr. 860 Terry Ave. N. ⌧ 206/324-1126. www.mohai.org. $20 adults, $16 seniors, $14 students, free ages 14 and under; free first Thursday of month. Daily 10am–5pm, Thurs until 8pm. See p. 24.

④ ★ Compass Cafe. Enjoy the fabulous view of Lake Union with fresh soup, a sandwich, or an espresso at this bright cafe in the northwest corner of MOHAI. 860 Terry Ave. N. ☎ 206/324-1126. $

The Center for Wooden Boats offers a fascinating boat collection, plus rentals and lessons.

⑤ ★★ Center for Wooden Boats. This unusual spot is basically an outdoor museum, where you can walk along the dock and enjoy a fascinating collection of historic and replica human- and wind-powered boats. You can also rent a sailboat or rowboat and take sailing lessons; old salts love the maritime library. 1010 Valley St. ☎ 206/382-2628. www.cwb.org. Free. Rowboats & sailboats from $25/hr (Sat-Sun). See p. 36.

⑥ ★★ Sunday Ice Cream Cruise. Capt. Larry (Kezner) is your congenial host for a 45-minute cruise of Lake Union on his charming ferryboat. The captain knows everything there is to know about Lake Union, its houseboat communities, and environs—and provides a lively, entertaining narrative while passengers enjoy chocolate ice cream floats. Other treats are also available. The boat—the m/v Fremont—leaves on the hour from 11am to 4pm year-round, rain or shine. Valley St. & Terry Ave. N. ☎ 206/713-8446, www.seattleferryservice.com. $12 adults, $11 seniors, $8 ages 5–13, $3 ages 4 & under.

⑦ ★★★ Seaplane Flights. What better way to see Seattle than from the air, and what more fitting takeoff and landing than the water? Seaplanes have been leaving from Lake Union since 1916, and Kenmore Air has been flying floatplanes in the Pacific Northwest for more than half a century. Its Lake Union facility is the busiest commercial seaplane terminal in the country. You can take the popular 20-minute City Explorer flightseeing excursion, or opt for a longer flight to a private beach with a gourmet catered picnic, day trips to Mt. Rainier, Mt. St. Helens, and the San Juan Islands, or even a getaway to Victoria (don't forget your passport). 950 Westlake Ave. N. ☎ 425/486-1257.

Lake Union's charming houseboats

www.kenmoreair.com. *20-min. City Explorer tour: $99 per person; prices vary for longer tours.*

8 ★★★ **Argosy Cruises.** Year-round, Seattle's premier sightseeing cruise company offers a fun and informative 1½-hour narrated cruise of Lake Union. Along the way, you'll see the floating houseboat neighborhoods made famous in the movie "Sleepless in Seattle" and learn about the cultural and industrial history of the lake. *Departs from AGC Marina. 1200 Westlake Ave.* ☎ *888/623-1445. www.argosy-cruises.com. Mar–mid-May Fri–Sun 3pm; mid-May–June Mon–Fri 3pm, Sat–Sun 1pm and 3pm; July–Sept daily 11am, 1pm, 3pm; check website for details. $32 adults, $27 seniors, $13 ages 4–12.*

Mega-Makeover

South Lake Union is undergoing a major transformation, thanks in large part to Microsoft co-founder/real estate magnate Paul Allen's vision of the former warehouse and industrial area as tech hub and urban business center. It's easy to get there via the new, bright red or green South Lake Union Streetcar, which runs between this neighborhood and downtown every 15 minutes. In addition to the tech firms, online bookseller Amazon.com has built a huge campus in South Lake Union that includes futuristic biospheres, and the old Navy armory building has reopened as the new home of Seattle's much-loved Museum of History & Industry (MOHAI). Visitors can enjoy the wide variety of boating and other waterfront activities along South Lake Union. If you work up a hunger, grab a burger or taco—or dine at one of the stylish lakeside restaurants. Try **Daniels' Broiler** (809 Fairview Pl. N.), or watch the boats from the outdoor deck at **McCormick & Schmick's Harborside** (1200 Westlake Ave. N.).

Hiram M. Chittenden Locks

① Visitors Center
② Carl S. English, Jr. Botanical Garden
③ Fish Ladder
④ Hiram J. Chittenden Locks
⑤ Lockspot Café

Watching the boats navigate the locks is a fascinating enough way to spend an afternoon, but at Hiram M. Chittenden, there's much more: those amazing climbing fish, the impressive botanical gardens, and the best grassy hills in town for kids to roll down. (Do keep an eye out for goose droppings.) You'll find lots of prime picnic spots where you can munch as you watch the boats go by. START: **Bus 44 to Northwest 54th Street & 30th Ave. NW.**

① ★ **Visitors Center.** Stop here first for free brochures on the locks and garden, and watch the informational video shown every half-hour. Free hour-long guided tours of both the locks and the garden are offered March through November (call for tour times). *3015 NW 54th St.* ☎ *206/783-7059. May–Sept: Daily 10am–6pm; Oct–April: Thurs–Mon 10am–4pm.*

② ★ **Carl S. English, Jr. Botanical Garden.** Building and dredging the locks produced a vast

The Carl S. English Jr. Botanical Garden is one of Seattle's best-kept secrets.

Come watch the salmon head upstream at the Fish Ladder.

amount of empty space. Botanist Carl S. English Jr., came to the rescue, transforming the grounds into a splendid English-style garden with plants from around the globe. This fragrant, blooming quilt is a little-known Seattle secret. *3015 NW 54th St.* ☎ *206/783-7059. Daily 7am–9pm.*

❸ ★ Fish Ladder. Salmon have got to be the most inspirational fish

Take a seafood break at casual Lockspot Café.

in the sea. They hatch in streams, swim out to the ocean, and then years later manage to swim upstream, against the odds, back to their exact birthplace to start the cycle again. Here, they swim from the ocean into Puget Sound, leap up a 21-"step" ladder to get up to freshwater Lake Washington level, then head home. It takes a lot of energy for a salmon to swim and flop its way up the ladder, but persistence pays. At different times during the summer you might see sockeye, Chinook, Coho, and steelhead salmon. Watch them climbing the ladders outdoors, and then head down to an underwater viewing room for a different perspective. Though it's open year-round, you won't find much but water from October through May. Call ahead to see what's running. *3015 NW 54th St.* ☎ *206/783-7059. http://www.govlink.org/watersheds/8/action/salmon-seeson/ballard.aspx. Free admission. Daily 7am–9pm.*

❹ Hiram M. Chittenden Locks. I never tire of watching the boats of all shapes and sizes make their ascent from salty Puget Sound up into the fresh waters of Lake Washington. Some pretty magnificent boats come through here. You might spot one of billionaire Paul Allen's mega-yachts. You might also spot a sea lion or harbor seal, hopping for a tasty salmon lunch. *3015 NW 54th St.* ☎ *206/783-7059. www.ballardlocks.org. Daily 7am–9pm.*

❺ Lockspot Cafe. You can't miss this eatery at the entrance to the locks: Just look for the undersea mural, complete with mermaid and orca. Grab some fish 'n chips at the outside counter and have a picnic at the locks. You can also dine inside in a pub-like atmosphere, but if it's a nice day, opt for the picnic. *3005 NW 54th St.* ☎ *206/789-4865. $*

Green Lake Park

1. Green Lake Path
2. Swimming Pools
3. Playground
4. Tennis Courts
5. Boating
6. 72nd Street Café
7. Seattle Public Theater at the Bathhouse

Rain or shine, the locals put their babies in a stroller and their dogs on a leash and head here for their daily dose of fresh air. The path, nearly 3 miles long, winds around a beautiful glacier-carved lake ringed by spectacular trees and Northwest plants. Cars zoom past on busy State Road 99, but the highway is just far enough away from this evergreen oasis that you barely notice. For more on the park, **visit** https://www.seattle.gov/parks/.

find/parks/green-lake-park.
START: Bus 16 or 316 to Woodlawn Avenue & NE 71st St., walk to East Green Lake Drive North.

1 ★★★ **Green Lake Path.** This 2.8-mile trail around the lake has a crushed granite inner lane for walkers, joggers, and strollers; an outer asphalt lane for bicyclists and skaters. The bird-watching is great! 7201 E. Green Lake Dr. N.

2 ★ **Swimming Pools.** In addition to an outdoor wading pool and indoor heated pool, there is a beach on the lakefront with lifeguards and diving boards in the summertime. Note: Green Lake has frequent algae blooms when the weather turns warm, which means the lake will be closed to swimmers, so check for informational signs before you go for a dip. See p 37, ⑩.

3 ★★ **Playground.** Parents and kids alike can take a break at this terrific play area, which offers some cool features not found in other parks. Younger kids love the sand

Scenic Green Lake Path is great for birdwatching.

pit with the sand-digging machine, and canoe for imaginary trips. If the weather turns nasty, the park's nearby community center has an indoor playroom for the younger set. *E. Green Lake Way & Latona Ave. NE (near the main entrance).*

4 ★ **Tennis Courts.** You'll find some just inside the main entrance, at 7201 E. Green Lake Dr. N., and also at W. Greenlake Way & Stone Ave. N. To reserve a court, call ☎ 206/684-4075. Fees to rent the tennis courts are $32 for singles and $40 for doubles, for a 1¼-hour reservation.

Canoe rentals on Green Lake

5 ★★ **Boating.** Take a canoe out on the lake—or a kayak or paddle boat. Or try out one of the stand-up paddleboards. You can rent them north of the main entrance, from Green Lake Rentals, and launch from there or the boat launch on the southwest side of the lake. *7351 E. Green Lake Dr. N. ☎ 206/527-0171. Rentals start at $18/hour.*

6 **72nd Street Café.** Genial baristas, rich Zoka coffee beans—what more could you ask for? Maybe some tasty pastries, or a grilled panini from Mike's East Coast Sandwiches. The kids can chomp on PB&Js while you sit back and smell (and sip) the coffee. *308 NE 72nd St. ☎ 206/523-5623. $*

7 ★★★ **Seattle Public Theater at the Bathhouse.** This 1920s-era bathhouse has been converted into a popular playhouse on the west side of the lake. Here, tucked away in the middle of Green Lake Park, Seattle Public Theater presents shows that are sometimes controversial and usually worth watching. *7312 W. Greenlake Dr. N. ☎ 206/524-1300. www.seattlepublictheater.org.*

Washington Park **Arboretum**

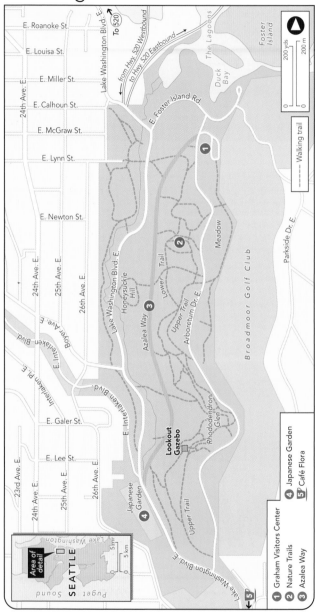

- **1** Graham Visitors Center
- **2** Nature Trails
- **3** Azalea Way
- **4** Japanese Garden
- **5** Café Flora

Walking trail

Lookout Gazebo

Broadmoor Golf Club

Foster Island

The Lagoons

Duck Bay

Meadow

Lower Trail

Upper Trail

Arboretum Dr. E.

Honeysuckle Hill

Azalea Way

Rhododendron Glen

Japanese Garden

E. Foster Island Rd.

Lake Washington Blvd. E.

To 520

from Hwy 520 Westbound

to Hwy 520 Eastbound

Parkside Dr. E.

E. Roanoke St.

E. Louisa St.

E. Miller St.

E. Calhoun St.

E. McGraw St.

E. Lynn St.

E. Newton St.

E. Galer St.

E. Lee St.

24th Ave. E.

25th Ave. E.

26th Ave. E.

Boyer Ave. E.

Interlaken Blvd

E. Interlaken Blvd.

Interlaken Pl. E.

23rd Ave. E.

24th Ave. E.

25th Ave. E.

26th Ave. E.

Lake Washington Blvd. E.

200 yds

200 m

SEATTLE

Lake Washington

Puget Sound

Area of detail

5 km

5 mi

This is Seattle's garden, spread out along 200 acres of lush property, with Lake Washington winding its way around the northern edge. Breathtaking any time of year, the arboretum is especially stunning in the spring and early summer. Thousands of exotic plants have been gathered from every corner of the world. START: **2300 Arboretum Dr.**

❶ ★ Graham Visitors Center. Stop here for a map of the trails and then wander among the trees, ponds, and shrubs of the Arboretum (open daily dawn to dusk) at your leisure. *2300 Arboretum Dr.* ☎ *206/543-8800. www.botanicgardens.uw.edu. Daily 9am–5pm.*

❷ ★★★ Nature Trails. Pick a trail on your map and start hiking! It's a good idea to bring along a light backpack for snacks and water. These trails are all easy walks with no hills to scale. My favorite is the 3.5-mile Foster Island trail, which winds along a boardwalk through an emerald-green wetland area and leads to two islands. You'll be rewarded with spectacular views of Lake Washington. *2300 Arboretum Dr.*

❸ ★★★ Azalea Way. This garden near Graham Visitors Center comes alive in the springtime, when it is transformed into a spectacular ¾-mile promenade of azaleas and cherry blossoms. *2300 Arboretum Dr.*

❹ ★★★ Seattle Japanese Garden. The centerpiece of the

The Seattle Japanese Garden is the centerpiece of Washington Park Arboretum.

Arboretum, this exquisite garden is the perfect place to slow your pace and contemplate life. World-famous Japanese garden designer Juki Iida designed it with sublime beauty. Formal tea ceremonies cost $10 per person and are held at the Shoseian Teahouse inside the garden, from April to October (check dates on the Urasenke Foundation's website: www.urasenkeseattle.org). *1075 Lake Washington Blvd. E.* ☎ *206/684-4725. www.seattlejapanesegarden.org. $6 adults, $4 seniors & ages 6–17. Open Mar–Nov. Mon noon–5pm, Tues–Sun 10am–6pm (closed Mon Mar & Oct–Nov; closing time changes seasonally, check website for hours).*

Spring is the best time to catch Washington Park Arboretum's Azalea Way in full bloom.

5️⃣ Café Flora. Located less than a half-mile from the Arboretum, this popular spot offers a host of delicious vegetarian, vegan and gluten-free dishes. It's a nice spot to share and sample "alternative" cuisine. Reserve on weekends. *2901 E. Madison St.* ☎ *206/325-9700. $*

Woodland Park

1. Woodland Park Zoo
2. Woodland Park Rose Garden
3. ZooTunes
4. Woodland Park

The focal point of this park, of course, is the Woodland Park Zoo, a must stop for families with kids. It's surrounded by grassy hills that are perfect for picnics and afternoons of fun. The part west of S.R. 99 (Aurora Avenue) is occupied mainly by the zoo; to the east of the highway stretch the parklands, which adjoin Green Lake Park. START: **Bus 5 or 82 to Phinney Ave. N. & N. 50th Street, walk to 750 N. 50th St.**

1 ★★★ Woodland Park Zoo.
There's never a dull moment at this zoo, where the tenants range from red pandas to Komodo dragons and giraffes. Though a zoo of some sort has occupied Woodland Park since the 1890s, the animal habitats today are on the cutting edge of zoo technology. Humboldt penguins and playful meerkats are among the most popular members of the menagerie. *750 N. 50th St.* ☎ *206/684-4800. www.zoo.org. May–Sept: $21 ages 13–64, $19 ages*

Local and exotic species are in residence at the Woodland Park Zoo.

The Woodland Park Rose Garden

65 & older, \$13 ages 3–12; Oct–Apr: \$15 ages 13–64, \$ 13 ages 65 & older, \$10 ages 3–12. May–Sept daily 9:30am–6pm; Oct–Apr: daily 9:30am–4pm. See p 37.

② ★★ Woodland Park Rose Garden. Roses love the Pacific Northwest, and even non-flower-lovers will be captivated by the beauty and diversity packed into this 2½-acre garden started in the 1920s. Although it's no longer an All-America Rose Selections test site, the Woodland Park Rose Garden displays the very latest prize-winning varieties. It's no wonder the garden is always in great demand for weddings. You'll find it east of the zoo's south entrance gate, but in the summertime your nose will lead you there. *700 N. 50th St. Free. Daily 7am–dusk.*

③ ★★ ZooTunes. Summertime means outdoor concert season at Woodland Park Zoo, and they're always great fun, whether it's a time-honored act like Pat Benatar or something a edgier, like the Violent Femmes. Bring a blanket or a low beach chair—yours might actually be measured if it looks too tall—and settle in on the meadow just inside the zoo's north entrance. Kids are welcome and dancing is encouraged! If you plan to visit Seattle from mid-June through August, check the schedule (www.zoo.org/zootunes) in early May. If you see a concert you like, book early because they sell out fast. The website explains how to buy tickets online. The prices are quite reasonable compared to most venues, averaging around \$25 a ticket, plus service fee for web sales. *N. 59th & Evanston Ave.* ☎ *206/615-0076.*

④ ★ Woodland Park. This large urban park is a favorite picnic spot. It's not the most beautiful park in Seattle but it is one of most used, because it offers so many recreational opportunities. You'll find tennis courts, horseshoes, a ball field, playground, and an off-leash dog area. *Aurora Ave. N. & N. 59th St.* ☎ *206/684-4081.*

Seattle Center

1. Seattle Center Armory
2. Space Needle
3. Chihuly Garden and Glass
4. Movies at the Mural
5. Seattle Children's Museum
6. Winterfest
7. Museum of Pop Culture (MoPOP)
8. International Fountain
9. Pacific Science Center
10. Seattle Fudge
11. Seattle Children's Theatre

This is where Seattle comes to party. From the spectacular fountain—where Northwesterners "cool off" as soon as it hits the 60s—to the myriad festivals that mark summertime in Seattle, there's always indoor and outdoor fun to be had here. Even in the winter, the grounds are a lovely place to enjoy a book on a sunny day. If it gets too chilly, pop into the Center House for a hot chocolate. START: Monorail or bus 3, 4, 8, 16 or 30 to Seattle Center.

① ★ **Seattle Center Armory.** This huge building is a focal point of Seattle Center, offering indoor activities that go hand-in-hand with the festivities outside, often hosting art shows and cultural activities, and musical performances on stage. The inside perimeter is lined with restaurants, cafes, and a candy shop. There are indoor tables, but on a nice day, it's much more fun to take your food outside and people-watch while you eat! *See p 35.*

② ★★★ **Space Needle.** Take a ride to the observation deck. On a clear day, you'll see all of Seattle (and Mt. Rainier) at your feet. Book online for discount. ⏱ *1 hr. Summer weekends are busiest. 400 Broad St.* ☎ *206/905-2100. Observation deck tickets: $19-$29 adults, $16-$22 seniors, $13-$18 ages 4-13. Mon–Thurs 10am-9pm; Fri-Sat 9:30am-10:30pm; Sun 9:30am-9:30pm. See p 48,* **⑮**.

③ ★★★ **Chihuly Garden and Glass.** This museum and landscaped garden showcases the extraordinary glass art of Tacoma native Dale Chihuly. *See p 27,* **③**.

④ ★★★ **Movies at the Mural.** Every August weekend, families bring their blankets and low folding chairs to the Mural Amphitheatre, to lounge on the lawn and watch a free movie projected onto a giant screen. Outdoor cinema on a perfect Seattle evening with the Space Needle

as a backdrop is a little slice of heaven. Check the website for the schedule (www.seattlecenter.com; click "Events," then "Film and Movies").

⑤ ★ **Seattle Children's Museum.** Crafts and exhibits for the younger set transform education into playtime, curiosity into creativity. ⏱ *1 hr. 305 Harrison St.* ☎ *206/441-1768. www.thechildrens museum.org. $11.50 adults & children, free under age 1. Mon–Fri 10am-5pm; Sat–Sun 10am-6pm. See p 35,* **④**.

⑥ ★★ **Winterfest.** From Thanksgiving weekend through December, this celebration puts a

The Frank Gehry–designed Museum of Pop Culture

The Best of the Outdoors

little magic into the cold, wet season. An antique carousel is set up outside the Center House, and rides are just $1. There are also bonfires, choirs, ice sculpting, and storytelling. If you get chilly, duck inside and admire the model train, complete with an oversized turn-of-the-20th-century village, set up in the Center House. Outside, Fisher Pavilion becomes an ice rink (Sun–Thurs 11am–8pm; Fri–Sat 11am–10pm. $5 adults, $3 ages 6–12), open through the first weekend of January. *305 Harrison St.* ☎ *206/684-7200. www.seattlecenter.com.*

⑦ ★ **Museum of Pop Culture (MoPOP).** It's the old Experience Music Project rebranded with expanded Star Trek and Sci-Fi museums, plus music-themed activities. ⓵ *1 hr. 325 5th Ave. N. (at Seattle Center).* ☎ tel] **206/770-2700**. *$28 adults, $25 seniors, $19 ages 5–17. Daily summer 10am–7pm, winter 10am–5pm. See p 13,* ③.

High-tech fun at The Pacific Science Center

⑧ ★ **International Fountain.** For sheer joy, it's hard to beat Seattle on a clear, warm summer day, and you'll see plenty of it (joy, that is) on the faces of kids, grownups, and a dog or two at this colossal fountain just north of the Center House. Water-lovers charge down the concrete ramp to splash through the spray, while sunbathers arrange themselves around the fountain to soak up the rays. At night, the waters dance to rainbow colors.

⑨ ★★ **Pacific Science Center.** Spend some time with the cool outdoor exhibits before you go inside. Walk through a giant water wheel, spin a 2-ton granite ball, or ride a high-rail bicycle (weather permitting). This hands-on approach to science is fun for everyone. ⓵ *2 hr. 200 2nd Ave. N.* ☎ *206/443-2001. www.pacific sceiencecenter.org. (including IMAX): $31 adults, $28 seniors, $23 ages 6–15, $19 ages 3–5. About $10 less without IMAX. Daily 10am–6pm. See p 36,* ⑤.

⑩' ★ **Seattle Fudge.** Don't even pretend to look for a healthy snack here (unless popcorn counts). Just go ahead and indulge in the rich, creamy fudge. The kids can watch taffy being pulled—hey, consider it an educational experience! *Center House.* ☎ *206/441-0524. www.seattlefudge.com. $*

⑪ ★★★ **Seattle Children's Theatre.** The shows at this first-rate playhouse are based on beloved classic and contemporary books and movies. *201 Thomas St. at Seattle Center.* ☎ *206/441-3322. www.sct.org. Ticket prices vary. See p 35,* ②. ●

Dining Best Bets

Best **French**
★★ Café Campagne $$–$$$
1600 Post Alley (p 124)

Best Weekend **Brunch**
★★ Salty's on Alki Beach $$$
1936 Harbor Ave SW. (p 131)

Best **Special Occasion**
★★★ Canlis $$$–$$$$$
2576 Aurora Ave N. (p 124)

Best **Steak**
★★★ Metropolitan $$$$
820 2nd Ave. (p 129)

Most Exciting **Fusion Cuisine**
★★★ Poppy $$–$$$
622 Broadway E. (p 130)

Best **Waterfront Dining**
★★★ Aqua $$$–$$$$$
2801 Alaskan Way, Pier 70. (p 123)

Best for **Vegetarians**
★★ Carlile Room. $$
93 Yesler Way. (p. 124)

Best **Dim Sum**
★ Jade Garden $–$$
424 7th Ave S. (p 127)

Best **Hotel Fine Dining**
★★ Tulio $$$ *1100 5th Ave. (p 134)*

Best **Pre-Theater**
★★ Wild Ginger $$–$$$
1401 3rd Ave. (p 134)

Best **Sushi**
★★ Shiro's $$ *2401 2nd Ave. (p 132)*

Best **Tapas**
★★ List $$–$$$
2226 1st Ave. (p 128)

Best **Italian**
★★★ Assaggio $$–$$$
2010 4th Ave. (p 123)

Best **Late-Night**
★★ Ten Mercer $$–$$$
10 Mercer St. (p 134)

Best **Fine Dining with Kids**
★★ Cutters Crabhouse $$$
2001 Western Ave. (p 124)

Best **Seafood Spot**
★★ Blueacre $$–$$$
1700 7th Ave., Ste. 100 (p 123)

Most Fun **Near the Market**
★★ Steelhead Diner $$–$$$ *95
Pine St. (p 133)*

Best **Organic**
★★★ Tilth $$–$$$ *1411 N. 45th St.
(p 134)*

Best **Mediterranean Menu**
★★ Andaluca $$$–$$$$ *407 Olive
Way.* ☎ *206/382-6999. (p 123)*

Best **Pizza**
★★ Serious Pie $$ *316 Virginia St.
(p 131)*

Best **Greek Meets the
Northwest**
★★★ Lola *2000 4th Ave.* $$–$$$
☎ *206/441-1430. (p 128)*

*Salty's on Alki offers a waterfront setting and a sumptuous seafood brunch buffet.
Previous page: An entrée from Andaluca restaurant at the Mayflower Park Hotel*

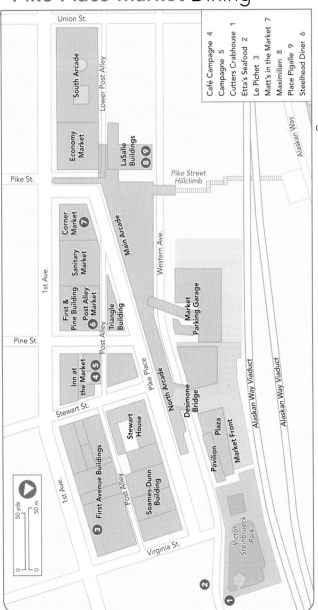

Pike Place Market Dining

Café Campagne 4
Campagne 5
Cutters Crabhouse 1
Etta's Seafood 2
Le Pichet 3
Matt's in the Market 7
Maximilien 8
Place Pigalle 9
Steelhead Diner 6

Downtown/Pioneer Square Dining

Andaluca **22**
Aqua **5**
Assaggio **15**
Blueacre **19**
Café Paloma **31**
Carlile Room **20**
Dahlia Lounge **14**
Dick's Drive-In **38**
Dunbar Room **34**
El Gaucho **7**
Elliott's Oyster
   House **28**
Il Fornaio **21**
Ivar's Fish Bar **29**
Jade Garden **33**
Lark **35**
List **11**
Lola **16**
Marrakesh Moroccan
   Restaurant **9**
Metropolitan Grill **30**
Miller's Guild **18**
MistralKitchen **17**
O'Asian Kitchen **27**
Osteria La Spiga **36**
Pagliacci Pizza **39**
Poppy **40**
Purple Café
   and Wine Bar **26**

Racha Thai
   Asian Kitchen **2**
Salty's on Alki **32**
Serious Pie **13**
Shaker + Spear **12**
Shiro's **8**
Shuckers **25**
Sitka & Spruce **37**
Six Seven **6**
SkyCity
   at the Needle **3**
Tavolata **10**
Ten Mercer **1**
Tulio Ristorante **24**
Wild Ginger **23**
Zeek's **4**

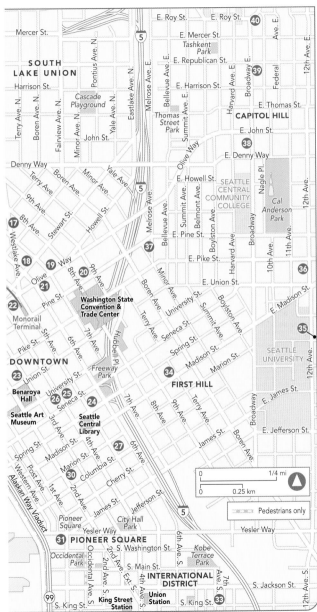

North Seattle Dining

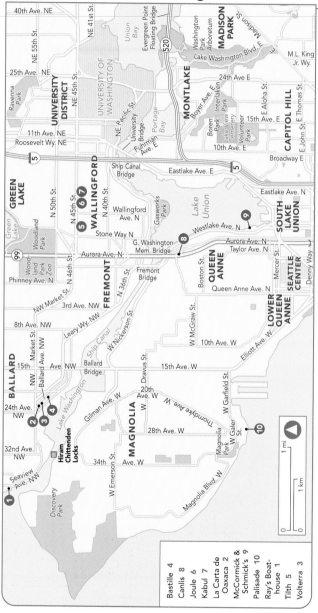

★★ **Andaluca** DOWNTOWN
MEDITERRANEAN Spain meets
the Northwest in perfectly spiced
paellas and other Mediterranean-
influenced choices. The romantic
Andaluca is at the Mayflower Park
Hotel. *407 Olive Way.* ☎ *206/382-
6999. www.andaluca.com. Entrees
$25–$39. Breakfast daily, lunch Mon–
Fri, dinner Tues–Sun. Bus: 25, 79,123,
202. Map p 121.*

★★★ **Aqua** WATERFRONT
SEAFOOD From a seasonal variety
of local oysters to crispy-skinned
salmon, Chef Wesley Hood's seafood is always fresh and delicious.
As the sister restaurant to El Gaucho steakhouse, this is one seafood
spot where landlubbers are just as
happy. The views of Elliott Bay add
romance to the flavors. *2801 Alaskan Way, Pier 70.* ☎ *206/956-9171.
www.elgaucho.com. Entrees $28–
$89. Dinner daily. Bus: 99.*

★★★ **Assaggio** DOWNTOWN
NORTHERN ITALIAN From the
Michelangelo-inspired art (look up!)
to the personal welcome by gregar-
ious owner/chef Mauro Golmarvi
to the handmade pastas and

melt-in-your-mouth veal dishes,
there's no doubt you've entered a
world where food is a passion.
Everything from the simple Margar-
ita pizza and baked lasagna to the
sophisticated osso buco is fresh and
memorable. Gluten-free versions of
the pastas are available. *2010 4th
Ave.* ☎ *206/441-1399. www.
assaggioseattle.com. Entrees $19–
$37. Lunch Mon–Fri, dinner Mon–Sat.
Bus: 1, 13, 15, 16, 17. Map p 120.*

★★ **Bastille** BALLARD *FRENCH*
The best choices at this fashionable
Parisian-style brasserie are the *plats
du jour* and the seasonal dishes
such as lamb Bolognese or Dungeness crab salad. This is a great spot
to come for Sunday brunch when
the Ballard Farmers' Market adds
spice to the scene and you can
people-watch from the enclosed
patio while enjoying a fluffy omelet.
5307 Ballard Ave. NW. ☎ *206/453-
5014. www.bastilleseattle.com.
Entrees $12–$33. Dinner Mon–Sat,
Sun brunch. See map p 122.*

★★ **Blueacre** DOWNTOWN
SEAFOOD Northwest cuisine
shines at this friendly but elegant

The artful setting for upscale Italian fare at Assaggio

spot, where the oyster bar serves up a variety of tender, buttery local offerings. The dinner menu offers inventively prepared, sustainably caught seafood. My favorite is the lemon-crusted salmon with horse-radish brown butter. When available, don't miss the lightly battered local chanterelle mushrooms in hot-sweet mustard vinaigrette. *1700 7th Ave., Ste. 100.* ☎ *206/659-0737. www.blueacreseafood.com. Entrees $20–$42. Lunch & dinner daily. Bus: 25, 66, 70, 73, 123. Map p 121.*

★★ **Café Campagne** PIKE PLACE MARKET *FRENCH* Come here for a casual, reasonably priced and oh-so-French bistro experience. You won't find a better *croque-monsieur* outside Paris and the *steak frites* and duck confit are always great. *1600 Post Alley.* ☎ *206/ 728-2233. www.cafecampagne.com. Entrees $17–$25.. Lunch Mon–Fri, brunch Sat–Sun, dinner daily. Bus: 10, 99, 113, 121, 122. Map p 119.*

★ **Café Paloma** PIONEER SQUARE *MEDITERRANEAN* At this intimate Turkish cafe, you'll find the Mediterranean standards, including the best falafel in town, plus some creative choices—think gorgonzola panini. *93 Yesler Way.* ☎ *206/405-1920. www.cafepaloma.com. Entrees $12–$16. Lunch Mon–Sat, dinner Tues–Sat, Sun brunch. Bus: 99, 143, 157, 158. Map p 121.*

★★★ **Canlis** DOWNTOWN *NORTHWEST* This is a dress-up place with mandatory jacket and tie for men and dining here is as much about the experience as it is about the meal. The food is fabulous—fresh and inventive, served as a 4-course meal or a la carte—and the wine list outstanding. But it's the service, impeccable without being stuffy, that makes this Relais & Chateaux restaurant perfect for a special occasion. Plan to spend longer than usual for dinner, because you won't

want the pampering—or the view of Lake Union—to end. *2576 Aurora Ave N.* ☎ *206/283-3313. www.canlis. com. Entrees $40–$80; 4-course fixed-price dinner $110. Dinner Mon–Sat. Bus: 5, 16, 28. Map p 122.*

★★ **Carlile Room** DOWNTOWN *PACIFIC NORTHWEST* Newly opened in 2016 but retro-fitted to look like the 1970s, this "plant-for-ward" restaurant cooks and serves up whatever products and produce come in fresh from their farms and local suppliers that day. Inventive and delicious vegetarian choices abound but meat and fish are also on the menu. *93 Yesler Way.* ☎ *206/946-9720. www.thecarlile. com. Entrees $14–$26. Dinner daily, brunch Sat-Sat. Map p 121.*

★★ **Cutters Crabhouse** PIKE PLACE MARKET *NORTHWEST* This lovely restaurant is just steps from Pike Place Market. With sweeping views of Elliott Bay and friendly service, it's the perfect place to relax after shopping—and you won't feel uncomfortable bringing the kids. (There's a children's menu.) The seafood shines; try the tasty crab cakes. *2001 Western Ave.* ☎ *206/448-4884. www.cuttersbayhouse.com. Entrees $25–$45. Lunch & dinner daily. Bus: 99, 113, 121, 122. Map p 119.*

High-end dining on innovative cuisine at Canlis

The focus at Dahlia Lounge is on local, sustainable, and organic ingredients.

★★ Dahlia Lounge BELLTOWN
NORTHWEST Local, sustainable
and organic are the catchwords for
the menu offerings at this ever-
popular Seattle restaurant. The
décor is reminiscent of an old-fashioned faux-Chinese restaurant, but
the food is as up-to-date as you
can be in Seattle, concentrating on
unique flavor combinations and a
seasonal "Fresh Tastes of the Market" approach. *2001 4th Ave.*
☎ *206/682-4142. www.dahlia
lounge.com. Entrees $21–$50. Lunch
Mon–Fri, brunch Sat–Sun, dinner
daily. Bus: 1, 13, 15, 26, 202. Map
p 120.*

★ Dick's Drive-In CAPITOL HILL
BURGERS Seattle's iconic burger
joint still has the orange awnings
from the '50s, though the drive-up
service has ended. Many locals
won't eat burgers anywhere else,
and I can't say that I blame them.
Of course there are also great fries,
hand-dipped shakes and root beer
floats. *115 Broadway Ave. E.*
☎ *206/323-1300. www.dicksdrivein.
com. Entrees $4–$6. Lunch & dinner
daily. Bus: 8, 43, 49, 60. Map p 121.*

★★ Dunbar Room FIRST HILL
NORTHWEST Formerly known as
the Hunt Club, this restaurant in the
historic Sorrento Hotel reinvented
itself and its menu in 2016 to reflect
a lighter, locavore philosophy. Try
the spicy tomato soup: it's been on
the menu for decades. This cozy,
wood-paneled sanctum is a great

place to come for happy hour
(4-6pm). *900 Madison St.* ☎ *206/
343-6156. www.hotelsorrento.com.
Entrees $18–$30. Breakfast, lunch &
dinner daily, brunch Sat–Sun. Bus: 12,
60. Map p 121.*

★★ El Gaucho BELLTOWN
STEAK The steaks are perfection and
the service attentive at this upscale,
supper-club-style steakhouse. For a
special occasion, order the cha-
teaubriand for two. *2505 1st Ave.*
☎ *206/728-1337. www.elgaucho.
com. Entrees $26–$75. Dinner daily.
Bus: 19, 24, 81, 99. Map p 120.*

★★ Elliott's Oyster House
WATERFRONT *SEAFOOD* This is
an oyster-lover's nirvana, with a
huge selection of local oysters, raw,
steamed, or pan-fried. The seafood
is fresh and local, with standouts
including the salmon (always non-
farmed) and the Dungeness crab
with chili-lime sauce. If it's a nice
day, dine outside on the deck overhanging Elliott Bay. *1201 Alaskan
Way, Pier 56.* ☎ *206/623-4340.
www.elliottsoysterhouse.com. Entrees
$18–$39. Lunch & dinner daily. Bus:
12, 99, 113, 121. Map p 120.*

★★★ Etta's Seafood PIKE
PLACE MARKET *SEAFOOD* Casual
but classy, Etta's caters to the tourist crowd but also has a loyal local
following. Etta's is my favorite destination for salmon—and for fresh
oysters and seafood in general,
because I've never had a less than
excellent meal here. Their

Seattle: A Locavore's Dream

Washington State's temperate climate is ideal for growing everything from apples to zucchinis. Small farms grow such a wide variety of fresh produce throughout the year that the locavore movement (eating locally as much as possible) has rapidly gained ground among chefs at top restaurants.

Seafood   Silvery salmon, hefty Dungeness crabs, clams, mussels, and dozens of varieties of oysters are the seafood stars in this city on the shores of Puget Sound. Salmon, although not always local, is a Northwest icon that shows up both fresh and smoked on Seattle menus. Wish you could take some home? Not a problem. Pike Place Market fishmongers will pack fresh salmon for you to take home on the plane, and some vacuum-packed smoked salmon doesn't even need to be refrigerated. You can sample fresh and relatively inexpensive oysters on the half-shell during happy hour at almost every Seattle restaurant, but be prepared to pay top dollar for freshly caught salmon and other local fish.

Chocolate   Seattle's **Theo Chocolate** (☎ **206/632-5100;** www. theochocolate.com), a company that gives tours of its chocolate factory, roasts its own organic and fair-trade cocoa beans. Finally, guilt-free chocolate!

Meat   Organic farms and cattle ranches in Washington State have seen a surge of interest in their grass-fed beef and organically raised chicken and pork products. You will now find delicious cuts of meat and chicken raised without antibiotics at just about every good restaurant in Seattle.

Coffee   Of course, as nearly everyone on the planet knows, Starbucks got its start in Seattle, and espresso here has been raised to an art form. Even espresso stands around town have jumped on the wagon, serving organic, fair-trade, and shade-grown coffees.

Wine & Beer   Many of Washington state's best and biggest wineries are in the town of Woodinville, just a 30-minute drive north of Seattle. Washington wineries are best known for their cabernet sauvignon and merlot, but you should also keep an eye out for excellent Syrahs and Semillons. Seattle is also home to quite a few craft breweries. Check out **Big Time Brewery & Alehouse** (☎ **206/ 545-4509;** www.bigtimebrewery.com) and the **Elysian Brewing Company** (p 140).

Vegetarian, Vegan, and Gluten-free   Seattle restaurants are at the top of the class when it comes to special dietary needs and preferences. Almost every restaurant has at least one vegetarian or vegan offering, and gluten-free options are available as well, sometimes for a small additional charge.

Dungeness crab cakes are a famous signature dish. On my last visit, I enjoyed a fabulous seafood stew. *2020 Western Ave.* ☎ *206/443-6000. www.tomdouglas.com. Entrees $16–$36. Lunch Mon–Fri, brunch/ breakfast Sat–Sun, dinner daily. Bus: 19, 21, 99, 113. Map p 119.*

★★ **Il Fornaio** DOWNTOWN *ITALIAN* By exploring a different region of Italy each month, this stylish eatery (yes, it is a chain) keeps things fresh. The breads, baked on site, are *fabuloso*; the pastas *deliciosa*; and many of the wines come from Il Fornaio's own vineyard in Tuscany. My favorite dish: the simple but satisfying *linguini di polpettine* (linguine with meatballs). The bakery and cafe are downstairs; climb up the spiral staircase to the classy dining room. *600 Pine St., Ste. 132.* ☎ *206/264-0994. www. ilfornaio.com. Entrees $18–$37. Breakfast, lunch & dinner daily. Bus: 10, 11, 14, 43, 49. Map p 121.*

★ **Ivar's Fish Bar** WATERFRONT *SEAFOOD* This iconic Seattle establishment perched on Pier 54, is part of a local seafood chain and has been in business in various forms since 1947. Come here for takeout fish and chips, made with fresh cod or halibut, and a cup of thick, creamy clam chowder. It's a great place to eat fresh, inexpensive seafood and watch the ferries crossing Elliott Bay. *1001 Alaskan Way.* ☎ *206/624-6852. www.ivars. com. Entrees $8–$15. Lunch & dinner daily. Bus: 16, 66, 99. Map p 120.*

★ **Jade Garden** INTERNATIONAL *ASIAN* In a town blessed with a number of good dim sum spots, this is one of the best for variety, freshness, and ambience. If you're new to dim sum, start with some basics like *hum bao* (steamed buns stuffed with sweet barbecued pork), *ha gao* (shrimp dumpling) and

sticky rice wrapped in lotus leaves. *424 7th Ave. S.* ☎ *206/622-8181. Entrees $8–$13. Lunch & dinner daily. Bus: 7, 14, 36, 99. Map p 121.*

★★★ **Joule** WALLINGFORD *KOREAN/FRENCH FUSION* Joule is a reasonably priced Korean steakhouse, with innovative dishes that blend Asian and American flavors and ingredients using classic cooking techniques. Try a short rib steak with grilled kimchi, or a wagyu hanger steak with smoky pineapple There are also rice and noodle dishes, plus a great and inexpensive weekend brunch. *1913 N. 45th St.* ☎ *206/632-1913. www. joulerestaurant.com. Entrees $17– $32.. Brunch Sat–Sun, dinner daily. Bus: 16, 44. Map p 122.*

★ **Kabul** NORTH SEATTLE *AFGHAN* If you've ever been curious about Afghan food, or know it and love it, this unpretentious restaurant in North Seattle is definitely worth trying. Kabul transforms the humble eggplant and other fresh veggies into flavorful dishes served over rice; there are also kebabs and salads. *2301 N. 45th St.* ☎ *206/545-9000. www.kabulrestaurant.com. Entrees $17–$25. Dinner Weds-Mon. Bus: 16, 44. Map p 122.*

★★ **Lark** CAPITOL HILL *INTERNATIONAL* Lark encourages family-style sharing and features only locally produced seasonal and organic grains, cheese, vegetables, fish, charcuterie, and meats. The fresh fish plates might include wild salmon with nasturtium, baby summer squash and cucumber wasabi emulsion. Vegetables and grains selections, depending on the season, could be farro with foraged chanterelle mushrooms or potato gnocchi with porcini mushrooms. The artisan cheeses are outstanding. *926 12th Ave.* ☎ *206/323-5275. www.larkseattle. com. Entrees $17–$32. Dinner daily, Sun brunch. Bus: 2, 9, 12. Map p 121.*

★★ La Carta de Oaxaca

BALLARD MEXICAN Seattle's most authentic Mexican restaurant is known for its yummy, hand-mashed guacamole with house-fried tortilla chips and the tender chicken in Oaxaca's signature sweet-spicy black mole. Tacos, empanadas, tamales, chile rellenos—they're all here, they're all excellent. 5431 Ballard Ave NW. ☎ 206/782-8722. www.lacartadeoaxaca.com. Entrees $14–$20. Lunch Tues–Sat, dinner Mon–Sat. Map p 122.

★★ Le Pichet PIKE PLACE MARKET FRENCH This casual bistro serves a classic French menu that would make a Parisian feel right at home. The ingredients are simple and fresh, the sauces superb. 1933 1st Ave. ☎ 206/256-1499. Entrees $12–$25. Lunch & dinner daily. Bus: 10, 99, 113, 121. Map p 119.

★★ List BELLTOWN TAPAS/ITALIAN There's a nice, relaxed vibe to this affordable wine bar and tapas spot. Share a few small plates—maybe the delectable gnocchi with black truffle cream, or the sea salt and pepper calamari—with a bottle of your favorite vintage (they also have good and inexpensive bottles of house red and white) and go on from there. During Happy Hour (all day Sun–Mon, 4–6:30pm & 9pm–midnight Tues–Thurs, 4–6:30pm Fri–Sat) many dishes are half price. 2226 1st Ave. ☎ 206/441-1000. www.listbelltown.com. Tapas $8–$18. Dinner daily. See map p 120.

★★★ Lola BELLTOWN GREEK If you love Greek food, you probably love lamb, and if you're a lamb fan, well, you're going to love Lola. Try the lamb ravioli with yogurt, Aleppo pepper, and pine nuts; lamb kebab with caramelized garlic and red wine; lamb burger; or the slow-cooked and succulent lamb shank. And if you're just hankering for a fresh Greek salad with tomatoes, olives, and feta cheese, this is the place to find it. I have never had a less than wonderful meal here. 2000 4th Ave. ☎ 206/441-1430. Entrees $14–$33. Breakfast Mon–Fri, brunch daily, lunch Mon–Fri, dinner daily. Bus: 1, 13, 15, 26, 202. Map p 120.

★ Marrakesh Moroccan Restaurant BELLTOWN MOROCCAN This cozy spot has the exotic feel of an Arabian tent. Diners sit on cushions or benches at round tables as tantalizing aromas and belly dancers (Wed–Sun) drift through the room. You can order fa la carte or from a fixed-price menu. 2334 2nd Ave. ☎ 206/956-0500. Entrees $12-$15, fixed-price menus $22–$32. Dinner daily. Bus: 1, 13, 15, 19, 24. Map p 120.

★★ Matt's in the Market PIKE PLACE MARKET NORTHWEST Chef Jason McClure doesn't have far to go to get market-fresh produce and seafood. Matt's expanded location is right above Pike Place Market; it's been around for over 20 years and should be around for at least 20 more. Winter cassoulet with duck confit leg, Arctic char with wild mushrooms, house-made charcuterie, falafel, catfish—there's something for every taste. The menu tends to go where the market (as in Pike Street) goes. This is a great lunch spot. 94 Pike St., Ste. 32. ☎ 206/467-7909. www.mattsinthemarket.com. Entrees $15–$30. Lunch & dinner Mon–Sat. Bus: 99, 113, 121, 122. Map p 119.

★★ Maximilien PIKE PLACE MARKET FRENCH Watch the sun set over Elliott Bay through panoramic windows as you dine on classic French fare. Diners have been doing just that here for more than 30 years. 81A Pike St. ☎ 206/682-7270. www.maximilien restaurant.com. Entrees $20–$37. Lunch & dinner daily, brunch Sun. Bus: 99, 113, 121, 122. Map p 119.

★ **McCormick & Schmick's**
LAKE UNION *SEAFOOD* With a spectacular view of Lake Union and an outside deck, this restaurant is a great spot for dinner. But it's also popular at lunchtime, when you can watch the seaplanes take off. Seafood is the star, and the "fresh list" is impressively long. Don't miss the bay shrimp cake appetizers. *1200 Westlake Ave. N.* ☎ *206/270-9052. www.mccormickandschmicks.com. Entrees $16–$34. Lunch & dinner daily. Bus: 17, 30. Map p 122.*

★★★ **Metropolitan Grill**
DOWNTOWN *STEAKS* This historic Seattle restaurant could make a beef-eater out of anyone. If you're in the mood for extravagance, order the prized wagyu beef. But the steak on the regular menu is so flavorful, and cooked to such perfection, there's no need to look further. At lunchtime, it's very popular with the business crowd. *820 2nd Ave.* ☎ *206/624-3287. www.the metropolitangrill.com. Entrees $20–$74. Lunch Mon–Fri, dinner daily. Bus: 143, 157, 158, 159. Map p 121.*

★★ **Miller's Guild** DOWNTOWN *PACIFIC NORTHWEST* A giant mesquite-burning stove in the open

A dessert flambé at the Metropolitan Grill

kitchen grills ribs, steaks, chops, and seafood at this spot, connected to Hotel Max. Maybe start with some Shigoku oysters. Then, if you're an unabashed carnivore, go for the meat, and especially the juicy chops and steaks from Niman Ranch. Order a couple of sides, like creamy mashed potatoes and crispy Brussels sprouts, and a glass of Oregon pinot noir, and you're set. *612 Stewart St.* ☎ *206/ 443-3663. www.millersguild.com. Entrees $26–$63. Breakfast, lunch & dinner daily. Map p 118.*

★★ **MistralKitchen** DOWNTOWN *CONTEMPORARY AMERICAN/GLOBAL* They say you can't please everyone, but chef/owner William Belickis does his best, mingling influences from Africa, France, Spain, Japan, and the U.S. Food is prepared at four stations: a wood-fired/tandoor oven, a traditional kitchen, a pastry kitchen, and a high-tech kitchen. The menu changes daily and seasonally, but might include short ribs with lentils, braised veal shank, or lamb with couscous, plus fresh fish, of course. *2020 Westlake Ave.* ☎ *206/623-1922. www.mistral-kitchen.com. Entrees $20–$38. Lunch Mon–Fri, dinner daily. Bus: 25, 98, 250, 252, 257. Map p 121.*

★ **O'Asian Kitchen** DOWNTOWN *CHINESE* The best thing at this stylish restaurant is the dim sum, which comes delicious and steaming-hot from the kitchen on traditional carts. This is a popular spot with the office lunch crowd, *800 5th Ave.* ☎ *206/264-1789. Dim sum $4–$8. Lunch, dinner & dim sum daily. Bus: 250, 252, 257, 260. Map p 121.*

★★ **Osteria La Spiga** CAPITOL HILL *NORTHERN ITALIAN* Lovingly prepared Northern Italian cuisine takes the spotlight at this contemporary, inviting spot. The daily selection of handmade pastas are standouts. Even a simple dish like

Meat is definitely on the menu at Miller's Guild.

gnocchi al pomodoro (gnocchi with tomatoes), with the restaurant's signature tomato sauce, is wonderful. *1429 12th Ave.* ☎ *206/323-8881. www.laspiga.com. Entrees $17–$34. Lunch Mon–Fri, dinner daily. Bus: 2, 12. Map p 121.*

★★ **Pagliacci Pizza** CAPITOL HILL *PIZZA* The pies here come with thin, crunchy crusts and bold, tasty toppings. Pizza comes in three sizes to accommodate your group—or appetite. Gluten-free crusts are available, and they deliver. *426 Broadway Ave. E.* ☎ *206/726-1717. www.pagliacci. com. Entrees $14–$24. Lunch & dinner daily. Bus: 9, 49. Map p 121.*

★★ **Palisade** NORTH SEATTLE *NORTHWEST/POLYNESIAN* This landmark Seattle restaurant has a Polynesian influence. The panoramic views of Elliott Bay, Mt. Rainier, and the city are stunning, and the seafood is fresh and expertly prepared. There's a great raw bar, delicious sushi selection, and a seafood tower heaped with chilled delights from the sea. In addition to fish entrees there are juicy steaks and herb-crusted prime rib. *2601 W. Marina Place.* ☎ *206/285-1000. www.palisade restaurant.com. Entrees $28–$79. Lunch Mon–Fri, dinner daily, brunch Sat-Sun. Bus: 19, 24, 33. Map p 122.*

★★ **Place Pigalle** PIKE PLACE MARKET *FRENCH* I have a soft spot for classic French restaurants with real tablecloths and wine by the glass. You can't beat the steamed mussels at this romantic spot perched above the Sound, or dining to the strains of Edith Piaf. Lovely in a lovely, old-fashioned Seattle way. *81 Pike St.* ☎ *206/624-1756. www. placepigalle-seattle.com. Entrees $26–$38. Lunch & dinner daily. Bus: 99, 113, 121, 122. Map p 119.*

★★★ **Poppy** CAPITOL HILL *PACIFIC NORTHWEST/INDIAN* A foodie mecca in Capitol Hill, this innovative, award-winning restaurant created by Chef Jerry Traunfeld presents a fresh local take on the Indian *thali*, a compartmentalized platter holding various dishes with many different tastes. The extraordinary medley of textures, herbs, and spices is surprising and satisfying. *622 Broadway E.* ☎ *206/324-1108. www.poppyseat-tle.com. Thalis $28–$32. Dinner daily. Bus 8, 49. See map p 121.*

★★ **Purple Café and Wine Bar** DOWNTOWN *PACIFIC NORTHWEST/INTERNATIONAL* With its huge glass windows and floor-to-ceiling wine storage tower, the dining room dwarfs the diners, but no one seems to mind because the food is always good and the atmosphere is lively and loud. Wine is a big feature here, and wine pairings with your various plates can be surprisingly inexpensive compared to other Seattle restaurants. The menu makes abundant use of the bounty of the Pacific Northwest in dishes like Dungeness crab and chanterelle mushroom pasta. You can also order crispy-crust pizzas or a burger made from free-range beef. *1225 4th Ave.* ☎ *206/829-2280. www.purplecafe.com. Entrees $16–$40. Lunch & dinner daily. Map p 121.*

★★ Racha Thai & Asian Kitchen QUEEN ANN *ASIAN*
Sure, you can get a delicious pad Thai at this elegant spot, but with so many more inventive items on the menu, consider branching out. The catfish Panang and Golden Duck with ginger sauce are real standouts. Everything can be ordered online and delivered. *23 Mercer St.* ☎ *206/281-8883. www. rachathaiasianseattle.com. Entrees $10–$15. Lunch & dinner daily. Bus: 1, 8, 13, 15, 18. Map p 120.*

★★ Ray's Boathouse NORTH SEATTLE *SEAFOOD* An iconic seafood restaurant in the Ballard neighborhood, Ray's menu is as fresh and delicious as ever. The view, looking out over Puget Sound, is jaw-dropping. Families with kids may opt for the more casual and inexpensive café upstairs; the main Boathouse dining room is dressier, dinner-only, and more romantic. Up and down, the seafood is great. Many gluten-free dishes available. *6049 Seaview Ave. NW.* ☎ *206/789-3770. www. rays.com. Entrees $15–$46. Lunch & dinner daily cafe, dinner daily Boathouse. Map p 122.*

★ Salty's on Alki WEST SEATTLE *SEAFOOD* The panoramic view looking across the bay at Seattle is what makes Salty's so popular—but so is the brunch buffet, laden with fresh seafood, pasta and omelets to order, meats, and more. The gingerbread pancakes are addictive! Save room for the dessert buffet,

starring a chocolate fountain. *1936 Harbor Ave. SW.* ☎ *206/937-1600. www.saltys.com/seattle. Brunch $59. Entrees $14–$5946 Lunch Mon–Fri, dinner daily, brunch Sat–Sun. Bus: 37 or water taxi from Seattle Pier 50. Map p 120.*

★★ Serious Pie DOWNTOWN *PIZZA* Chef Tom Douglas is serious about food, and that includes pizza. His applewood-burning oven turns out artisan-quality pies. My mouth waters for the Yukon gold potato pizza with rosemary and pecorino. Of course, you can order a gourmet appetizer and wine. Reservations are not accepted, so arrive early or late. *316 Virginia St.* ☎ *206/838-7388. www.tomdouglas.com. Entrees $17–$19. Lunch & dinner daily. Bus: 1, 13, 15, 16, 17. Map p 120.*

★★ Shaker + Spear BELLTOWN *PACIFIC NORTHWEST* This inviting restaurant in the new Palladian Hotel opened in 2017 and quickly became a favorite dinner spot. But I like it for lunch, when you can get a crispy rockfish or chicken sandwich. The dinner menu is alert to current tastes and trends and usually has 4 to 5 fresh fish dishes plus steak and salads, all expertly prepared. *2000*

Ray's Boathouse offers a stunning waterfront setting and either casual or upscale dining rooms.

Second Ave. www.shakerandspear. com. ☎ 206/448-1111. Entrees $15–$30. Bus: 1, 13, 15, 26, 202. Map p. 120.

★★★ Shiro's BELLTOWN SUSHI
Try to get a seat at the sushi bar, where you can watch legendary sushi Chef Shiro Kashiba work his genial magic. Sushi-loving Seattle-ites say this is the best in town. 2401 2nd Ave. ☎ 206/443-9844. www.shiros.com. Entrees $7–$20; assortments $25 & up. Dinner daily. Bus: 19, 24, 116, 118. Map p 120.

★★ Shuckers DOWNTOWN SEAFOOD
The world can be your oyster at Shuckers, and I hope it will be, because oysters are what this long-established oyster bar is known for. Come during happy hour (3-6pm) and enjoy fresh oysters for $2 each. Every day, besides about 8 varieties of oysters, four or five fresh fish choices are available. The service is impeccable but the ambience is relaxed and the interior clubby with an old-fashioned "nautical" theme. 411 University St. (in the Fairmont Olympic Hotel). ☎ 206/621-1700. Entrees $23–$43. Lunch Mon–Sat, dinner daily. Bus: 85, 143, 150. Map p 121.

★★ Sitka & Spruce MELROSE PACIFIC NORTHWEST
The lunches are great at Chef Matt Dillon's loca-vore hotspot, where the focus is on fine, local foods accented with North African, Spanish, and Persian seasonings. A good choice for veg-etarians. Reserve in advance or be prepared to wait. 1531 Melrose Ave. ☎ 206/324-0662. www.sitkaand spruce.com. Entrees $13–$32. Lunch Mon–Fri, brunch Sat–Sun, dinner Tues–Sun. Map p 121.

★★ Six Seven WATERFRONT SEAFOOD
Located in the fun- and food-loving Edgewater Hotel (where the Beatles once stayed), the Six Seven has gone upscale without los-ing its friendly ambiance. The res-taurant showcases the best of the region's seafood. Menus change with the seasons, but you can't go wrong with the cedar plank king salmon. I recommend Six-Seven for lunch because it's less expensive and there's a spectacular view of Elliott Bay (you can sit outside in the summertime). If you want a good lunch to go, order the Deli Board Bento Box with soup and your choice of sandwich ($18). 2411 Alas-kan Way. ☎ 206/269-4575. www. edgewaterhotel.com. Entrees lunch $14–$28, dinner $36–$48. Breakfast & dinner daily, lunch Mon–Sat, brunch Sun. Bus: 19, 24, 99. Map p 120.

★ SkyCity at the Needle
DOWNTOWN NORTHWEST It's high and high-priced dining, to be sure, since the restaurant sits atop the Space Needle's observation deck. The 3-course fixed-price brunch and dinner menus are the way to go here. But let's be honest: the real main course is the view.

Lunch at stylish Six Seven lets diners appreciate its excellent view of Elliott Bay.

You'll see Seattle from every angle as SkyCity slowly revolves. Your expensive meal includes observation deck admission. *400 Broad St. ☎ 206/905-2100. www.spaceneedle. com/restaurant. Entrees $42–$69; 3-course brunch $53; 3-course dinner $79. Admission to Observation Deck included with meal. Lunch, brunch & dinner daily. Monorail or Bus: 3, 4, 8, 16 or 30. Map p 120.*

★★ **Steelhead Diner** PIKE PLACE MARKET *SEAFOOD/NEW AMERICAN* No ordinary diner, this lively spot overlooking Post Alley features the cooking of Kevin Davis, who brings together influences of New Orleans, France, California, and the Northwest. For an appetizer, try the crab and bay shrimp tater tots. Other standouts: kasu-marinated Oregon black cod, and a fabulous veggie "meatloaf." *95 Pine St. ☎ 206/625-0129. www. steelheaddiner.com. Entrees $19–$45. Lunch & dinner daily, brunch*

A creative, internationally influenced menu makes Steelhead Diner a standout near Pike Place Market.

Sat–Sun. Bus: 10, 99, 113, 121, 122. Map p 119.

★★ **Tavolata** BELLTOWN *ITALIAN* This hip urban eatery is all about the pasta, made fresh daily and served up with mouthwatering sauces and toppings. Take your pick: spaghetti, rigatoni, tonnarelli, or bucatini. The pasta menu changes daily, but other classic Italian starters remain

Dining Out of Town

Located in Woodinville, about 30 miles north of Seattle, The Herbfarm (☎ 425/485-5300; www.theherbfarm.com) is known for its lavish, themed meals that feature Pacific Northwest goods and wines that change with the seasons. Wild gathered vegetables, seafood from regional waters, Washington State meats, organic produce, foraged mushrooms, and, of course, fresh herbs from the Herbfarm gardens are the ingredients from which the restaurant creates its culinary extravaganzas. Nine-course dinners are paired with complementary Northwest wines. There is only one seating a night. Cost for the 9-course dinner with 5 paired wines is between $205 and $265.

A recent "Knife, Fork, Smoke" themed dinner featured grilled and smoked foods: a rye cracker with wood-oven vegetables; corn soup with lemon and thyme; grilled skewers with spot prawn, mussels, rabbit and chanterelles, all smoked with different flavors; a croissant with caramelized eggplant and garlic; vine-ripened tomatoes with beef drippings; grilled lamb loin; grilled cheese on fermented potato bread, and melon sorbet. If you're a foodie, you need to have a dinner experience like this at least once in your life. The restaurant is in a country inn beside a contemporary Northwest-style lodge.

constant. The mozzarella is home-made too. *2323 2nd Ave.* ☎ *206/838-8008. www.tavolata.com. Entrees $18–$24. Dinner daily. Bus: 1, 15, 27, 19, 24. Map p 120.*

★★ **Ten Mercer** QUEEN ANNE *CONTEMPORARY AMERICAN* Upstairs is elegantly formal; down-stairs is more casual. Either way, it's a great spot for dinner before or after the opera or a play at Seattle Center—they're open 'til midnight! You can't beat the garlic-crusted pan-roasted Washington chicken, juicy and tender with a perfect, crisp skin. *10 Mercer St.* ☎ *206/691-3723. www.tenmercer.com. Entrees $16–$38. Dinner daily. Bus: 1, 8, 13, 15, 18. Map p 120.*

★★★ **Tilth** NORTH SEATTLE *ORGANIC/NEW AMERICAN* This cozy restaurant in a Craftsman house showcases the organic and wild bounty of the region. Renowned chef Maria Hines whips up a mouth-watering array of seasonal delicacies. There's a tasting menu for every appetite, preference, and allergy: 5 course, 8 course, 5-course vegan, 5- and 8-course vegetarian, and 5-course gluten-free. *1411 N. 45th St.* ☎ *206/633-0801. www.tilthres-taurant.com. Entrees $16–$35, tast-ing menus $73–$95. Dinner daily, brunch Sat–Sun. Bus: 16, 44. Map p 122.*

★★ **Tulio Ristorante** DOWN-TOWN *ITALIAN* The pasta is pains-takingly handmade at this warm, inviting spot, which I love to visit before a show at the 5th Avenue Theatre. Chef Walter Pisano is a maestro at Italian cooking with con-temporary flair. One customer comes from Canada just for the sweet potato gnocchi, and when you taste it, you'll know why. *1100 5th Ave. (at the Hotel Vintage).* ☎ *206/624-5500. www.tulio.com. Entrees $18–$35. Breakfast & lunch Mon–Fri,* dinner daily, brunch Sat–Sun. Bus: 12, 143, 157, 158, 545. Map p 121.

★★ **Volterra** NORTH SEATTLE *ITALIAN* The rich flavors of a Tuscan village meld with the bounty of the Northwest on Don Curtiss' inventive menu. The signature dish, wild boar tenderloin with gorgonzola sauce, is rich and creamy. The polenta with wild mushrooms is a standout appetizer. Don't pass on the choco-late orange cake. (Trust me.) *5411 Ballard Ave NW.* ☎ *206/789-5100. www.volterrarestaurant.com. Entrees $28–$34. Dinner daily, brunch Sat–Sun. Bus: 17, 18, 44. Map p 122.*

★★ **Wild Ginger** DOWNTOWN *PAN-ASIAN* This perennially popular restaurant is sophisticated without being stuffy, and boasts a tempting menu that emphasizes satays, or skewers. You can't go wrong with the Wild Ginger fragrant duck. There's a terrific vegetarian menu. *1401 3rd Ave.* ☎ *206/623-4450. www.wildginger.net. Entrees $14–$28. Lunch & dinner Mon-Sat, dinner Sun. Bus: 1, 13, 14, 16, 17. Map p 121.*

★★ **Zeeks** BELLTOWN *PIZZA* The crust is to die for; the toppings unconventional. Try the Tree-Hugger, with mozzarella, sun-dried tomato, spinach, mushroom, artichoke hearts, broccoli, tomato, garlic, and olives. *419 Denny Way.* ☎ *206/285-8646. Entrees $18–$26. Lunch & din-ner daily. Bus: 8, 30. Map p 120.* ●

The tasting menus at Tilth are foodie favorites.

7

The Best Nightlife

Nightlife **Best Bets**

Best **Fine-Dining Wine Bar**
★★ Purple Café and Wine Bar, *1225 4th Ave. (p 141)*

Best **Place to Dance with the Beautiful People**
★★ Baltic Room, *1207 Pine St. (p 143)*

Best **Bartenders**
★★ ZigZag Café, *1501 Western Ave. (p 142)*

Best **Date Spot**
★★ Chinese Room, *506 2nd Ave. (p 140)*

Best **Brewpub**
★★ Elysian Brewing Company, *1221 E. Pike St. (p 140)*; and
★ Pike Brewing Company, *1415 1st Ave. (p 141)*

Best **Mariners Game-Day Hangout**
★ Pyramid Alehouse, *1201 1st Ave. S. (p 142)*

Best **Jazz Club**
★★★ Dimitriou's Jazz Alley, *2033 6th Ave. (p 144)*

Best **Happy Hour**
★★★ Oliver's Lounge, *405 Olive Way (p 141)*

Best **Hotel Bar**
★★ Fireside Room, *900 Madison St. (p 140)*

Best **Bar Burger**
Two Bells, *2313 4th Ave. (p 142)*

Best **After-Work Bar**
★★ W Bar, *1112 4th Ave. (p 142)*

Best **Spot for a Romantic Cocktail**
★★ The Sitting Room, *108 W. Roy (p 142)*

Best **Bavarian-style Beer Hall**
★★ Rhein Haus, *912 12th Ave. (p 142)*

Best **(and Only) Lesbian Bar**
Wild Rose, *1021 E. Pike St. (p 143)*

Best **Place to See & Be Seen**
★★ Black Bottle Gastro-Tavern, *2600 1st Ave. (p 139)*

Best **Martinis**
★★★ Oliver's Lounge, *405 Olive Way (p 141)*

Best **Gay-Friendly Bar**
★★ Neighbours, *1509 Broadway (p 143)*

A beer-tasting flight at Elysian Brewing Company
Previous page: A dinner performance at renowned Dimitriou's Jazz Alley

Pioneer Square

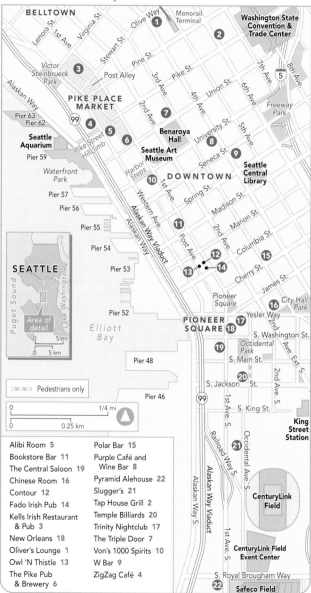

Alibi Room 5

Bookstore Bar 11

The Central Saloon 19

Chinese Room 16

Contour 12

Fado Irish Pub 14

Kells Irish Restaurant
& Pub 3

New Orleans 18

Oliver's Lounge 1

Owl 'N Thistle 13

The Pike Pub
& Brewery 6

Polar Bar 15

Purple Café and
Wine Bar 8

Pyramid Alehouse 22

Slugger's 21

Tap House Grill 2

Temple Billiards 20

Trinity Nightclub 17

The Triple Door 7

Von's 1000 Spirits 10

W Bar 9

ZigZag Café 4

Downtown

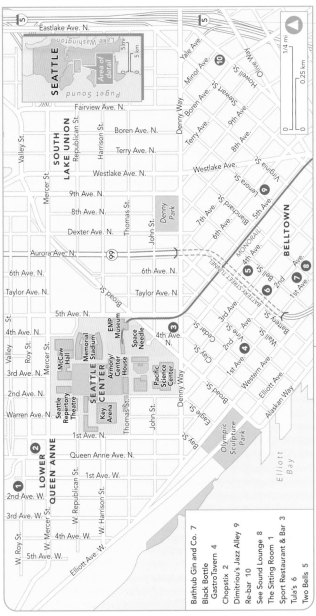

Bathtub Gin and Co. 7
Black Bottle GastroTavern 4
Chopstix 2
Dimitriou's Jazz Alley 9
Re-bar 10
See Sound Lounge 8
The Sitting Room 1
Sport Restaurant & Bar 3
Tula's 6
Two Bells 5

Capitol Hill

Artusi 9	Elysian Brewing Company 11	Raygun Lounge 3
Baltic Room 2	Fireside Room 1	Rhein Haus 13
Cha Cha Lounge 5	Madison Pub 12	The Wild Rose 6
Chop Suey 10	Neighbours 4	
The Cuff Complex 7		

Seattle Nightlife A to Z

Bars/Lounges

★★ **Alibi Room** PIKE PLACE MARKET Tucked away underneath the market, right across from the famous Gum Wall on cobblestoned Post Alley, this pub has long been a fave with Northwest literary types who like potent drinks and very good food. Club nights with dance DJs are Fridays and Saturdays, in the downstairs room. *85 Pike St., Ste. 410.* ☎ *206/623-3180. www.seattlealibi.com. Bus: 19, 21, 99, 113, 157. Map p 137.*

★★ **Artusi** CAPITOL HILL When you need a hit of Italy, head for this lively, minimalist *aperitivo* bar for a grappa or amaro accompanied by excellent *stuzzichini* ("little nibbles"). Sunday and Monday are

pasta and wine nights (2 pastas and bottle of wine for $35). *1535 14th Ave.* ☎ *206/678-2516. www.artusibar.com. Bus: 2, 10, 11. Map p 139.*

★★ **Bathtub Gin and Co.** BELLTOWN All that's missing in this dimly lit, speakeasy atmosphere is the cigarette smoke. Come here for a great cocktail or, on a chilly evening, a signature hot toddy. *2205 2nd Ave.* ☎ *206/728-6069. www.bathtubginseattle.com. Bus: 19, 24, 99. Map p. 138.*

★★ **Black Bottle Gastro-Tavern** BELLTOWN Seattleites make the scene here as much for the food as for the drinks. Lots of small plates, meant to be eaten as soon as they arrive, add to the loud, convivial, atmosphere. *2600 1st Ave.*

☎ 206/441-1500. www.blackbottle seattle.com. Bus: 1, 13. Map p 138.

★★ **Bookstore Bar** DOWN-TOWN This elegant bar at the Alexis Hotel makes you feel like you're enjoying old-fashioned drinks like Bloody Marys and Screwdrivers in a well-read friend's private library, before the advent of the Internet and craft cocktails. *1009 1st Ave.* ☎ *206/624-3646. www.librarybistro. com. Bus: 12, 16, 66, 99. Map p 137.*

★ **The Central Saloon** PIONEER SQUARE The oldest saloon in Seattle, the Central is a slice of gritty old Seattle but remains a favorite neighborhood hangout. The food is good, and the live rock can be fabulous. *207 1st Ave. S.* ☎ *206/622-0209. www.centralsaloon.com. Cover $5–$10 (or joint Pioneer Square cover $12 and up Fri–Sat. Bus: 85, 99, 143, 157, 158. Map p 137.*

★ **Cha Cha Lounge** CAPITOL HILL Potent margaritas and salty nachos augment the red lighting, kitschy velvet paintings, and piñatas hanging from the ceiling. Punk and heavy metal shake the rafters. Or get those nachos upstairs at Bimbo's Cantina. *1013 E. Pike St.* ☎ *206/ 322-0703. www.chachalounge.com. Bus: 2, 10, 11. Map p 139.*

★★★ **Chinese Room** PIONEER SQUARE The historic Chinese Room on the 35th floor of Smith Tower is a great spot for sunset cocktails and spectacular views.

You have to pay $19 to get up t0 the Observation Deck, but your date will be impressed. *506 2nd Ave.* ☎ *206/624-0414. www.smith tower.com. Bus: 85, 99, 143, 157, 158. Map p 137.*

★★ **Elysian Brewing Company** CAPITOL HILL This award-winning microbrewery concentrates on great beer and offers food as an afterthought. A customer favorite is the Avatar Jasmine, an Indian pale ale brewed with jasmine flowers. *1221 E. Pike St.* ☎ *206/860-1920. www.elysianbrewing.com. Bus: 2, 10, 11. Map p 139.*

★ **Fado Irish Pub** DOWNTOWN Seattle meets Dublin, or maybe it's the other way around at this Irish pub, started by real Irish entrepreneurs. Throw back a pint of Irish ale with the regulars at this popular after-work tavern, chomp down corned beef and cabbage, and enjoy the Irish bands that frequently play the hearty and heartrending tunes of Eire. *801 1st Ave.* ☎ *206/264-2700. www.fadoirishpub.com/seattle. Bus: 99, 143, 157, 158. Map p 137.*

★★★ **Fireside Room** FIRST HILL This elegant lounge at the Sorrento Hotel is a romantic spot to stop for a cocktail and some whispered sweet nothings, especially on Friday and Saturday nights, when you can make amorous eye contact to the soft, sexy sounds of live jazz. *900 Madison St.* ☎ *206/622-6400. Bus: 12. Map p 139.*

The Central Saloon is a Seattle institution.

Kells Irish Pub is a great place to raise a pint on Post Alley.

★ Kells Irish Restaurant & Pub

PIKE PLACE MARKET If it's a nice day, settle in on the patio with a shepherd's pie and a pint, and enjoy the lively mixed crowd of tourists and students. Live Irish music will set your feet to tappin'. *1916 Post Alley.* ☎ *206/728-1916. www.kells irish.com. Cover free to $5. Bus: 10, 99, 113, 121, 122. Map p 137.*

★★★ Oliver's Lounge

DOWNTOWN This time-honored and traditionally minded bar at the elegant Mayflower Park Hotel serves award-winning martinis and upscale bar food. Try it at Happy Hour. *405 Olive Way.* ☎ *206/623-8700. Bus: 25, 79, 123, 355. Map p 137.*

★★ Owl 'N Thistle

DOWNTOWN This popular Irish bar kicks up a ruckus with an eclectic mix of bands, including its own house Irish folk band, and has a dance area where you can kick off your heels and kick up your heels. *808 Post Ave.* ☎ *206/621-7777. www.owln thistle.com. Cover free to $5. Bus: 12, 16, 66, 99. Map p 137.*

★ Pike Brewing Company

PIKE PLACE MARKET One of the largest breweries in the state, Pike keeps customers coming back for labels like the Scotch Style Pike Kilt Lifter and Naughty Nellie. You get the idea. *1415 1st Ave.* ☎ *206/622-6044. Bus: 99, 113, 121, 143, 157. Map p 137.*

★★ Polar Bar

PIONEER SQUARE Watched over by a rearing polar bear (don't worry, it's art), this Art Deco lobby bar in the wonderfully restored Arctic Club Hotel, once an exclusive men's club, is a cool and civilized place for evening drinks and conversation beside the fireplace. *700 3rd Ave.* ☎ *206/340-0340. Bus: 99, 143. Map p 137.*

★★ Purple Café and Wine Bar

DOWNTOWN A soaring wine tower with wraparound spiral staircase dominates the Purple and signals that an impressive selection of vino is on hand. If you're hungry, order a cheese and wine flight, or try several small plates. *1225 4th Ave.* ☎ *206/829-2280.*

Elegant ambiance at Oliver's Lounge in Mayflower Park Hotel

www.thepurplecafe.com. Bus: 14, 21, 22, 202, 210. Map p 137.

★ **Pyramid Alehouse** PIONEER SQUARE There are two big draws here: the location (across the street from Safeco Field) and the beer (including the award-winning Pyramid Hefe Weizen). On Mariners game days, it fills up fast. *1201 1st Ave. S.* ☎ *206/682-3377. Bus: 12, 21, 54, 56, 99. Map p 137.*

★ **Raygun Lounge** CAPITOL HILL It looks kind of unfinished, but that's part of the brainy charm of this super-friendly spot offering dozens of board games, gaming games and fun events for all ages. While you're playing, you can order food, sip a spirit (if you're old enough) or something non-alcoholic (if you're not), and never feel like you're being rushed. *501 E. Pine St.* ☎ *206/852-2521. Bus: 2, 10, 11. Map p 139.*

★★ **Rhein Haus** CAPITOL HILL Beer, brats ,and bocce are the three Bs that make this Bavarian-inspired beer hall and garden so popular and fun. The wursts and breads are made from scratch daily. *912 12th Ave.* ☎ *206/325-5409. www.rheinhausseattle.com. Bus 2, 10, 11. Map p 139.*

★★ **See Sound Lounge** BELL-TOWN Trendy and lively, See Sound's crowd tends toward the younger, Instagramming set that comes to hear DJs from around the world and enjoy the cool visual projections on the walls. *115 Blanchard St.* ☎ *206/374-3733. Bus: 19, 24, 99. Map p 138.*

★★ **The Sitting Room** QUEEN ANNE A cozy spot with more than a dash of Francophile style, the Sitting Room serves yummy specialty drinks and gourmet eats at intimate candlelit tables where you can actually hear what your date is saying. *108 W. Roy.* ☎ *206/285-2830.*

www.the-sitting-room.com. Bus: 1, 2, 8, 13, 15. Map p 138.

★ **Smith** CAPITOL HILL This dark, rustic tavern is a fave with locals who come for a beer or cocktail and appetizers like salted cod fritters. *332 15th Ave E.* ☎ *206/709-1900. Bus: 99, 143.*

★ **Tap House Grill** DOWNTOWN With more than 150 beers on tap and a menu that includes steaks and sushi, this upscale spot is a fun place to watch a game or the other patrons. *1506 6th Ave.* ☎ *206/816-3314. www.taphousegrill.com. Bus: 10, 11, 14, 43, 545. Map p 137.*

★ **Two Bells** DOWNTOWN A favorite neighborhood hangout, Two Bells serves beer, wine, and some of the best burgers in Seattle. *2313 4th Ave.* ☎ *206/441-3050. www.thetwobells.com. Bus: 1, 13, 15, 16, 17. Map p 138.*

★★ **Von's 1000 Spirits** DOWN-TOWN Von's famous Scratch Martini is reason enough to visit this purveyor of fine handcrafted spirits and fab finger foods (plus primo burgers and pizzas baked over almond wood). But the tequila and bourbon are equally famous. *1225 1st Ave.* ☎ *206/621-8667. Bus: 12, 16, 99. Map p 137.*

★★ **W Bar** DOWNTOWN With a classy decor, great happy hour, and gourmet bar food, the W is a favorite after-work gathering spot. *1112 4th Ave.* ☎ *206/264-6000. Bus: 202, 210, 214, 215, 554. Map p 137.*

★★ **ZigZag Café** PIKE PLACE MARKET The bartenders at this friendly lounge and snackery are practically magicians and more than happy to fill you in on all their amazing cocktails, many made with fresh-squeezed juices. The food is simple and good, with oysters on the half-shell and many Greek-inspired dishes. *1501 Western Ave.*

☎ 206/625-1146. www.zigzag seattle.com. Bus: 12, 99, 113, 121, 122. Map p 137.

Dance Clubs

★★ Baltic Room CAPITOL HILL This classy, romantic club plays themed music from around the globe. A fun clientele of various ethnicities and sexual persuasions packs the small dance floor. *1207 Pine St.* ☎ *206/625-4444. Cover free to $10. Bus: 10, 11, 14, 43, 49. Map p 139.*

★ Chop Suey CAPITOL HILL The dance floor is usually packed at this eclectic bar. Bands and DJs range from punk to techno. *1325 E. Madison.* ☎ *206/324-8005. www.chop suey.com. Cover free to $30. Bus: 2, 10, 11, 12. Map p 139.*

★ Contour DOWNTOWN This is where serious partiers dance till dawn to DJs and live bands. On Friday, Saturday and Sunday, the happiest Happy hour in Seattle lasts 6 hours, ending at 9pm, otherwise it's 3 to 8pm. *807 1st Ave.* ☎ *206/447-7704. www.clubcontour.com. Cover free to $10. Bus: 12, 16, 66. Map p 137.*

★★★ Trinity Nightclub PIONEER SQUARE A young Dionysian clientele dances its way through three areas, each with a different type of music, at this multi-level dance club. The dance floor is one of the

Disco balls light up the dancefloor at Trinity.

largest in town. *111 Yesler Way.* ☎ *206/447-4140. Cover free to $15. www.trinitynightclub.com. Bus: 99, 143, 157, 158, 161. Map p 137.*

Gay & Lesbian-Friendly

★ The Cuff Complex CAPITOL HILL This popular gay bar draws mostly men into leather and fetish scenes (the cuffs referred to in the name are not shirt cuffs). It has pool tables, pinball, a small dance floor, and nice outdoor deck in the back. *1533 13th Ave.* ☎ *206/323-1525. www.cuffcomplex.com. Bus: 2, 10, 11, 12. Map p 139.*

★ Madison Pub CAPITOL HILL The crowd at this low-key pub is mixed, but mostly gay and male. It's a down-to-earth place with friendly bartenders who make everyone feel welcome. *1315 E. Madison St.* ☎ *206/325-6537. www.madisonpub. com. Bus: 2, 10, 11, 12. Map p 139.*

★★ Neighbours CAPITOL HILL This longtime favorite disco is gay-friendly but attracts a mixed group to bump and grind on its large, popular dance floor. *1509 Broadway.* ☎ *206/324-5358. Bus: 2, 10, 11, 49. Map p 139.*

★ Re-bar BELLTOWN There's always something going on at this funky club, which attracts a mixed straight/younger gay (some in drag) clientele. There's dancing every night. *1114 Howell St.* ☎ *206/233-9873. www.rebarseattle.com. Bus: 70, 71, 72, 73, 83. Map p 138.*

★★ The Wild Rose CAPITOL HILL Everyone is welcome at Seattle's only real lesbian bar, as long as they're tolerant and don't gawk at the gals. The drinks are strong, the bar food is good, and the atmosphere is lady-back at this women-owned bar that's been around since 1984. *1021 E. Pike St.* ☎ *206/324-9210. www.thewildrose bar.com. Bus: 2, 10, 11. Map p 139.*

World-class acts play at Dimitriou's Jazz Alley.

Live Jazz & Blues

★★★ Dimitriou's Jazz Alley

BELLTOWN With consistently great acts from around the globe, this beautiful club is Seattle's premier jazz spot. *2033 6th Ave. ☎ 206/441-9729. www.jazzalley.com. Ticket prices vary; check website. South Lake Union Street Car 98, Bus: 25, 66, 70, 73, 250. Map p 138.*

★ New Orleans PIONEER

SQUARE The New Orleans is hopping every night with live jazz, zydeco, and blues. Chow down on some Cajun food while you listen. Kids are allowed until 10pm. *114 1st Ave. S. ☎ 206/622-2563. www. neworleanscreolerestaurant.com. Cover free to $14 Fri–Sat. Bus: 99, 143, 157, 158, 159. Map p 137.*

★★★ The Triple Door DOWN-

TOWN This former vaudeville theater attracts an upscale, friendly crowd. Hear music from around the world upstairs in the Musiquarium (a bar with a huge fish tank) or buy a ticket to watch the show in the Mainstage Theatre. Shows that start before 9pm are open to children. *216 Union St. ☎ 206/838-4333. www. tripledoor.com. Ticket prices vary. Bus: 143, 157, 158, 159, 162. Map p 137.*

★★★ Tula's BELLTOWN You'll

find live jazz nightly at this intimate club, plus a tasty Mediterranean menu. All ages welcome until 10pm. Best to make a reservation. *2214 2nd Ave. ☎ 206/443-4221. www.tulas.com. Cover $10–$15. Bus: 19, 21, 24, 56. Map p 138.*

Sports Bars

★ Slugger's PIONEER SQUARE

Across from CenturyLink Field, this neighborhood joint draws lots of pre- and post-game fans in addition to those watching the game on the giant screens. Popular Mon-Fri 3-6pm Happy Hour. *538 1st Ave. S. ☎ 206/654-8070. www.sluggers seattle.com. Bus: 13, 70, 85, 99, 522. Map p 137.*

★★ Sport Restaurant & Bar

QUEEN ANNE This place is so big it's a world unto itself. If you get a booth, you can control your own TV screen. If not, you'll have plenty of options, including the gargantuan HD screen in the lounge. Good food and good service to go with the endless physical activity. *140 4th Ave. N., Ste. 130. ☎ 206/404-7767. www.sportrestaurant.com. Bus: 3, 8, 13, 16, 30. Map p 138.*

★ Temple Billiards PIONEER

SQUARE A friendly place with great pool tables and sticks, Temple also has a DJ, dancing downstairs, and the second-longest Happy Hour in Seattle (daily 4-8pm). Oh, and it's open for lunch, too. Ladies play free on Weds. *126 S. Jackson St. ☎ 206/682-3242. www.templebillianrds.com. Bus: 10, 13, 99. Map p 137.* ●

8

The Best Arts & Entertainment

Arts & Entertainment Best Bets

Most **Jaw-Dropping Show with Dinner**
★★★ Teatro ZinZanni, *222 Mercer St. (p 150)*

Best **Place to Go for a Guffaw**
★ The Comedy Underground, *109 S. Washington St. (p 148)*

Best **Family Entertainment**
★★ Zootunes, *N. 59th St. and Evanston Ave. (p 148)*

Best **Popular Music**
★★★ Showbox, *1426 1st Ave. (p 152)*

Best **Orchestra**
★★★ Seattle Symphony, *200 University St. (p 148)*

Most **Eclectic Theater Calendar**
★★ The Moore Theatre, *1932 2nd Ave. (p 152)*

Best **Place to Hear Chamber Music One Night and a Talk on Religion in Politics the Next**
★★ Town Hall, *1119 8th Ave. (p 148)*

Best **Theater to Take Your Sweetheart before Popping the Question**
★★★ Paramount Theatre, *911 Pine St. (p 152)*

Best **Place to Watch an Arabesque**
★★★ Pacific Northwest Ballet, *321 Mercer St. (p 149)*

Most **Eclectic Musical Lineup**
★★★ The Triple Door, *216 Union St. (p 151)*

A performance at The Triple Door
Previous page: Pacific Northwest Ballet dancers

Seattle Arts & Entertainment

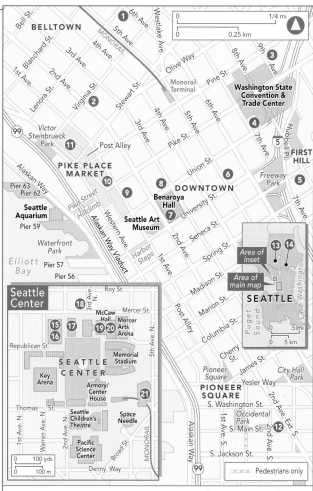

ACT (A Contemporary Theatre) **4**

Can Can **10**

The Comedy Underground **12**

Cornish Playhouse **17**

Dimitriou's Jazz Alley **1**

Experience Music Project **21**

5th Avenue Theatre **6**

The Moore Theatre **2**

Pacific Northwest Ballet **19**

Paramount Theatre **3**

The Pink Door Cabaret **11**

Seattle Gilbert & Sullivan Society **16**

Seattle Opera **20**

Seattle Repertory Theatre **15**

Seattle Symphony/ Benaroya Hall **7**

Showbox **9**

Teatro ZinZanni **18**

Town Hall **5**

The Triple Door **8**

UW World Series **14**

Zootunes **13**

Seattle Arts & Entertainment A to Z

Classical Music

★★★ Seattle Symphony

DOWNTOWN The 85-person orchestra is beloved in the community, and has been going strong for more than a century. The Seattle Symphony is internationally respected and known for pushing the envelope musically and showcasing contemporary as well as classical works. It performs in the beautiful and acoustically outstanding Benaroya Hall downtown. *200 University St.* ☎ *206/215-4800. www.seattlesymphony.org. Ticket prices vary. Bus: 212, 216, 217, 218, 225. Map p 147.*

★★★ The Comedy Underground

PIONEER SQUARE Comics from around the country keep the audience in stitches here every night of the week. The roster includes winners of regional comedy contests, late-night TV guests, and up-and-comers. The historic club is headquarters for the Seattle International Comedy Competition. *109 S. Washington St.* ☎ *206/628-0303. www.comedyunderground.com. Ticket prices vary. Bus: 85, 99. Map p 147.*

Concert Venues

★★★ Benaroya Hall

DOWNTOWN This gorgeous concert hall built in 1998 in the heart of downtown is the home of the Seattle Symphony, but it's not just classical music they play and you might be surprised at the performers they partner with. *200 University St.* ☎ *206/215-4800. www.seattle symphony.org. Ticket prices vary. Bus: 212, 216, 217, 218, 225. Map p 147.*

★★★ Town Hall

FIRST HILL From chamber music to science lectures to political discussions, you never know what you might hear at Town Hall, Seattle's cultural gathering place—despite the name, it is not connected to city government. The beautifully restored Roman-revival building houses two performance halls. *1119 8th Ave.* ☎ *206/652-4255. www.townhallseattle.org. Ticket prices vary. Bus: 2, 12. Map p 147.*

★★ Zootunes

FREMONT Every summer, locals head to Woodland Park Zoo one evening during the week to lounge on a grassy meadow and hear concerts by old favorites and new groups. You might hear anyone from Ziggy Marley and the Seattle Symphony to the Violent Femmes. The concert starts at 6pm, just inside the northern zoo gate. Lots of folks bring picnic baskets and low chairs or towels, but food is also available. You can buy tickets at the zoo, but many concerts

The Seattle Symphony Orchestra performs in Benaroya Hall.

Can Can cabaret shows range from mild to wild.

sell out, so check the website in advance. *N. 59th St. & Evanston Ave.* ☎ *206/548-2500, ext.1164. www.zoo.org/zootunes. Prices vary but are reasonable; kids 12 & under free. Bus: 5, 82. Map p 147.*

Dance

★★★ Pacific Northwest Ballet QUEEN ANNE One of the country's largest and most acclaimed ballet companies, the PNB gives more than 100 performances a year, mostly at the beautiful Marion Oliver McCaw Hall, culminating in the beloved *Nutcracker*—complete with spectacular Maurice Sendak sets—over the holidays. *321 Mercer St.* ☎ *206/684-7200. www.pnb.org. Ticket prices vary. Bus: 3, 16, 82. Map p 147.*

★★ UW World Series UNIVERSITY DISTRICT The University of Washington brings in world-class dancers, musicians, and other artists from around the globe to perform at Meany Hall on the UW campus. The season runs October through May. UW Arts Ticket Office: 3901 University Way NE.

Meany Hall is on the west side of the UW campus. *15th Ave. NE & NE 40th.* ☎ *206/543-4880. www. uwworldseries.org. Ticket prices vary. Bus: 25, 43, 49, 70. Map p 147.*

Dinner Theatre

★★ Can Can PIKE PLACE MARKET This creative cabaret venue is sometimes for the nostalgic, sometimes for the daring and open-minded, and always enjoyable. Some shows are on the cutting edge of neo-burlesque and for adults only, others for 17 and up, but minors must always leave by 10pm. Dinner/show packages are available, and there is also a midnight show on weekends. Can Can brings in local and national acts, and also has its own house cabaret troupe. Almost anything can happen here! *94 Pike St.* ☎ *206/652-0832. www. thecancan.com. Show $35–$65. Bus: 19, 99, 113, 121, 122. Map p 147.*

★★ The Pink Door Cabaret PIKE PLACE MARKET Since 1981 there's always been something out of the ordinary going on behind the pink doors of The Pink Door, be

Cheap Tickets

If you want to catch a show in town but don't have tickets, try the theater box office—you can sometimes score a great deal an hour before a performance. Many Seattle theaters also have special discounted seats for seniors and under-25s. You can also try www.goldstar.com (click on "Seattle" at the bottom of the page after you sign up), where you can get discounted deals on many local shows, as well as on lake and harbor cruises. Comedy Clubs.

Dinner shows at Teatro ZinZanni are a mix of acrobatics, circus acts, cabaret, and comedy.

it a trapeze artist above the dining room, a strolling accordion player or a wandering Tarot card reader. Saturday nights are reserved for the fun and naughty burlesque show in the lounge, which starts at 11pm and incorporates cross-dressing and elements of striptease. Come earlier and you can enjoy a delicious Italian meal in the dining room before the show. Refrain from arriving in grungy gym shorts or touristy sports attire; there isn't a dress code (especially for the performers) but the management would like you to dress up a bit. *1919 Post Alley.* ☎ *206/443-3241. www.thepinkdoor.net. Cover for burlesque show $25. Bus: 10, 99, 113, 121, 122. Map p 147.*

★★★ **Teatro ZinZanni** QUEEN ANNE Talk about overstimulation! This incredible spectacle of sights and sounds, set inside a huge tent, is accompanied by a first-class five-course meal created for every new show by a renowned chef. This 3-hour mix of acrobatics, circus acts, cabaret, comedy, and audience interaction must be experienced to be believed. Teatro is housed in a spectacular building just across from McCaw Hall; shows tend to sell out, so reserve as far in advance as you can. *222 Mercer St.* ☎ *206/802-0015. www.zinzanni.com. Showtimes 6:30pm Thurs–Sat (& some Wed); 5:30pm Sun. Tickets $99–$185 depending on day & seating area. ($10 more in Dec.) Bus: 1, 2, 8, 13, 15. Map p 147.*

Jazz

★★★ **Dimitriou's Jazz Alley** BELLTOWN If you're a jazz-lover, don't miss Dimitriou's while you're in town. The lineup of world-class performers at this large, yet somehow intimate, dinner/jazz club never fails to amaze. *2033 6th Ave.* ☎ *206/441-9729. www.jazzalley. com. Ticket prices vary; check website. South Lake Union Street Car 98, Bus: 25, 123, 250, 252. Map p 147.*

Dimitriou's Jazz Alley attracts internationally renowned talents.

★★★ The Triple Door DOWN-TOWN Jazz is just part of the attraction at this hot club, known for its eclectic roster of performers. Its offerings even include chamber music by a group of musicians from the Seattle Symphony. *216 Union St. ☎ 206/838-4333. www.tripledoor. com. Ticket prices vary. Bus: 143, 157, 158, 159, 161. Map p 147.*

Opera
★★ Seattle Gilbert & Sullivan Society FIRST HILL This is an amateur group, but it does the Victorian pitter-pattering opera writers of classics like HMS Pinafore proud. The shows are fun, colorful, and fast-paced. The group uses different venues and ticket prices vary; check the website. *☎ 206/682-0796. www.pattersong.org. Map p 147.*

★★★ Seattle Opera QUEEN ANNE Housed in the Marion Oliver McCaw Hall, this fine company performs the great operatic repertoire and an acclaimed "Ring" cycle by Richard Wagner every 4 years. *321 Mercer St. ☎ 206/389-7676. www. seattleopera.org. Ticket prices vary. Bus: 3, 16, 82. Map p 147.*

Plays
★★★ 5th Avenue Theatre DOWNTOWN This elegant play-house produces some of the liveliest theater in Seattle, including original and Broadway-bound shows and traveling productions of Broadway musicals. *1308 5th Ave. ☎ 206/625-1900. www.5thavenue. org. Ticket prices vary. Bus: 250, 252, 257, 260, 261. Map p 147.*

★★ ACT (A Contemporary Theatre) DOWNTOWN The energetic productions staged at this venue is are a mix of re-imagined classics and newer plays, plus a yearly *Christmas Carol* for the family. *700 Union St. ☎ 206/292-7676. www.acttheatre.org. Ticket prices vary. Bus: 306, 312, 522. Map p 147.*

★★ Intiman Theatre Serious drama-lovers will love the Tony award–winning Intiman. This gem of a regional theater, on the north side of Seattle Center, has produced international classics as well as contemporary plays—including some world premieres—for over 4 decades. Prices vary; check box office and website. *201 Mercer St. ☎ 206/443-2222. www.intiman.org. Bus: 1, 2, 8, 13.*

The Seattle Opera stages Wagner's epic Ring cycle every four years.

A performance of The Women at ACT

★★ The Moore Theatre

DOWNTOWN Seattle's oldest theater dates from 1907but hosts some of the edgiest acts in town. It's always a diverse lineup; you might see anyone from Bill Maher to Apocalyptica to Art Garfunkle. *1932 2nd Ave. ☎ 206/467-5510. www. stgpresents.org. Ticket prices vary. Bus: 10, 25, 99, 113, 121. Map p 147.*

★★★ Paramount Theatre

DOWNTOWN From Broadway to rock shows, the Paramount offers great entertainment with high

The glamorous Paramount Theatre

production values in a glamorous historic setting. *911 Pine St. ☎ 206/467-5510. www.stgpresents.org. Ticket prices vary. Bus: 10, 11, 14, 43, 49. Map p 147.*

★★ Seattle Repertory Theatre

The Rep's offerings tend to be important, beautifully performed literary and artistic productions, including Broadway hits and world premieres. The theater itself is an elegant venue, located at Seattle Center. *155 Mercer St. ☎ 206/443-2222. www.seattlerep.org. Prices vary; check with box office or on the website. Bus: 1, 2, 8, 13, 15. Map p 147.*

Popular Music
★★★ Showbox PIKE PLACE

MARKET One of Seattle's premier music clubs, the legendary Showbox has a lot going for it: great bands, elbowroom, good acoustics, and lots of all-ages shows. (The under-21s have their own section.) Around since 1939, the ballroom has hosted everyone from Duke Ellington to Pearl Jam. There is also a Showbox in the Sodo district. *Market location: 1426 1st Ave. Sodo: 1700 1st Ave. S. Info line for both: ☎ 206/628-3151. www.showboxon-line.com. Ticket prices vary by event; check website. Bus: 99, 113, 121, 122, 143. Map p 147.* ●

Seattle **Lodging**

The Best Lodging

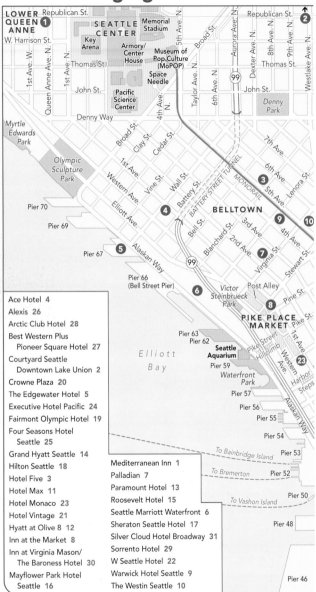

Ace Hotel 4
Alexis 26
Arctic Club Hotel 28
Best Western Plus
  Pioneer Square Hotel 27
Courtyard Seattle
  Downtown Lake Union 2
Crowne Plaza 20
The Edgewater Hotel 5
Executive Hotel Pacific 24
Fairmont Olympic Hotel 19
Four Seasons Hotel
  Seattle 25
Grand Hyatt Seattle 14
Hilton Seattle 18
Hotel Five 3
Hotel Max 11
Hotel Monaco 23
Hotel Vintage 21
Hyatt at Olive 8 12
Inn at the Market 8
Inn at Virginia Mason/
  The Baroness Hotel 30
Mayflower Park Hotel
  Seattle 16

Mediterranean Inn 1
Palladian 7
Paramount Hotel 13
Roosevelt Hotel 15
Seattle Marriott Waterfront 6
Sheraton Seattle Hotel 17
Silver Cloud Hotel Broadway 31
Sorrento Hotel 29
W Seattle Hotel 22
Warwick Hotel Seattle 9
The Westin Seattle 10

Previous page: The lobby at the iconic Edgewater Hotel

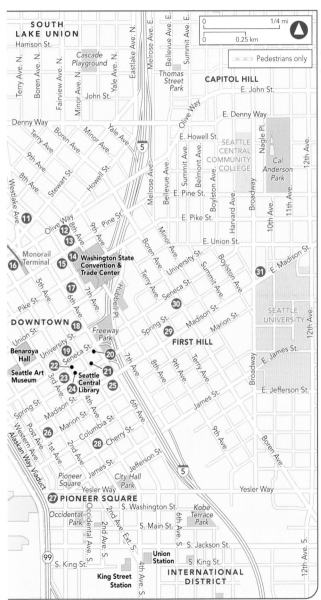

SOUTH LAKE UNION

Harrison St.

Terry Ave. N.

Boren Ave. N.

Fairview Ave. N.

Minor Ave. N.

Cascade Playground

John St.

Yale Ave. N.

Eastlake Ave. N.

Melrose Ave. E.

Bellevue Ave. E.

Summit Ave. E.

Thomas Street Park

0   1/4 mi

0   0.25 km

Pedestrians only

CAPITOL HILL

E. John St.

E. Denny Way

Denny Way

Terry Ave.

Boren Ave.

Minor Ave.

9th Ave.

8th Ave.

Stewart St.

Howell St.

Yale Ave.

Olive Way

5

E. Howell St.

Summit Ave.

Belmont Ave.

Bellevue Ave.

E. Pine St.

Boylston Ave.

Harvard Ave.

Broadway

Nagle Pl.

SEATTLE CENTRAL COMMUNITY COLLEGE

Cal Anderson Park

12th Ave.

Westlake Ave.

⑪

⑫ 8th Ave.

⑬

Olive Way

9th Ave.

Pine St.

Melrose Ave.

E. Pike St.

E. Union St.

10th Ave.

11th Ave.

⑯ Monorail Terminal

⑮ ⑭ Washington State Convention & Trade Center

5th Ave.

7th Ave.

Hubbell Pl.

Boren Ave.

Minor Ave.

University St.

Terry Ave.

Seneca St.

Summit Ave.

Boylston Ave.

⑰

6th Ave.

Pike St.

DOWNTOWN

Union St.

University St.

⑱

Freeway Park

Spring St.

Madison St.

Marion St.

⑳

⑲

⑰

Benaroya Hall

Seattle Art Museum

⑳

㉒

㉓ Seattle Central Library

㉔

㉑

㉕

7th Ave.

8th Ave.

9th Ave.

Terry Ave.

James St.

㉚

㉙

FIRST HILL

㉛ E. Madison St.

SEATTLE UNIVERSITY

12th Ave.

Broadway

E. James St.

E. Jefferson St.

Spring St.

Madison St.

Marion St.

3rd Ave.

Western Ave.

Post Ave.

1st Ave.

2nd Ave.

4th Ave.

Columbia St.

Cherry St.

㉖

㉘

6th Ave.

9th Ave.

Jefferson St.

5

City Hall Park

Alaskan Way Viaduct

Pioneer Square

James St.

Yesler Way

Yesler Way

Boren Ave.

㉗ PIONEER SQUARE

Occidental Park

Occidental Ave. S.

2nd Ave. S.

S. Washington St.

S. Main St.

6th Ave. S.

Kobe Terrace Park

S. Jackson St.

12th Ave. S.

99

S. King St.

King Street Station

4th Ave. S.

2nd Ave. Ext. S.

Union Station

S. King St.

INTERNATIONAL DISTRICT

Lodging **Best Bets**

Most **Authentic Seattle Experience**
★★★ The Edgewater $$$–$$$$
2411 Alaskan Way (p 158)

Best **Panoramic City Views**
★ The Westin Seattle $$$–$$$$
1900 5th Ave. (p 162)

Most **Romantic**
★★★ Inn at the Market $$$–$$$$
86 Pine St. (p 160)

Most **Traditionally Elegant**
★★★ Mayflower Park Hotel
Seattle $$–$$$ 405 Olive Way (p 160)

Most **Whimsical**
★★ Hotel Monaco $$$–$$$$
1101 4th Ave. (p 159)

Most **Elegant European Style**
★★★ Sorrento $$–$$$
900 Madison St. (p 162)

Best **Location**
★★ Alexis $$$–$$$$
1007 1st Ave (p 157)

Best **Choice for Wine-Lovers**
★★ Hotel Vintage $$–$$$$
1100 5th Ave. (p 159)

Greenest Hotel
★★ Hyatt at Olive 8 $$$–$$$$
1635 8th Ave. (p 160)

Hippest Hotel
★★★ W Seattle Hotel $$$–$$$$
1112 4th Ave. (p 162)

Hottest New Hotel
★★★ Palladian $$$–$$$$
2000 2nd Ave. (p 160)

Most **Stunning Lobby**
★★★ Fairmont Olympic Hotel
$$–$$$$$ 411 University St. (p 158)

Artsiest Hotel
★★ Hotel Max $$–$$$
620 Stewart St. (p 159)

Best **Seattle History**
★★ Arctic Club $$$–$$$$
700 3rd Ave. (p 157)

Best **Pool with a View**
★★★ Four Seasons $$$$–$$$$$
99 Union St. (p 159)

Best **Reasonably Priced Hotel**
★★★ Inn at Virginia Mason/
Baroness Hotel $–$$$
1006 Spring St. (p 160)

The 1927 Mayflower Park Hotel is one of Seattle's grand dames.

Seattle **Hotels A to Z**

When you're searching for a place to say in Seattle, don't forget to check out Airbnb (www.airbnb.com), HomeAway (www.homeaway.com), and VRBO (www.vrbo.com) for some unique Seattle-stay possibilities. These websites, offering rooms in private homes and sometimes entire apartments, are legal to use in Seattle and can provide a unique neighborhood experience that you wouldn't find in a downtown hotel. Prices are approximately $50–$75 less than you'd pay for a mid-range hotel room in central Seattle.

If you're driving to Seattle and staying downtown, parking is going to be an issue. All downtown Seattle hotels offer valet parking in protected garages, but valet-parking services are not cheap: expect to pay anywhere from $40 to $55 per night to safely stow your car. Some hotels, especially those away from the city center, have self-service parking options or can recommend nearby parking lots or garages.

★★ **Ace Hotel** BELLTOWN You'll need to climb stairs to reach it, but at the top you'll find a unique, European-style hotel where some rooms cost less because they share a bathroom. The Ace was fashioned from a historic brick building in Belltown so no two rooms are alike, but they are all comfortable in an unconventional way. There are hip cafes, bars and restaurants right outside the door. *2423 1st Ave.* ☎ *206/448-4721. www.acehotel. com. 28 units, 14 with shared bathroom. $129–$140 double w/shared bath; $219–$239 double w/bath. Bus: 99. Map p 154.*

★★ **Alexis** DOWNTOWN Just north of Pioneer Square, this cozy boutique hotel is luxurious and romantic, pampering guests with Egyptian-cotton sheets, comfy beds, complimentary wine hour and a spa. Jetted tubs and wood-burning fireplaces are available in some suites. Unwind and/or dine at the Bookstore Bistro & Bar. *1007 1st Ave. (at Madison).* ☎ *866/356-8894 or 206/624-4844. www.alexishotel. com. 121 units. Doubles $175–$465. Bus: 12, 16, 66, 99. Map p 155.*

★★★ **Arctic Club Hotel** DOWNTOWN Once an exclusive club for gold prospectors who struck it rich, this historic building now houses the luxurious Doubletree Arctic Club Hotel. The warmth and glamour remains, from the beautiful onyx bar and fireplace in the lobby to the sculpted walruses that wrap around the outside of the building to the Northern Lights Dome Room, with its spectacular stained-glass dome. The rooms have a sturdy masculine flavor that suits the period and the place. *700 3rd Ave. (at Cherry St.)* ☎ *800/600-7775 or 206/340-0340. www.arcticclubhotel. com. 120 units. Doubles $229–$369. Bus: 11, 15, 18, 121, 122, Map p 155.*

★★ **Best Western Plus Pioneer Square Hotel** PIONEER SQUARE Set in the midst of Seattle's historic Pioneer Square district, this hotel brings history to life in a century-old Romanesque Victorian building but provides all the services travelers need today, plus it's within walking distance of the waterfront and downtown. *77 Yesler Way.* ☎ *800/800-5514 or 206/340-1234. www.pioneersquare.com. 72 units.*

Doubles $140–$350, includes continental breakfast. Bus: 99, 143, 157, 158, 159. Map p 155.

★ Courtyard Seattle Downtown Lake Union LAKE UNION

This Marriott-brand hotel is on Lake Union, not in downtown, but a nearby streetcar runs downtown every 15 minutes until 9pm (11pm on weekends). Try to book a room overlooking the lake with its houseboats, sailboats, steamers and kayaks. The hotel also has a pool. *925 Westlake Ave. N.* ☎ *800/321-2211 or 206/213-0100. www.courtyard lakeunion.com. 250 units. Doubles $215–$379, includes continental breakfast. Bus: 26, 28. Map p 154.*

★★ Crowne Plaza DOWNTOWN

Two blocks from the convention center and a few blocks from Pike Place Market, this comfortable, sleek, and slightly anonymous-feeling hotel is also near the theaters and downtown shops. *1113 6th Ave.* ☎ *800/770-5675 or 206/ 464-1980. www.cphotelseattle.com. 415 units. Doubles $185–$370. Bus: 3, 5, 16, 82. Map p 155.*

★★★ The Edgewater Hotel

WATERFRONT This landmark Seattle inn, now a fun boutique hotel, is the only hotel in town directly on the waterfront. Perched on a pier over Elliott Bay, view rooms at the Edgewater put you right on the water looking west to the Olympics. The hotel's Six-Seven restaurant serves great food with the same great view. The Beatles stayed here on their 1962 world tour and famously fished from their window. *2411 Alaskan Way, Pier 67.* ☎ *800/624-0670 or 206/728-7000. www.edgewater hotel.com. 223 rooms. Doubles $223–$415. Bus: 19 24, 99. Map p 154.*

★★ Executive Hotel Pacific

DOWNTOWN A true find, this hotel is one of the best deals in downtown Seattle. Fashioned from a 1920s building, it has a modest but comfortable appeal with small, nicely done rooms and baths. It's like an unpretentious city hotel you'd find in Europe and you can walk everywhere in downtown and vicinity. *400 Spring St.* ☎ *888/388-3932 or 206/623-3900. www.executivehotels. net. Doubles: $118–$219. Bus: 12, 16, 66, 99. Map p 155.*

★★★ Fairmont Olympic Hotel

DOWNTOWN Traditional elegance is the theme at this classic luxury hotel, a palace-sized landmark that's been part of Seattle's consciousness since 1926. The rooms have been updated, but remain steadfastly traditional and eminently comfortable. The Georgian Room is a magnificent spot for breakfast or lunch, and oysters and seafood are on the menu at Shuckers. A welcome package is available for children, as is every amenity you can possibly think of. *411 University St.* ☎ *800/257-7544 or 206/621-1700. www.fairmont.com/ seattle. 452 units. Doubles $229–$329. Bus: 85, 143, 150, 157, 158. Map p 155.*

The lushly elegant lobby at the Fairmont Olympic

★★★ Four Seasons Hotel

DOWNTOWN Though it's practically next door to bustling Pike Place Market, the spacious Four Seasons retains an air of quiet luxury that sets it apart from the street scene. But it's not stuffy, and it's extremely comfortable. The large, big-windowed rooms look out on expansive bay or city views. Marble-clad bathrooms are like mini-spas, and there's also a real spa and state-of-the-art fitness center if you want it, and the city's only rooftop infinity pool overlooking Elliott Bay. *99 Union St.* ☎ *206/749-7000. www.fourseasons.com/seattle. 149 rooms. Doubles $409–$1,019. Bus: 12, 99, 121, 122, 125. Map p 155.*

★★ Grand Hyatt Seattle

DOWNTOWN This high-tech high-rise hotel has comfy beds, good work spaces and oversized bathrooms with soaking tubs. Check out the local art throughout the hotel, including a glass "waterfall" sculpture in the lobby. Adjacent is Ruth's Chris Steak House. *721 Pine St.* ☎ *888/591-1234 or 206/774-1234. www.grandseattle.hyatt.com. Doubles $281–$405. Bus: 10, 11, 14, 43, 49. Map p 155.*

★ Hilton Seattle

DOWNTOWN Conveniently connected by tunnel to both the convention center and 5th Avenue shopping area, the Hilton is especially popular with business travelers and groups. The rooms have great views, and they come with large HDTVs with music channels and Nintendo systems. Some have fridges and free breakfast is included in many of the room rates. *1301 6th Ave.* ☎ *800/HIL-TONS or 206/624-0500. www.seattle-hilton.com. Doubles $202–$369. Bus: 2, 250, 306, 312, 522. Map p 155.*

★ Hotel FIVE Seattle

DOWNTOWN The iconic Seattle monorail runs directly in front and above his former Ramada Inn, now a Hotel Five with completely reimagined décor. While not right in the central core of downtown, you can easily walk there and to Seattle Center and all the happening scenes in Belltown. Max's Café serves breakfast and lunch. *2200 5th Ave. (at Blanchard St.).* ☎ *206/441-9785. www.hotelfiveseattle.com. Doubles $140–$240. Bus: 56, 202. Map p 154.*

★★ Hotel Max

DOWNTOWN A sexy boutique hotel with dark walls and eye-popping red accents, Hotel Max occupies a former 1927 office building located just a couple of blocks from downtown. Rooms are on the small side with snug bathrooms but they have the kind of personality that's missing from many hotels. Rooms have vintage vinyl LPs that you can play on a turntable. There a free, nightly craft-beer hour and Miller's Guild restaurant (p 155) on site. *620 Stewart St. (at 6th Ave.).* ☎ *866/833-6299 or 206/728-6299. www.hotelmax seattle.com. 163 units. Doubles $179–$249. S. Union Street Car 99, Bus: 25, 123, 250, 252, 257. Map p 155.*

★★ Hotel Monaco

DOWNTOWN The whimsical decor at this lovely boutique hotel makes it an inviting place for kids and adults. Kids get their own welcome gift and special programs, but there's ample pampering for grown-ups, too, including a complimentary evening wine hour. You can bring your dog—and even order dinner and a free pillow for him—or just borrow a goldfish overnight. *1101 4th Ave.* ☎ *800/ 715-6513 or 206/621-1770. www. monaco-seattle.com. 189 units. Doubles $235–$425. Bus: 202, 210, 214, 215, 554. Map p 154.*

★★ Hotel Vintage

DOWNTOWN In this romantic, wine-themed hotel, each room is named for a different Washington winery, and guests are treated to a nightly wine reception. The comfy rooms are larger than

The cozy Hotel Monaco is kid- and pet-friendly.

average, with a tasteful and quietly contemporary décor. In-room spa services are available, The wonderful Tulio Ristorante (p 134) excels at handmade pasta, and the Fifth Avenue Theatre and shops are steps away. *1100 5th Ave.* ☎ *800/853-3914 or 206/624-8000. www.hotelvintage-seattle.com. 125 units. $149–$349. Bus: 12, 143, 157, 18, 159. Map p 155.*

★★ **Hyatt at Olive 8** DOWNTOWN This is one of Seattle's greenest hotels—it's LEED-certified for energy efficiency. Rooms may be a bit smaller than at the Grand Hyatt around the corner, but prices are lower and the service is excellent. There's a nice pool in a glass-walled room with views of Seattle, and Urbane is a great choice from breakfast to dinner. *1635 8th Ave.* ☎ *206/695-1234. www.olive8.hyatt.com. Doubles $289–$384. Bus: 10, 11, 14, 43. 49. Bus: 12, 21, 99, 120. Map p 155.*

★★★ **Inn at the Market** PIKE PLACE MARKET A romantic hideaway right across from Pike Place Market, this charming boutique hotel offers spectacular views of Elliott Bay and the mountains. The rooms offer a crisp, spare sophistication. Best-kept secret: the 5th-floor roof garden. Take a bottle of wine, a couple of glasses, and enjoy! Room service is from the nearby Café Campagne (p 124). *86 Pine St.* ☎ *800/446-4484 or 206/443-3600. www.innatthemarket. com. 70 units. Doubles $350–$475. Bus: 10, 99, 113, 121, 122. Map p 154.*

★★★ **Inn at Virginia Mason/ The Baroness Hotel** FIRST HILL These two wonderfully restored

apartment buildings from the 1920s offer comfortable, reasonably priced rooms next to the hospitals on First Hill and within walking distance of downtown. You'll find a rare kind of authentic period charm here, and you can dine at the onsite Rhododendron Cafe. *86 Pine St.* ☎ *800/446-4484 or 206/443-1006 Spring St.* ☎ *800/283-6453 or 206/583-6453. www.innatvirginiamason. com. www.baronesshotel.com. Doubles $119–$229. Bus: 2. Map p 155.*

★★★ **Mayflower Park Hotel Seattle** DOWNTOWN, This elegantly restored gem from 1927 may be the easiest hotel to reach in all of Seattle, since it connects to Westlake Center, a stop on the light-rail system to and from Sea-Tac airport. Traditional comfort is the key here, both in furnishings and the top-notch service. Oliver's Lounge (p 141) is one of Seattle's great cocktail bars and Andaluca restaurant (p 123) serves exceptional cuisine. *405 Olive Way.* ☎ *800/426-5100 or 206/623-8700. www.mayflowerpark. com. 171 units. Doubles $179–$419. Bus: 25, 79, 123, 202, 355. Map p 155.*

★ **Mediterranean Inn** QUEEN ANNE A sunny yellow building in a quiet neighborhood houses this moderately priced hotel. Rooms come with kitchenettes. A short stroll takes you to Seattle Center, where you can catch the monorail downtown. *425 Queen Anne Ave. N.* ☎ *866/525-4700 or 206/428-4700. www.mediterranean-inn.com. Doubles $139–$249. Map p 154.*

★★ **Palladian** BELLTOWN Seattle's newest boutique hotel

was created from one of its oldest, a century-old hotel in Belltown. There are playful contemporary touches throughout, such as celebrity portraits on the pillows, but the overall feeling in the rooms is one of sexy comfort. No views, to speak of, but there's a complimentary wine hour and a great new restaurant called Shaker + Straw. *2000 2nd Ave. (at Virginia St.).* ☎ *858/808-0900 or 206/448-1111. 97 units. Doubles: $165–$455. Bus: 116, 118, 119, 120, 202. Map p 154.*

★★ **Paramount Hotel** DOWN-TOWN Across the street from the Paramount Theatre and minutes from the convention center and all things downtown, this mid-size hotel offers contemporary rooms that are briskly stylish if not particularly memorable. The staff is great. *724 Pine St.* ☎ *800/663-1144 or 206/292-9500. www.paramounthotelseattle. com. 146 units. Doubles $278–$448. Bus: 10, 11, 14, 43, 49. Map p 155.*

★ **Roosevelt Hotel** DOWN-TOWN This lovely old hotel has personality, and it's right across from Pacific Place, in the heart of downtown. The rooms have an updated but old-fashioned charm, in keeping with the overall historic flavor. *1531 7th Ave.* ☎ *206/621-1200. www.rooseveltlhotel.com. 151 units. Doubles $189–$259. Bus: 10, 11, 14, 43, 49. Map p 155.*

★★ **Seattle Marriott Water-front** WATERFRONT A short walk from Pike Place Market and across the street from the waterfront, this hotel was built with dramatic views in mind: water, cityscape, mountains. Half the rooms have balconies, and the indoor/outdoor pool has a sweeping view of Elliott Bay and the Olympic Mountains. *2100 Alaskan Way.* ☎ *800/455-8254 or 206/443-5000. www.marriott.com/hotels/travel/seawf-seattle-marriott-waterfront. 358 units. Doubles $289–$439. Bus: 99. Map p 154.*

★★ **Sheraton Seattle Hotel** DOWNTOWN One of the city's larges and greenest hotels, the Sheraton has a pool and workout center. Near the convention center and downtown shops, it offers both views and convenience. The beds are comfy, and the Pike Street Cafe and Gallery Lounge are great for relaxing and dining. Cribs and video games are a help for families. *1400 6th Ave.* ☎ *206/621-9000. www.starwoodhotels.com/sheraton/seattle. 1,258 units. Doubles $159–$350. Bus: 312, 522. Map p 155.*

★★ **Silver Cloud Hotel Broadway** CAPITOL HILL Situated in the funky-around-the-edges Capitol Hill district, the Silver Cloud offers a range of large, comfortable rooms, all with refrigerators and microwaves, plus an indoor pool and fitness center. A shuttle gets you

The elegant lobby of the Mayflower Park Hotel

The sleek and stylish W Seattle Hotel

downtown. *1100 Broadway.* ☎ *800/590-1801 or 206/325-1400. www.silvercloud.com/seattlebroadway. 179 units. Doubles $129–$259. Bus: 12. Map p 155.*

★★★ Sorrento Hotel FIRST

HILL This luxury boutique hotel's first guest was Teddy Roosevelt, and it's been pampering travelers ever since with European style and service. Original features abound. Spacious bathrooms feature Italian marble, and the rooms have been smartly refreshed with colors that add snap to the sedate elegance of the period. The wood-paneled lobby with a fire crackling in the fireplace is a cozy spot to enjoy the complimentary nightly wine hour, and the Dunbar Room serves breakfast, lunch and dinner. *900 Madison St. (at Terry).* ☎ *800/426-1265. www.hotelsorrento.com. 76 units. Doubles $179–$359. Bus: 12. Map p 155.*

★★★ W Seattle Hotel DOWN-

TOWN Sleek, contemporary, and youthful, the W is trendy in a good way. The rooms are warmly inviting, and you can choose from a "Wonderful" room to an "Extreme Wow" suite (on the 24th floor with more than 1,000 square feet of space). Get a shiatsu massage in your room—or most anything (legal!) your heart desires, via the Whatever/Whenever service. Dine at the

palate-pleasing Trace. *1112 4th Ave.* ☎ *206/264-6000. www.hotels.com/Seattle. 417 units. Doubles $276–$395. Bus: 202, 210, 214, 215, 554. Map p 155.*

★★ Warwick Hotel Seattle

BELLTOWN This French-owned Belltown property is an easy walk from downtown and Pike Place Market. It features bright, contemporary-styled rooms, an indoor pool, accommodating staff, and a balcony on every room. Dine at the excellent Brasserie Margaux. *401 Lenora St.* ☎ *206/443-4300. www.warwickwa.com. 230 units. Doubles $249–$357. Bus: 116, 118, 119, 120, 202. Map p 154.*

★★ The Westin Seattle

DOWNTOWN Located in twin landmark round towers from the World's Fair era of 1962, the 47-story Westin offers breathtaking views of the Space Needle, Puget Sound and the downtown cityscape. Rooms come with the Westin Heavenly Bed but don't offer much in the way of personality. Kids get a special welcome kit and will enjoy the roomy indoor pool. *1900 5th Ave.* ☎ *800/WESTIN or 206/728-1000. www.westin.com/seattle. 891 units. Doubles $250–$400. South Lake Union Street Car 98, Bus: 25, 79, 123. Map p 154.* ●

Check out the Space Needle from your room—views from the Westin are spectacular.

Tacoma

1. Tacoma Art Museum
2. Hello, Cupcake
3. Tacoma Union Station
4. Washington State History Museum
5. Chihuly Bridge of Glass
6. Museum of Glass
7. W.W. Seymour Botanical Conservatory
8. Point Defiance Zoo & Aquarium

True, it has no Space Needle, but the old port and lumber town of Tacoma, 30 miles south of its glitzy northern neighbor, has spruced up its image by redeveloping its downtown into a charming area with free light rail, an esplanade along the Thea Foss Waterway, a convention center, and major cultural facilities as anchors. It's worth checking out. START: **1701 Pacific Ave.**

① ★★ Tacoma Art Museum.

The building is itself a work of art, with a ramp that spirals up through galleries, arranged around an atrium with a stone garden. The museum houses a fine collection of works by Northwest artists, including one of the world's largest collection of Tacoma native Dale Chihuly's glass, and has consistently interesting thematic shows. In addition to American art, you'll find European and Asian works. ⏱ 1 hr. 1701 Pacific Ave. ☎ 253/272-4258. www. tacomaartmuseum.org. $15 adults,

Previous page: Hikers on Mt. Rainier

$13 seniors & students, $40 family (2 adults & up to 4 children), free ages 4 & under, Tues–Sun 10am–5pm, 3rd Thurs 10am–8pm (free 5–8pm).

② Hello, Cupcake. Just look for

the pink bicycle outside. This charming little spot serves the tastiest cupcakes around. Try the red velvet and the vanilla vanilla. The décor's as playful as the cupcakes. *1740 Pacific Ave.* ☎ *253/383-7772.* $

③ Tacoma Union Station. The

former terminus of the Northern

Tacoma

Pacific Railroad, this grand station was abandoned for many years, then renovated in the 1990s and turned into rental space. There are no more trains, but it's worth a stop to admire the magnificent 90-foot-tall rotunda dome, now decorated with a splendid 20-foot Chihuly chandelier. ⏱ *15 min. 1717 Pacific Ave.* ☎ *253/863-5173, ext. 223. www.unionstationrotunda.org. Free to the public. Mon–Fri 8am–5pm.*

④ ★★★ **Washington State History Museum.** History comes to life here via high-tech interactive displays. Engaging for all ages, these exhibits make learning history not only painless but terrific fun. "Meet" characters from Washington's past—like Lewis & Clark—in the Great Hall of Washington history. ⏱ *1½ hr. 1911 Pacific Ave.* ☎ *253/272-3500. www.washingtonhistory.org. $14 adults, $11 seniors/ages 6–17, $40 families (2 adults & up to 4 children), Tues–Sun 10am–5pm, third Thurs 10–8pm (free 2–8pm).*

⑤ ★★★ **Chihuly Bridge of Glass.** Connecting the revitalized downtown to Tacoma's waterfront and the Museum of Glass is a spectacular 500-foot pedestrian bridge by Chihuly and architect Arthur Andersson. It rises 70 feet into the air as it crosses Interstate 705, and features a ceiling of "seaform" glass, blue crystal towers, and a variety of glass sculptures. *1801 Dock St.*

⑥ ★★ **Museum of Glass.** Here you'll find works by world-famous contemporary glass artists, and you can stop at the hot shop to watch artisans at work. ⏱ *1hr. 1801 Dock St.* ☎ *253/284-4750. www.museumofglass.org. $15 adults, $12 seniors, $5 ages 6–12, Summer: Mon–Sat 10am–5pm, Sun noon–5pm, third Thurs 10am–8pm (free 5–8pm). Fall/Winter/Spring: Wed–Sat 10am–5pm,* Sun noon–5pm, third Thurs 10am–8pm (free 5–8pm).

⑦ ★★ **W.W. Seymour Botanical Conservatory** Now more than a century old, the graceful W. W. Seymour Conservatory in historic Wright Park is one of only 3 glasshouses on the West Coast. Enjoy colorful seasonal floral displays, exotic orchids and tropical plants, and then stroll in the park, home to some of Washington's largest and oldest specimen trees. ⏱ *½ hr. 316 South St.* ☎ *253/591-5330. Admission by donation. Tues–Sun 10am–4:30pm.*

⑧ ★★ **Point Defiance Zoo & Aquarium.** This terrific little zoo is best known for its marine exhibits, including walruses, brightly colored tropical fish and five species of sharks. There are also camel rides. ⏱ *1½ hr. 5400 N. Pearl St.* ☎ *253/404-3689. www.pdza.org. $16 adults, $15 seniors, $12 ages 5–12, $8 ages 3–4. Daily 9:30am (8:30am July to early Sept), closing hours vary.*

The Chihuly Bridge of Glass connects Tacoma's waterfront to the downtown area.

San Juan Islands

1. Friday Harbor Ferry Dock
2. Whale Watch
3. Pelindaba Lavender Gallery
4. San Juan Coffee Roasting Co.
5. Whale Museum

Just a few hours from Seattle, these small islands are a quiet world unto themselves. The quaint portside town of Friday Harbor, at the tip of San Juan Island, is lined with interesting shops, art galleries, shops and cafes. The islands are a popular getaway for both tourists and local residents. You won't need a car, unless you want to drive around the islands and do some exploring. Even then, you can rent bikes or mopeds when you get there. START: **Friday Harbor Ferry Dock.**

1 Friday Harbor Ferry Dock. This landing, with its stunning views of the surrounding hilly islands, is where your adventure begins. You can get here from the Seattle waterfront, via the *Victoria Clipper* (☎ 206/448-5000; www.victoria clipper.com; operates daily May-Oct), or you can drive up I-5 to Anacortes (about a 2-hr. trip), then follow the signs to the Washington State ferry dock. You can take your car on the boat, but it costs quite a bit more. Long-term parking at the dock is cheaper, and you can walk right onto the boat. Car lines get long in the summertime. For Anacortes–San Juan Islands ferry schedules, check the website (www. wsdot.wa.gov/ferries). This 1½-hour ferry ride is one of the prettiest in the world, winding its way among enchanting emerald islands. It's spectacular on a sunny day, but dreamy in the mist as well. ① *2 hr., 45 min. each way on Victoria Clipper* from Seattle (round trip $149–$185 adults, $74.50–$92.50 children; discounts if purchased in advance); or 2 hr. by car, then about 1½ hr. excluding wait time on Washington State ferry, each way (current Anacortes–Friday Harbor round-trip Washington State ferry fares: passenger-only $13.25 adults, $6.60 seniors/ages 6–18. For car under 22-ft. long, add $63.75, which includes driver's fare).

② ★★★ Whale Watch. A number of whale-watching cruises leave from Friday Harbor. If you get there via the Victoria Clipper, whale-watch tickets can be purchased as a package. Most companies won't guarantee you'll see sleek black-and-white orcas leaping out of the water, but chances are good in the summer. Most boats have knowledgeable guides who recognize the individual whales in the resident pods. *Victoria Clipper:* ⏱ *2½ hr. from the port. Friday Harbor Port.*

An Orca surfaces during a whale-watching trip off San Juan Island.

☎ *800/888-2535. www.clipper vacations.com. Prices vary, depending on date, how far in advance purchased & whether purchased separately or as package from Seattle. Check website for options. Victoria Clipper round-trip with whale watch: $219–$261 per person.*

❸ ★ Pelindaba Lavender Gallery. FRIDAY HARBOR Who knew there were so many uses for lavender—from cooking ingredients to pet-odor spray? Pelindaba grows its own lavender right on San Juan Island. *150 1st St., Friday Harbor.* ☎ *866/819-1911. www.pelindaba lavender.com.*

❹ San Juan Coffee Roasting Co. For a great cup of island-roasted coffee, made with estate-grown beans from around the world, pop into San Juan Coffee and sample their smooth java. While you're there, give in to your sweet tooth; their chocolates are the melt-in-your-mouth variety. The shop is right beside the ferry dock. *18 Cannery Landing.* ☎ *800/624-4119. $*

❺ ★ Whale Museum. FRIDAY HARBOR Three blocks from the harbor, this unusual little museum is chock full of information on these huge sea mammals, especially the three orca pods that spend their summers around the San Juan Islands. Exhibits include a whale skeleton. ⏱ *1 hr. 62 1st St. N.* ☎ *360/378-4710. www.whale museum.org. $6 adults, $5 seniors, $3 ages 5–18. Daily summer 10am–6pm, winter 10am–4pm.*

Bellevue

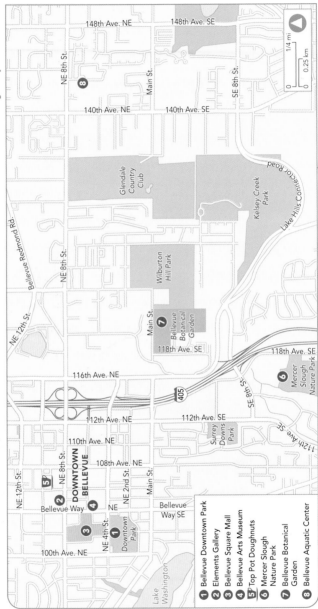

1/4 mi

0.25 km

148th Ave. NE

148th Ave. SE

NE 8th St.

Main St.

SE 8th St.

140th Ave. NE

140th Ave. SE

Glendale
Country
Club

Kelsey Creek
Park

Lake Hills Connector Road

Bellevue Redmond Rd.

NE 8th St.

Wilburton
Hill Park

NE 12th St.

Main St.

Bellevue
Botanical
Garden

118th Ave. SE

118th Ave. SE

116th Ave. NE

405

Mercer
Slough
Nature Park

112th Ave. NE

112th Ave. SE

SE 8th St.

110th Ave. NE

Surrey
Downs
Park

108th Ave. NE

112th Ave. SE

NE 8th St.

DOWNTOWN
BELLEVUE

Main St.

NE 12th St.

Bellevue Way

NE 2nd St.

Bellevue
Way SE

100th Ave. NE

NE 4th St.

Downtown
Park

Lake
Washington

1 Bellevue Downtown Park
2 Elements Gallery
3 Bellevue Square Mall
4 Bellevue Arts Museum
5 Top Pot Doughnuts
6 Mercer Slough
   Nature Park
7 Bellevue Botanical
   Garden
8 Bellevue Aquatic Center

Shooting for the stars across the lake from Seattle is the city of Bellevue, which has quietly boomed from a sleepy Eastside suburb into one of the richest towns in Washington, with an overall per capita income nearly twice that of Seattle. Along with a thriving population comes high-end shopping, high-rise buildings teeming with shops and offices, and lots of great activities. Some areas have taken on a suburban, corporate look, but Bellevue also boasts miles of beautiful parks and waterfront. Just a short drive from downtown Seattle—across Lake Washington on either of two floating bridges—Bellevue has its own personality: less eccentric and more well-heeled than its counterpart on the west side of the lake.

START: **Bus 233, 234, or 249 to NE 10th Street & 110th Avenue, walk to 108th Avenue NE., or drive across SR 520 floating bridge, left on NE 12th Street, right on 108th Avenue NE, to 1116 108th Avenue NE.**

❶ **Bellevue Downtown Park.** This 21-acre park in the heart of downtown Bellevue is a good spot to start your tour of Bellevue, a city that has experienced explosive growth in the last 20 years as a result of high-tech industries like Microsoft. Bellevue Downtown Park, with its circular promenade and encircling water channel that ends in a splashing waterfall, reflects something of Bellevue's nouveau upmarket aesthetic. Only a block from the legendary Bellevue Mall and close to new residential towers and rowhouses, the park is an oasis with a big green central lawn for volleyball and Frisbee, and plenty of benches for relaxing. ⏱ *30 min. 10201 NE Fourth St. Dawn to 11pm.*

The canal at Bellevue Downtown Park

An exhibit at Bellevue Arts Museum

2 Elements Gallery. Visitors can take home a treasured souvenir or just enjoy gazing at the exquisite art, much of it created in the Northwest. Brilliantly colored glass, elegant sculptures, gleaming carved wood, and stunning jewelry share the space here. ⏱ *30 min. 10500 NE 8th St.* ☎ *425/454-8242.*

3 ★ Bellevue Square Mall. A shopping excursion at Bellevue Square is not your ordinary mall experience. With about 200 upscale shops and restaurants to explore, and a multiplex for movies, it's easy to get lost—which usually translates into more shopping bags. Tenants now include an Amazon Books, a Microsoft outlet (giving the existing Apple store a little competition), Nordstrom, Crate & Barrel, Harry & David, Macy's, Once Upon a Time (quality toys), Something Silver, True Religion, Zumiez, and Tiffany & Co. If the little ones get antsy, head up to the Kids' Cove play area

on the third floor. Mom and Dad can grab a latte while the tots scramble across a Washington ferryboat and other brightly colored climbing toys. Mall parking is free. Try to find *that* in Seattle. ⏱ *1 hr. 1086 Bellevue Sq.* ☎ *425/646-3660. www.bellevuecollection.com. Mon–Sat 9:30am–9:30pm, Sun noon–5pm.*

4 ★ Bellevue Arts Museum. With a focus on fine crafts and design, BAM is appropriately housed in an eye-catching red building by contemporary architect Steven Holl. Exhibits are usually inventive and thoughtful, showcasing Northwest and international artists. ⏱ *1 hr. 510 Bellevue Way NE.* ☎ *425/519-0770. www.bellevuearts. org. $10 adults, $8 students & seniors, free for kids 5 & under. Hours: Weds–Sun. 10am–5pm.*

5 Top Pot doughnuts. This local Seattle chain has a little satellite right in Bellevue Mall, but head 3 blocks away to find a roomy place with lots of tables, great coffee, and the doughnuts that made their name. ⏱ *15 min. 10600 NE 9th Pl. NE.* ☎ *425/457-7440. $*

6 ★ Mercer Slough Nature Park. Explore 320 acres of hiking trails, wetlands, and wildlife habitat along beautiful Lake Washington. Be sure to stop by the environmental education center's visitor center, where you'll find interpretive displays, trail maps and nature-inspired art exhibits. The treehouse offers a bird's-eye view of the park, and free nature walks leave from the center at 2pm on selected Sundays (call for dates). From May to September, 3-hour guided canoe trips ($18 per person; ☎ 425/452-6885) leave at 8:45am every

Saturday (and Sundays in July and August) from Enatai Beach Park, 3519 108th Ave. SE. Advance registration and canoeing experience are required. ⏱ *1 hr. Environmental Education Center, 1625 118th Ave. SE. Free admission. Daily 10am–4pm.*

7 ★★★ **Bellevue Botanical Garden.** One of the great gardens of Washington, the glorious Bellevue Botanical Garden should definitely be on your list of Bellevue must-sees. The scope and variety of the land and display gardens found on these 53 acres near downtown Bellevue comes as an eye-opening surprise and provides a glimpse of the Bellevue landscape before development took over. A paved pathway winds through seven display gardens, including an award-winning and eye-popping perennial garden, and natural areas. From Thanksgiving through New Year, more than a half-million lights lend a festive glow to the garden from 5 to 10pm daily during Garden d'Lights. It is not to be missed. Stop in first at the Visitor Center for maps and info. ⏱ *1 hr. 12001 Main St.* ☎ *425/452-2750. www.bellevue botanical.org. Free ($5 adults for Garden d'Lights). Daily dawn to dusk, Visitor Center daily 9am–4pm.*

8 ★ **Bellevue Aquatic Center.** With two large indoor pools, the Blue Lagoon and Warm Springs, this is a great place for a refreshing workout, rain or shine. You can also dive off diving boards into the tank or head down the 10-foot slide. The Warm Springs is heated to a balmy 91 degrees for therapy, but it's also open to the public several times a day (check website for times)—and perfect for the younger set. *601 143rd Ave. NE.* ☎ *425/452-4444. www.ci.bellevue.wa.us/aquatic_ center.htm. Open swim sessions $7 adults, $6 ages 12 & under. Mon–Fri 8am–8pm, Sat 8am–2:30pm, Sun 9am–2:30pm.*

An aerial view of Bellevue and Lake Washington

Mount Rainier National Park

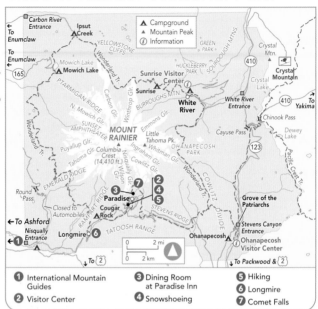

- **1** International Mountain Guides
- **2** Visitor Center
- **3** Dining Room at Paradise Inn
- **4** Snowshoeing
- **5** Hiking
- **6** Longmire
- **7** Comet Falls

Seattleites can go for weeks without seeing the sun, and they're pretty OK with that. What gets them down is when the gray skies blanket their beloved Mount Rainier, which soars—on a clear day—a mile-and-a-half above the surrounding Cascade peaks. When it breaks through the clouds, you're likely to hear someone say, "The mountain's out!" Less than 3 hours from the city, Mt. Rainier is considered somewhat of a backyard by Seattleites, who love to hike it, climb it, picnic on it, and marvel at its wildflowers. START: **The Nisqually Entrance.**

1 ★★★ **Go Mountain Climbing.** Several mountain-climbing organizations offer programs for various levels of climbers (including novices). A popular one is International Mountain Guides. *31111 S.R. 706, Ashford.* ☎ *360/569-2609. www. mountainguides.com. Prices start at $219 for 1-day mountaineering school.*

2 **Paradise Jackson Visitor Center.** From Seattle, drive south on I-5, east on SR 512, south on SR 7 to Elbe, then east on SR 706 through Ashford to reach the Nisqually Entrance of Mount Rainier National Park. This entrance is open year-round, as is the ride along the Nisqually-Paradise Road to Paradise. The drive is spectacular, winding through old-growth forest as the road climbs the mountain. At Paradise, stop at the Visitor Center for maps of the park and its many trails. Free nature walks also leave from the center. *At Paradise.* ☎ *360/569-6971. Single-vehicle fee (with all passengers,* *valid for 7 consecutive days) $25; one-year unlimited entrance fee $50. May–Sept daily 10am–4:30pm, Oct–Apr Sat-Sun only 10am–4:30.*

3 **Dining room at Paradise Inn.** A dramatically beautiful mountain lodge and hotel made of Alaskan cedar, Paradise Inn is a national historic building with a huge fireplace. In the dining room (closed in the winter months), you can enjoy fabulous views with your sit-down meal; in the Tatoosh Café you can grab a burger or a smoked salmon Caesar salad to go. ☎ *360/569-2275. www.mtrainierguestservices.com. $*

4 ★★★ **Try Snowshoeing.** Snowshoeing is a popular sport on Mount Rainier, and no wonder: The variety of trails is endless, from very easy to super challenging. Beginners might want to try the half-mile Myrtle Falls trail, which starts near the Paradise Inn and leads to a lovely view of Myrtle Falls and the Paradise Valley. From mid-December through March, rangers lead free 1.8-mi 2-hour snowshoe walks for kids and adults; rental snowshoes available on-site, or bring your own. Sign up in the Visitors Center 1 hr. before. ⏱ *2 hr. Visitors Center. ☎ 360/569-6971. Free. Walks leave from Visitors Center Sat–Sun at 11am and 1:30pm mid-Dec-Mar.*

5 ★★★ **Take a Hike.** The park maps will help you decide which trails will suit you best. There are plenty of easy hikes, and lots of tougher ones as well. Watch for wildlife and dramatic mountain vistas. Or continue driving up the Nisqually-Paradise Road to Kautz Creek (plowed in winter but chains may be required on some heavy snowfall days), where you can park and enjoy the view of Mount Rainier. You can also hike along the Kautz Creek trail to Indian Henry's Hunting Ground.

6 ★★ **Longmire.** Nisqually-Paradise Road takes you next to Longmire, a town about 12 miles from Paradise, where you will find the **Longmire Museum** (☎ 360/569-6650; usually open year-round, daily 9am–4:30pm, free), a repurposed homesteader's cabin from 1916 with exhibits about the land's history and geology. Longmire is also where you'll find the **National Park Inn** (☎ 360/569-2275) and hiking trails that lead you to nearby mineral springs bubbling out of the earth as a result of volcanic processes deep underground. The springs are most visible in spring and sometimes dry up entirely by late summer. For environmental protection reasons, visitors are not allowed to soak in them.

7 ★★ **Comet Falls.** About 10 miles from the entrance to the park, Nisqually-Paradise Road takes you to a Comet Falls, a 300-foot waterfall, the most dramatic waterfall on Mt. Rainier. You can hike there or drive to the viewing area, just past Christine Falls.

A view of Mt. Rainier

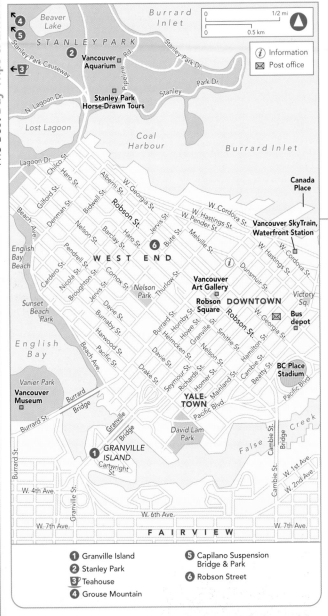

Vancouver, B.C.

Burrard Inlet

| 0 | | 1/2 mi |
| 0 | 0.5 km | |

Beaver Lake

STANLEY PARK

Stanley Park Dr.

ℹ️ Information
✉️ Post office

4 **5** ↖️

Stanley Park Causeway

2 **Vancouver Aquarium**

Pipeline Rd.

Park Dr.

Stanley

←**3** 🚌

N. Lagoon Dr.

Stanley Park Horse-Drawn Tours

Lost Lagoon

Coal Harbour

Burrard Inlet

Lagoon Dr.

Chilco St.

Haro St.

Gilford St.

Canada Place

W. Georgia St.

W. Cordova St.

W. Hastings St.

W. Pender St.

Vancouver SkyTrain, Waterfront Station

W. Cordova St.

Alberni St.

Bidwell St.

Robson St.

Haro St.

Jervis St.

Bute St.

Melville St.

Beach Ave.

Denman St.

Nelson St.

Barclay St.

W. Hastings St.

Dunsmuir St.

English Bay Beach

Cardero St.

Pendrell St.

Comox St.

WEST END

Thurlow St.

ℹ️

Vancouver Art Gallery

Victory Sq.

Nicola St.

Broughton St.

Nelson Park

Robson Square

DOWNTOWN

Robson St.

W. Georgia St.

✉️

Bus depot

Sunset Beach Park

Jervis St.

Davie St.

Burnaby St.

Burrard St.

Hornby St.

Howe St.

Granville St.

Smithe St.

Hamilton St.

Cambie St.

English Bay

Harwood St.

Pacific St.

Davie St.

Helmcken St.

Nelson St.

BC Place Stadium

Seymour St.

Richards St.

Homer St.

Beatty St.

Pacific Blvd.

Vanier Park

Vancouver Museum

Beach Ave.

Drake St.

Burrard

YALE-TOWN

Mainland St.

Burrard St.

Burrard Bridge

Granville Bridge

Pacific Blvd.

Cambie St.

Bridge

Creek

False

Burrard St.

Granville St.

1 *GRANVILLE ISLAND*

Cartwright St.

David Lam Park

Cambie St.

W. 1st Ave.

W. 2nd Ave.

W. 4th Ave.

W. 6th Ave.

W. 7th Ave.

FAIRVIEW

W. 7th Ave.

1 Granville Island
2 Stanley Park
3 Teahouse
4 Grouse Mountain

5 Capilano Suspension Bridge & Park
6 Robson Street

So close to Seattle it's considered a neighbor, Vancouver is a sophisticated city with lots to offer. The people are friendly, the shopping and dining top-notch, the skyline dramatic—no wonder it's consistently ranked as one of the most livable cities in the world. Set on the Pacific Ocean, with the majestic Coast Mountains looming in the background, Vancouver is breathtakingly beautiful and very much oriented to the outdoors. But it's also the liveliest and trendiest Canadian city, and used so often as a setting for movies and TV shows that's sometimes called "Hollywood North." To get there, drive 2½ hours north from Seattle along I-5, over the Canadian border at Blaine or take the 4-hour Amtrak Cascades ride (☎ 800/USA-RAIL; www.amtrak.com). Passports are a must. Getting around town is a breeze—by light rail (The Vancouver Sky Train), bus, or ferry. START: **GRANVILLE ISLAND. Take the #50 False Creek bus from Gastown (downtown area), which stops just off Granville Island; walk toward the sign. Other city buses will take you to Granville & 5th Ave., and you can walk to the island. You can also take a ferry (continuous runs 7am to 10:30pm in the summer; until 8:30pm in the winter).**

❶ ★★★ Granville Island. If you have time for only one stop, make it lively, picturesque Granville Island. The public market is an almost overwhelming sensory experience of colors, smells, and tastes. The fish and produce are fresh and delicious. Just outside the market building, buskers and entertainers of all kinds are usually performing. Shops and galleries around Granville Market carry everything from custom-made jewelry and books to nautical gear and Pacific Northwest First Nation artwork. The Kids Market is an entire building of children's shops surrounding a three-story climbing ball pit. ⏲ *2 hr. www.granvilleisland.com/public-market. Market open daily 9am-7pm.*

The Public Market at Granville Island rivals Pike Place, but without the crowds.

❷ ★★★ Stanley Park. One of the world's most magnificent parks, Stanley is a 1,000-acre paradise of meadows, forests, and gardens surrounded on three sides by water. As if the natural beauty weren't enough, there's plenty to do here. The **Vancouver Aquarium ★★** (www.van aqua.org; C$39 adults, C$30 seniors and ages 13–18, C$22 ages 4–12; daily 10am–5pm) is one of the top-rated aquariums on the West Coast. The **Variety Kids Water Park** (open June-early Sept) is free—and teeming with little ones running and playing in the different water sprays. For more water fun, take a plunge into the heated seawater pool (late May through Labor Day) or bask on two bathing beaches. If you want to see and learn more about the park in a leisurely fashion, take one of the scenic 1-hr carriage rides offered by **Stanley Park Horse-Drawn Tours ★★★** (☎ 604/681-5115; C$42 adults, C$40 seniors and students, C$20 children 3–12). The tours depart from near the Georgia St. entrance to the park every 20 to 30 minutes (9:30am–4pm late-Feb-mid-Nov) and take you along the

The Best Day Trips & Excursions

The Capilano Suspension Bridge takes the daring high above the forest floor.

water's edge, through the forest, to the famous totem poles carved and painted by native artisans. ⏱ *2 hr. Georgia St. entrance, north end. www. stanleypark.com. Park is free. Bus: 19.*

3C Teahouse in Stanley Park. Elegant but never stuffy, the Teahouse is a landmark restaurant that serves lunch, brunch, and dinner and afternoon tea and wine. Try the smoked salmon, a perennial favorite. Reservations recommended. *Ferguson Point, Stanley Park Drive.* ☎ *604/669-3281. $–$$$*

4 ★ Grouse Mountain. Just a 15-minute drive from the city, Grouse Mountain offers snowshoeing, ice skating, and sleigh rides in the winter. In the summer, take the SkyRide cable car (all-day admission: C$49 adults, C$45 seniors, C$30 youth13–18, C$16 ages 5–12) up to

the top and enjoy the panoramic view. The price includes other activities, such as films about endangered animals, the Refuge for Endangered Wildlife, chairlift rides, and—in season—sleigh rides. Work up an appetite, then enjoy fine dining at the Observatory Restaurant, or a casual bite at the cafe or bistro. ⏱ *2 hr. 6400 Nancy Greene Way.* ☎ *604/ 980-9311. www.grousemountain.com. Take Bus 232 from Phibbs Exchange or Bus 236 from Lonsdale Quay. Or drive north across Lions Gate Bridge, take the North Vancouver exit to Marine Drive, then 3 mi. up Capilano Road. Daily 9am to 10pm.*

5 ★ Capilano Suspension Bridge & Park. This 443-foot swinging bridge gives you a breathtaking view of the rainforest and the Capilano River rushing along below. In the park, you can watch First Nation carving demonstrations and go on the Treetops Adventure, which takes you far above the forest floor on a separate series of suspension bridges. ⏱ *1½ hr. 3735 Capilano Rd.* ☎ *604/985-7474. www.capbridge.com. C$43 adults, C$39 seniors, C$27 ages 13–16, C$15 ages 6–12. Open daily, but check website for times.*

6 ★★★ Robson Street. The Rodeo Drive of Vancouver, with upscale shopping and lots of restaurants, cafes and coffee shops. *Btw. Burrard & Jervis sts.* ●

Olympic Gains

Vancouver and environs spruced up to the tune of US$6 billion for the 2010 Winter Olympics. That included improvements to the Sea to Sky Highway (99), a formerly challenging—and sometimes scary!—route from Vancouver north to the breathtaking ski town of Whistler. Now wider and safer, the road takes you there in less than 2 hours. You'll need an early start to fit this into your day trip, but it's worth it for the spectacular alpine scenery.

The **Savvy Traveler**

Before You Go

Tourist Offices

Need more information about Seattle? You can get all the details your heart desires by contacting **Seattle's Convention and Visitors Bureau,** 701 Pike St., Suite 800, Seattle, WA 98101 (☎ 206/461-5800; www.visitseattle.org; ☎ 206/461-5840), which operates the Seattle Visitor Center inside the Washington State Convention and Trade Center, 7th Avenue and Pike Street, Upper Pike Street Lobby). Or try the **Market Information Center** (☎ 206/461-5840), located at the southwest Corner of 1st Avenue and Pike Street in the Pike Place Market. For information on other parts of Washington, contact **Washington State Tourism** (☎ 800/544-1800; www.experiencewa.com).

The Best Times to Go

We always say that summer arrives in the Pacific Northwest on July 5th. From then through the end of September, the rain (for the most part) goes away and Seattleites come out to play. The picture-perfect weather means hotels and restaurants are crowded, so book as far in advance as possible. If you're not afraid of the rain—usually more of a mist than a downpour—come in the winter months, when rates are lower, crowds are thinner, and the theaters are in full performance mode. With Seattle's temperate climate, it will probably be warmer than wherever you started out.

Festivals & Special Events

SPRING. April brings the **Skagit Valley Tulip Festival** (☎ 360/428-5959; www.tulipfestival.org), in and around La Conner. An hour north of Seattle, enormous fields of tulips and daffodils blanket the Skagit Valley with a kaleidoscope of color for weeks, accompanied by festivities. May starts with a splash the first Saturday of the month with the **Opening Day of Boating Season** (☎ 206/325-1000; www.seattle yachtclub.org). It's held on Lakes Union and Washington. Next comes the first big street fair, the **U District Street Fair** (☎ 206/547-4417; www.udistrictstreetfair.org), in north Seattle's lively University District. Also in mid-May is Giant Magnet's **International Children's Friendship Festival** (☎ 206/684-7338), at Seattle Center, celebrating cultures from around the world. Then comes the world-famous **Seattle International Film Festival** (☎ 206/324-9996; www.seattlefilm. com), held at area theaters, mid-May through early June. On Memorial Day weekend, the **Northwest Folklife Festival** (☎ 206/684-7300; www.nwfolklife.org) at Seattle Center honors the many cultures that come together in the Northwest.

SUMMER. The third weekend in June is time for the wackiest festival of all, the **Fremont Fair** (☎ 206/694-6706; www.fremontfair.com), which welcomes the summer solstice with a quirky parade, complete with political satire and bicyclists in the buff. At the end of the month comes **Seattle Pride** (☎ 206/322-9561; www.seattlepride.org), the city's biggest annual gay, lesbian, bisexual, and transgender festival. On the Fourth of July, head for **Lake Union** (☎ 206/281-7788; www.familyfourth.org) to ooh and ahhh at fireworks over the lake. The biggest event of the season is **Seafair** (☎ 206/728-0123; www.seafair. com), which starts in early July and

Previous page: A ride on the Bainbridge ferry

SEATTLE'S AVERAGE TEMPERATURE & DAYS OF RAIN						
	JAN	FEB	MAR	APR	MAY	JUNE
Temp. (°F)	46	50	53	58	65	69
Temp. (°C)	8	10	12	14	18	21
Rain (days)	16	17	14	10	9	5
	JULY	AUG	SEPT	OCT	NOV	DEC
Temp. (°F)	75	74	69	60	52	47
Temp. (°C)	24	23	21	16	11	8
Rain (days)	7	9	14	18	20	19

lasts for a month. Highlights are the hydroplane boat races, the Navy's Blue Angels show and the Torchlight Parade. At **Bite of Seattle** in mid-July, crowds head to Seattle Center to hear live bands and sample treats and wine from local restaurants. Wrapping up the summer is **Bumbershoot, the Seattle Music & Arts Festival** (☎ 206/281-7788; www.bumbershoot.org), at Seattle Center on Labor Day weekend. It's a little bit crazy and a lot of fun.

FALL. Issaquah Salmon Days Festival (☎ 425/392-0661; www.salmondays.org) welcomes the salmon on their return to the lakes and streams. Issaquah, 15 miles east of Seattle, the first full weekend in October.

WINTER. Throughout December, the **Argosy Cruises Christmas Ships Festival** (☎ 888/623-1445 or 206/622-8687; www.argosycruises.com) takes place at various waterfront locations. Boats decked out with Christmas lights parade past a number of beaches. What better way to ring in the new year than with **New Year's at the Needle** (☎ 206/905-2100; www.spaceneedle.com), Seattle Center, December 31.

In January, Seattle celebrates the Chinese New Year in a big way, with dragon kites, music and dance. The **Chinatown/International District Lunar New Year Celebration** (☎ 206/382-1197; www.cidbia.org), is held at Hing Hay Park (423 Maynard Ave. S.).The next month,

gardening buffs head to the **Northwest Flower & Garden Show** (☎ 253/756-2121; www.gardenshow.com), at the Washington State Convention and Trade Center.

The Weather

Okay, so Seattle doesn't come to mind when you think of sunny destinations. But if you're here in July, August, or September, when those glorious summer days stretch lazily on 'til 10pm, you might think the city has an undeserved rap. Come back in November and you might change your mind. But even then, the rain is generally more drizzle than downpour. When they run the numbers, it turns out that Seattle gets 19 inches less rain every year than Miami—though it rains here 29 more days. Theirs is torrential downpour; ours is gentle mist. So Seattle has less rain but more gray days. No matter when you visit, bring an umbrella or hooded jacket for chilly nights. Winters seldom bring below-freezing temperatures in temperate Seattle, and snow is a rarity in the city.

Car Rentals

All the major car-rental agencies have offices in Seattle and at or near Seattle-Tacoma International Airport. These include the following:

• **Advantage** (☎ 800/777-5500 or 206/824-0161; www.advantage.com)

Useful Websites

- Seattle's Convention and Visitors Bureau (www.visitseattle.org)
- Seattle-Tacoma International Airport (www.portseattle.org/seatac)
- Public transportation: King County Metro (http://kingcounty.gov/depts/transportation/metro.aspx)
- *Seattle Times* (www.seattletimes.com)
- *Seattle Weekly* (www.seattleweekly.com)
- Universal Currency Converter (www.xe.com/ucc)
- Visa ATM Locator (www.visa.com), MasterCard ATM Locator (www.mastercard.com)
- Washington State Ferries (www.wsdot.wa.gov/ferries)
- Weather (www.intellicast.com and www.weather.com)

- **Alamo** (☎ 877/905-5555 or 206/433-0182; www.goalamo.com)

- **Avis** (☎ 800/331-1212 or 206/433-5231; www.avis.com)

- **Budget** (☎ 800/527-0700 or 206/444-7510; www.budget.com)

- **Dollar** (☎ 800/800-3665 or 206/433-5825; www.dollar.com)

- **Enterprise** (☎ 800/261-7331 or 206/246-1953; www.enterprise.com)

- **Hertz** (☎ 800/654-3131 or 206/248-1300; www.hertz.com)

- **National** (☎ 877/222-9058 or 206/433-5501; www.nationalcar.com)

- **Thrifty** (☎ 800/847-4389 or 877/283-0898; www.thrifty.com)

Cellphones

It's a good bet that your phone will work in well-wired Seattle, but take a look at your wireless company's coverage map on its website before heading out. If you need to stay in touch at a destination where you know your phone won't work, **rent** a phone that does from **InTouch USA** (☎ 800/872-7626; www.intouchglobal.com) or a rental car location, but beware that you'll pay by the minute for airtime.

Getting **There**

By Plane

Seattle is an international hub. The **Seattle-Tacoma International Airport** (☎ 206/433-5388; www.portseattle.org/seatac) is served by about 30 airlines.

Some international carriers fly direct from major European, and Asian cities to Seattle, others fly to Los Angeles and/or San Francisco and continue (sometimes on a partner airline) to Seattle.

From New Zealand and Australia, there are flights to San Francisco and Los Angeles on **Qantas (**www.qantas.com.au) and **Air New Zealand** (www.airnewzealand.co.nz).

Seaplane service between Seattle and the San Juan Islands; and Victoria, British Columbia, is offered by **Kenmore Air** (☎ 866/435-9524 or 425/486-1257; www.kenmoreair.com), which has its Seattle terminals at the south end of Lake Union and at the north end of Lake Washington.

By Car

There are two main exits from the airport: From the loading/unloading area, take the first exit if you're staying near the airport. Take the second exit (Wash. 518) if you're headed to downtown Seattle. Driving east on Wash. 518 will connect you to I-5, where you'll then follow the signs for Seattle. Generally, allow 30-45 minutes for the drive between the airport and downtown—longer during rush hour.

By Link Light Rail

The easiest and cheapest way to get from the airport to downtown Seattle is by taking **Link Light Rail** (☎ 800/201-4900 or 206/398-5000; www.soundtransit.org). The Link station is connected to the fourth floor of the airport's parking garage. Trains run between the airport and downtown (now going as far north as the U of Washington) every 7½ to 15 minutes, from 5am to 1am Monday through Saturday, and 6am to midnight Sunday, The trip takes about 35 minutes. The fare is $2.25 to $3.25 for adults, $1 to $1.75 for seniors ((fare is based on distance traveled). Buy your ticket from a vending machine on the platform before you board.

By Taxi, Uber, Lyft, Shuttle, or Bus

A taxi into downtown Seattle will cost you about $50 to $60. However, many companies now charge a lower fixed rate. **Yellow Cab** (www. yellowtaxi.net; ☎ 206/ 622-6500), available outside the baggage claim area, and **Horizon Car Service** (www.seattleairport-taxi.com; ☎ 206/306-2000) both charge a flat rate of $40 to downtown Seattle.

Both **Uber** (www.uber.com) and **Lyft** (www.lyft.com) car services are available in Seattle, including to

and from the airport. Cost is generally $32 to $40, plus a $5 airport surcharge.

Shuttle Express

Shuttle Express (☎ 800/487-7433 or 425/981-7000; www.shuttle express.com) provides 24-hour passenger-van service between Sea-Tac and Seattle and environs. Rates to downtown Seattle hotels are $18 for adults, children 17 and under ride free with paying adult. You need a reservation to get to the airport; to leave the airport, reservations are recommended, but walk-ups are welcome. Head to the Ground Transportation Center on the third floor of the parking garage.

By Ferry

Seattle is served by **Washington State Ferries** (☎ 888/808-7977 within Washington, or 206/464-6400; www.wsdot.wa.gov/ferries). Car ferries travel between downtown Seattle and both Bainbridge Island and Bremerton from Pier 52. Car ferries also connect Fauntleroy (in West Seattle) with Vashon Island and the Kitsap Peninsula; Tahlequah (Vashon Island) with Point Defiance in Tacoma; Edmonds with Kingston (on the Kitsap Peninsula); Mukilteo with Whidbey Island; Whidbey Island at Keystone with Port Townsend; and Anacortes with the San Juan Islands and Sidney, British Columbia (near Victoria).

If you're traveling between Victoria, British Columbia, and Seattle, several options are available through **Victoria Clipper,** Pier 69, 2701 Alaskan Way (☎ 800/888-2535, 206/448-5000, or 250/382-8100 in Victoria; www.victoriaclipper.com).

By Train

Amtrak (☎ 800/872-7245; www. amtrak.com) service runs from Vancouver, British Columbia, to Seattle and from Portland and as far south as Eugene, Oregon. The train takes about 4 hours from Vancouver and 3½ to 4 hours from Portland. There is also Amtrak service to Seattle from San Diego, Los Angeles, San Francisco, and from Spokane and points east. Amtrak also operates a bus between Vancouver and Seattle. Trains arrive and depart from **King Street Station,** 303 South Jackson St., near the Pioneer Square area of downtown Seattle.

By Bus
Greyhound (☎ **800/231-2222;** www.greyhound.com) bus service provides connections to almost any city in the continental United States. Seattle's Greyhound bus station is at 811 Stewart St., a few blocks northeast of downtown.

Bolt Bus (☎ 877/BOLTBUS; www.boltbus.com) offers an inexpensive, direct service between Portland and Vancouver, B.C., to Seattle several times a day, stopping in Seattle at King St. in the Chinatown/International District.

By Metro Bus King County's extensive **Metro** (☎ **206/553-3000;** http://metro.kingcounty.gov) bus system will get you anywhere you need to go in and around the city; adult fares range from $2.25 to $3.25 ($1 to $1.75 seniors) depending on distance and time of day. You need exact change; or an ORCA card (www.orcacard.com), which costs $5 ($3.50 seniors) and allows you to load fares and purchase $8 ($4 seniors) day passes.

Getting **Around** By Car

Seattle is 110 miles from Vancouver, British Columbia, 175 miles from Portland, 810 miles from San Francisco, 1,190 miles from Los Angeles, 835 miles from Salt Lake City, and 285 miles from Spokane. I-5 is the main north–south artery, running south to Portland and north to the Canadian border. I-405 is Seattle's eastside bypass and accesses Bellevue, Redmond, and Kirkland on the east side of Lake Washington. I-90, which ends at I-5, connects Seattle to Spokane in the eastern part of Washington. Wash. 520 connects I-405 with Seattle just north of downtown and also ends at I-5. Wash. 99, the Alaskan Way Viaduct, is another major north–south highway through downtown Seattle but it's slated to be removed and replaced by a tunnel. All the major car-rental agencies have offices in Seattle and at or near Sea-Tac International Airport.

Keep in mind that Seattle traffic congestion is bad, parking is limited (and expensive), and streets are almost all one-way. You'll avoid frustration by leaving your car in your hotel parking garage. You might not need a car at all. The city center is well served by public transportation. Plus, Seattle is very walkable. However, to get north of Seattle Center, east of Lake Washington, west of Puget Sound or south of the sports stadiums is a bit tricky without a car (of course, you can take the foot ferry for a trip to Bainbridge Island). You could certainly have a very fun trip to Seattle without renting a car.

Parking
On-street parking in downtown Seattle is expensive and extremely limited. Most downtown parking lots charge $20 to $25 per day, though many offer early-bird specials. Some lots near the Space Needle charge less, and you can leave your car there, then take the monorail downtown. Some restaurants and Pike Place Market merchants validate parking permits.

By Streetcar

One line of the **Seattle Streetcar** (www.seattlestreetcar.org) runs from downtown to Lake Union and a second line runs along Broadway in Capitol Hill. Fares are $2.50 for adults, $1.50 for seniors.

By Light Rail

The **Central Link Light Rail** (www.soundtransit.org) runs beneath 3rd Avenue from Westlake Station south to Sea-Tac airport, making key downtown stops along the way, and north to the University of Washington, making one stop at Capitol Hill. Adult fares range from $2.50 to $3.25 (depending on distance traveled); senior fares are $1.50.

Fast **Facts**

AREA CODE   The area code is 206 in Seattle, 425 for the Eastside (including Kirkland and Bellevue), and 253 for south King County (near the airport).

ATMS   Bank and street ATMs are located all throughout downtown Seattle and at major tourist attractions.

BUSINESS HOURS   The following are general guidelines. Banks are open Monday through Friday from 9am to 5pm (some also on Sat 9am–noon). Stores are open Monday through Saturday from 10am to 6pm and Sunday from noon to 5pm (malls usually stay open until 9pm Mon–Sat). Bars can stay open until 2am.

CURRENCY   The most common bills are the $1 (a "buck"), $5, $10, and $20 denominations. Coins: 1¢ (1 cent, or a penny); 5¢ (5 cents, or a nickel); 10¢ (10 cents, or a dime); 25¢ (25 cents, or a quarter); 50¢ (50 cents, or a half dollar); the gold-edged and rarely used Sacagawea coin, worth $1.

DENTIST   Contact the **Dental Referral Service** (☎ 800/510-7315).

DOCTOR   To find a physician, check at your hotel for a referral, contact **Swedish Medical Center** (☎ 800/833-8879; www.swedish.org), or call the referral line of the **Virginia Mason Medical Center** (☎ 888/862-2737; www.virginiamason.org).

DRINKING LAWS   The legal age for purchase and consumption of alcoholic beverages is 21; proof of age is required and often requested at bars and restaurants. Do not carry open containers of alcohol in your car or any public area. And nothing will ruin your trip faster than getting a citation for DUI ("driving under the influence"), so don't even think about driving while intoxicated.

CANNABIS LAWS   The legal age for purchase and use of cannabis ("pot") is 21; proof of age is required. The use of cannabis is prohibited in all public indoor and outdoor spaces including parks. It may be used on private property only, but that does not include your hotel.

EMBASSIES & CONSULATES   All embassies are located in the nation's capital, Washington, D.C., and some consulates are located in major U.S. cities. If your country isn't listed below, call for directory information in Washington, D.C. (☎ 202/555-1212) or log on to www.embassy.org/embassies.

The embassy of **Australia** is at 1601 Massachusetts Ave. NW, Washington, DC 20036 (☎ 202/797-3000; www.usa.embassy.gov.au). There are consulates in New

York, Atlanta, Chicago, Denver, Honolulu, Houston, Los Angeles, and San Francisco.

The embassy of **Canada** is at 501 Pennsylvania Ave. NW, Washington, DC 20001 (☎ **202/682-1740;** www. canadianembassy.com). Other Canadian consulates are in cities including Buffalo (New York), Detroit, Los Angeles, New York, and Seattle.

The embassy of **Ireland** is at 2234 Massachusetts Ave. NW, Washington, DC 20008 (☎ **202/462-3939;** www.embassy ofireland.org). Irish consulates are in Boston, Chicago, New York, San Francisco, and other cities. See website for complete listing.

The embassy of **New Zealand** is at 37 Observatory Circle NW, Washington, DC 20008 (☎ **202/328-4800;** www.nzembassy.com/usa). New Zealand consulates are in Los Angeles, Salt Lake City, San Francisco, and Seattle.

The embassy of the **United Kingdom** is at 3100 Massachusetts Ave. NW, Washington, DC 20008 (☎ **202/588-6500;** www.ukinusa. fco.gov.uk/en). Other British consulates are in Atlanta, Boston, Chicago, Cleveland, Houston, Los Angeles, New York, San Francisco, and Seattle.

EMERGENCIES For police, fire, or medical emergencies, phone ☎ **911.**

HOLIDAYS Banks, government offices, post offices, and many stores, restaurants, and museums are closed on the following legal national holidays: January 1 (New Year's Day), the third Monday in January (Martin Luther King, Jr., Day), the third Monday in February (Presidents' Day), the last Monday in May (Memorial Day), July 4 (Independence Day), the first Monday in September (Labor Day), the second Monday in October (Columbus Day), November 11 (Veterans' Day/Armistice Day), the fourth Thursday in November (Thanksgiving Day), and December 25 (Christmas).

The Tuesday after the first Monday in November is Election Day.

HOSPITALS Hospitals convenient to downtown include **Swedish Medical Center,** 747 Broadway (☎ 206/386-6000; www.swedish. org), and **Virginia Mason Medical Center,** 1100 9th Ave. (☎ **206/583-6433** for emergencies or 206/624-1144 for information; www. virginiamason.org).

INTERNET ACCESS Virtually all hotels now include free WiFi. If you need to use the internet are don't have a phone or device with you, the **Seattle Central Library,** 1000 4th Ave. (☎ 206/386-4636) has hundreds of online computer terminals.

LOST & FOUND Be sure to tell all of your credit card companies the minute you discover your wallet has been lost or stolen and file a report at a police precinct. Your credit card company or insurer may require a police report number or record of the loss. Most credit card companies have an emergency toll-free number to call if your card is lost or stolen. **Visa**'s U.S. emergency number is ☎ 800/847-2911. **American Express** cardholders should call ☎ 800/528-4800. **MasterCard** holders should call ☎ 800/627-8372. For other credit cards, call the toll-free number directory at ☎ 800/555-1212. You can have money wired to you via **Western Union** (☎ 800/325-6000; www. westernunion.com).

NEWSPAPERS & MAGAZINES The "Seattle Times" (www.seattletimes. com) is Seattle's daily newspaper. "Seattle Weekly" (www.seattle weekly.com) is the city's free arts-and-entertainment weekly. The city's best alternative newspaper is **The Stranger** (www.thestranger. com), which covers arts, politics and local news.

PHARMACIES Conveniently located downtown pharmacies include **Rite**

Aid, with branches at 319 Pike St. (☎ **206/223-0512**) and 2603 3rd Ave. (☎ **206/441-8790**). For 24-hour service, try **Bartell Drug Store,** 600 1st Ave. N. (☎ **206/284-1353**).

POLICE For police emergencies, phone ☎ **911.**

RESTROOMS There are public restrooms in Pike Place Market, Westlake Center, Pacific Place, Seattle Center, and the Washington State Convention and Trade Center. You'll also find restrooms in most hotel lobbies and coffee bars in downtown Seattle.

SAFETY Although Seattle is a relatively safe city, it has its share of crime. The most questionable neighborhood you're likely to visit is the Pioneer Square area. By day, this area is quite safe (though it has a contingent of street people), but when the bars are closing, stay aware of your surroundings. Also take extra precautions with your wallet or purse when you're in the crush of people at Pike Place Market. Try to park your car in a garage at night. If you must park on the street, make sure there are no valuables in view.

SMOKING Smoking (cigarettes and cannabis) is banned in public indoor spaces throughout the state of Washington, even in bars.

TAXES Seattle has a 9.5% sales tax. In restaurants, there's an additional .5% food-and-beverage tax. The hotel-room tax in the metro area ranges from around 10% to 16%. On rental cars, you pay an 18.6% tax, plus, if you rent at the airport, a 10% to 12% airport concession fee (plus other fees for a whopping total of around 45%!).

TELEPHONES Hotel surcharges can be astronomical, so use your cellphone. Many convenience groceries sell prepaid calling cards; for international visitors these can be the least expensive way to call home. For calls within the United States and to Canada, dial 1 followed by the area code and the seven-digit number. For other international calls, dial 011 followed by the country code, city code, and the number you are calling.

Calls to area codes 800, 888, 877, and 866 are toll-free. For local directory assistance ("information"), dial 411; for long-distance information, dial 1, then the appropriate area code and 555-1212.

TIME Seattle is in the Pacific Standard Time (PST) zone, making it 3 hours behind the East Coast of the U.S.

Daylight Saving Time is in effect from 1am on the second Sunday in March to 1am on the first Sunday in November. Daylight Saving Time moves the clock 1 hour ahead of standard time.

TIPPING Tips are the standard way of showing appreciation for services provided. In hotels, tip bellhops at least $1 per bag ($2–$3 if you have a lot of luggage) and tip the cleaning staff $1 to $2 per day (more if you've left a disaster area). Tip the doorman or concierge only if he or she has provided you with some specific service. Tip the valet-parking attendant $2-$3 every time you get your car. In restaurants, bars, and nightclubs, tip service staff 15% to 20% of the check, tip bartenders 10% to 15%, tip checkroom attendants $1 per garment, and tip valet-parking attendants $2–$3 per vehicle. Tip cab drivers 15% of the fare; tip skycaps at airports at least $1 per bag ($2–$3 if you have a lot of luggage); and tip hairdressers and barbers 15% to 20%. Note: some restaurants in Seattle now add an obligatory 20% tip to the bill.

TRANSIT INFO For 24-hour information on Seattle's **Metro bus system,** call ☎ **206/553-3000** or go to http://metro.kingcounty.gov. For information on the **Washington**

State Ferries, call ☎ 888/808-7977 within Washington, or 206/464-6400; www.wsdot.wa.gov/ferries.

TRAVELERS WITH DISABILITIES For anyone using a wheelchair, the greatest difficulty of a visit to Seattle is dealing with the city's steep hills. One solution for dealing with downtown hills is to use the elevator at Pike Place Market to get between the waterfront and 1st Avenue. There's also a public elevator at the west end of Lenora Street (just north of Pike Place Market). This elevator connects the waterfront with the Belltown neighborhood.

Organizations that offer assistance to disabled travelers include **MossRehab** (☎ 800/CALL-MOSS; www.mossresourcenet.org); the **American Foundation for the Blind (AFB)** (☎ 800/232-5463; www.afb.org); and **SATH (Society for Accessible Travel & Hospitality)** (☎ 212/447-7284; www.sath.org). **AirAmbulanceCard.com** is now partnered with SATH and allows you to preselect top-notch hospitals in case of an emergency.

WEATHER Check the "Seattle Times"newspaper for forecasts (or ask Siri for a 5-day Seattle weather report on your iPhone). If you want to know what to pack before you depart, go to www.wrh.noaa.gov/seattle, www.cnn.com/weather, or www.wunderground.com/US/WA.

A Brief **History**

1792 British Capt. George Vancouver explores and names Puget Sound.

1851 The Denny party makes land at Alki Point (now West Seattle) and endures a harsh first winter with the help of local Indian tribes.

1852 Denny and gang move their town to the more temperate east side of the Puget Sound; "Doc" Maynard names the town after Chief Sealth of the local Duwamish tribe.

1853 The Washington Territory is officially created; it includes what is now Idaho and part of Montana.

1853 Henry Yesler opens the first of many sawmills to be built in the Puget Sound area.

1855 The U.S. government signs treaties with several Native-American tribes in the Washington Territory, giving much of their land to the federal government.

1861 The University of Washington (then called Territorial University) opens its doors to students.

1863 Idaho Territory is separated from the Washington Territory.

1863 The "Gazette," later to become the "Seattle Post-Intelligencer," publishes its first newspaper.

1864 Cross-country Western Union telegraph line reaches Seattle.

1869 The City of Seattle incorporates.

1871 The Indian Appropriations Act says Indians are no longer sovereign but federal "wards."

1878 Seattle gets its first telephones.

1885 Chinese immigrants are forced out of Seattle.

1889 Twenty-five blocks of Seattle burn to the ground in the Great Fire, prompting a frenzy of building—several feet higher than the original shops had been.

1889 Washington becomes the nation's 42nd state.

1893 Transcontinental Great Northern Railway reaches Seattle.

1893 Great Panic delivers a punch to Washington's economy.

1896 Col. Alden Blethen buys *The Seattle Daily Times*. (The Blethen family still owns *The Seattle Times*.)

1897–1899 Seattle booms as a stopping-off point for Klondike gold-seekers.

1901 John Nordstrom opens his first shoe store.

1907 Pike Place Market brings farmers and customers directly together.

1910 Seattle women win their on-again-off-again right to vote once and for all.

1914 Smith Tower is completed in Seattle, becoming the tallest building west of the Mississippi.

1915 William Boeing goes for his first flight.

1916 A long, violent longshoremen's strike takes place.

1917 Construction is complete on the Lake Washington Ship Canal.

1917 Boeing Airplane Co. is launched.

1919 The nation's first general strike causes mayhem in Seattle.

1919 First international airmail delivery by Boeing and Hubbard.

1919 Eddie Bauer's first store opens.

1921 The Alien Land Law is passed in Washington, restricting Asian immigrants' rights to own or lease property.

1924 Native Americans are made U.S. citizens.

1926 Seattle elects the first woman mayor of any major U.S. city.

1940 Lake Washington Floating Bridge becomes the first of its kind in the world.

1940 Sen. Henry "Scoop" Jackson wins election to Congress, and later to the U.S. Senate.

1942 FDR signs order sending Japanese Americans from the West Coast to internment camps; thousands in the Seattle area are forced to abandon their homes and businesses.

1942 Seattle native Jimi Hendrix is born.

1949 Sea-Tac International Airport is opened.

1951 Washington State Ferries begin service on Puget Sound.

1954 First successful passenger jet, Boeing 707, takes off.

1962 Seattle builds Space Needle and monorail for the World's Fair.

1966 Boeing builds 747 assembly plant.

1970S Boeing layoffs devastate the local economy.

1971 Starbucks opens its first shop, and the rest is history.

1975 Microsoft is founded by Bill Gates and Paul Allen in Albuquerque; three years later it moves to Seattle area.

1976 First woman governor of Washington, Dixy Lee Ray, is elected.

1976 The new Seahawks football team plays its first game.

1977 The new Mariners baseball team throws its first pitch.

1979 The Seattle SuperSonics win the NBA Championship.

1999 A World Trade Organization conference in downtown Seattle prompts riots, property damage, and accusations of police misconduct.

2001 The Nisqually Earthquake causes extensive damage to many older Seattle buildings.

2004 Washington elects Christine Gregoire in tightest governor's race in U.S. history, giving Washington state three women in its powerful political positions—two U.S. senators and the governor.

2005 Smoking is banned in all public places in Washington.

2006 Starbucks CEO Howard Schultz sells the Seattle Super-Sonics team to an Oklahoma group after the city refuses to expand the basketball arena or build a new one. This leaves the Sonics' future in Seattle in doubt.

2007 The Washington state Legislature legalizes same-sex domestic partnerships.

2008 Seattle voters approve $73 million worth of renovations to their beloved but aging Pike Place Market.

2009 The Link light rail station opens at Sea-Tac Airport, providing rapid mass transportation from downtown Seattle to the airport.

2010 A new law makes it a primary offense to text-message or hold a cellphone to your ear while driving.

2010 The Seattle Storm women's basketball team win their second WNBA championship.

2012 Washington State legalizes same-sex marriage and possession of small amounts of marijuana for recreational use.

2013 Work begins on the demolition of Alaskan Way, a 1960s-era freeway that blights the downtown waterfront; a new tunnel will carry traffic and street adjacent to Seattle's waterfront will eventually be transformed into a park.

2014 Seattle Seahawks beat the Denver Broncos and win the Super Bowl. An estimated 700,000 people celebrate the event at a downtown parade. Refurbishment of Seattle Waterfront begins.

2015 Amazon opens its first corporate office tower in South Lake Union. When construction is completed in 2018 or later, Amazon will have three towers with plant-filled biospheres between them.

2016 The First Hill Streetcar line between E. Howell and Pioneer Square opens. Extension of Central Link light-rail from Sea-Tac to University of Washington in north Seattle begins service.

2017 2-mile tunnel beneath Alaskan Way Viaduct is completed after 4 years. It will be everal more years before the viaduct is removed and Seattle's Waterfront is turned into a park.

Index

See also Accommodations and Restaurant indexes

Photo **Credits**